T0247568

Unstressable

Also by Mo Gawdat

Solve for Happy

Scary Smart

Unstressable

A Practical Guide
to Stress-Free Living

Mo Gawdat
and Alice Law

ST. MARTIN'S
ESSENTIALS
NEW YORK

This book is dedicated to our loved ones lost
to the stresses of the modern world.
It's our mission to help one million people
to become unstressable every year.

First published in the United States by St. Martin's Essentials,
an imprint of St. Martin's Publishing Group

UNSTRESSABLE. Copyright © 2024 by Mo Gawdat and Alice Law. All rights reserved. Printed in the United States of America. For information, address St. Martin's Publishing Group, 120 Broadway, New York, NY 10271.

www.stmartins.com

The Library of Congress Cataloging-in-Publication Data is available upon request.

ISBN 978-1-250-31975-3 (hardcover)
ISBN 978-1-250-31976-0 (ebook)

Our books may be purchased in bulk for promotional, educational, or business use. Please contact your local bookseller or the Macmillan Corporate and Premium Sales Department at 1-800-221-7945, extension 5442, or by email at MacmillanSpecialMarkets@macmillan.com.

First Edition: 2024

10 9 8 7 6 5 4 3 2 1

Contents

This Is Not an Introduction

You are stressed. Aren't you? If you live in our modern world with all its madness and relentless pace, then you must be. If the title of this book got you to flip a page to read this, then you must really feel it. You did well. You acknowledged how you feel. You seem curious as to what you can do about it; being curious is the most crucial step on the path to recovery. Welcome! You're in the right place.

Yes. I did say *recovery* because stress, as in modern-day stress, truly is a disease. In fact, it is *the* most prominent disease, wearing humanity down and leading to many of the other diseases that we scramble to treat while letting their underlying cause thrive.

Unstressable is a book with a mission. We are not writing it to help you become calm regardless of what life throws at you. This is as much a book about prevention of future stress as it is about healing you from your current stresses. Alice and I have committed ourselves to creating a community that aims to help a million people every year live a life that is stress-free—#OneMillionUnstressable—a movement that we hope you will be a part of.

All of us—regardless of how easy or hard our lives may seem—face challenges every day. Whether it's a global economic crisis, an argument with a boss or loved one, or a bit of illness or hardship, we all face hardships, but our reactions differ. Some of us feel overwhelmed and stressed, even depressed, while others find a silver lining in their individual challenges.

Could reality actually be far more enlightening than what we were made to believe? Although the challenges that litter our path through life are forced upon us, could it be that feeling stressed is a choice? Could we develop skills and resources to de-stress? Could stress be prevented? The answer is a resounding *yes*.

 It's not the events of our lives that stress us. It is the way we deal with them that does.

Don't be alarmed if you're stressed. You're not alone! We're all entangled in this complicated, stressful, fast-paced modern world, expected to handle it flawlessly, without the simplest education on **how** to make the stressors work for us, not against us. This expectation is as silly as asking you to jump into a supercar, race it around a Formula One track in the pouring rain, win the title, and make it off the track alive without ever being taught how to drive.

SERIOUSLY EPIDEMIC

Most of us believe that the only pandemic we needed to face in our lifetimes so far was COVID-19, but this is not true. For many years now, the World Health Organization has dubbed stress as "the health epidemic of the 21st century."

Research shows that 70–90 percent of *all* doctors' visits in the US are reported to somehow be related to stress.[1] According to the American Institute of Stress, one of every three Americans lives in extreme stress, 77 percent suffer physical health issues due to the stress they feel, and stress negatively impacts the mental health of 73 percent of all Americans. One in every two Americans has trouble sleeping because of stress[2]—and those kinds of stats are surely not just a US-specific phenomenon. The global sleeping aids market was estimated at $64.29 billion in 2019 and is expected to reach $101.7 billion by 2026.[3]

In the UK, studies showed that 74 percent of Brits are so stressed that they feel unable to cope with life; 51 percent of those also reported feeling depressed, and 61 percent reported feeling anxious.[4] Stress has overtaken musculoskeletal problems (our aching backs from sitting at our desks too long) as the top reason for work-related absence, with 17.9 million working days lost in the UK alone to stress every year.

What is more concerning is that more than 120,000 people in the US *die* every year due to work-related stress, and this is despite spending more than $190 billion on treating illnesses that are associated with stress at work.[5]

How about the rest of the world? Tokyo has been reported as the most stressed city in the world, and Greece, a place we normally associate with a relaxed lifestyle, fresh food, and sunshine, has taken the prize for the most stressed country. Though we couldn't find stats there, it is fair to expect they will be worse than the US and the UK.

Gone are the days when youth was carefree. The younger you are, the more stressed you are likely to be: 61 percent of Gen Z adults (ages 18–23) report they felt stressed during the immediate prior month. This is significantly higher than for all other generations: 56 percent for millennials (ages 24–41), 52 percent for Gen X (ages 42–55), 40 percent for boomers (56–74), and 33 percent for older adults (75+).[6] This could be attributed to the fact that we learn to deal with stress better as we age or that we become more established in terms of resources to make our lives a bit easier.

No matter if you're young or old, if you live in the sunshine or in the cold, it seems that . . .

Remember! If you're part of today's modern world, stress will have somehow found a way to reach you.

There is no doubt that stress has affected us since the cave-human years. The difference, however, is that it has gone from being the very thing that allowed our ancestors to survive in a life-or-death situation to becoming the silent killer of our health, happiness, and well-being in the civilization we have created.

If we are to view stress as a pandemic, I believe it would be very interesting to trace its roots in an attempt to find . . .

PATIENT ZERO

If our ancestors—the cave people—were not regularly stressed, we would not be here today. Stress was a necessary ingredient of life to avoid danger and keep safe. If a saber-toothed tiger were lurking in the bushes and ready to pounce on you, your stress response was what stopped you from approaching it with a smile, saying, "Aww, cute kitty." Instead, stress would have set off your fight-or-flight response, which made you run for your life or attack to save it.

Those split-second responses were, and still are, the result of a highly orchestrated set of biological machinery. The amygdala detects the threat and alerts the hypothalamus, which then activates the sympathetic nervous system by sending signals to the adrenal glands, which instantly release the stress hormone cortisol into your bloodstream, acting like the extra octane you need to prime your body to do whatever it must to deal with the present danger.

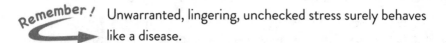 Unwarranted, lingering, unchecked stress surely behaves like a disease.

But it is not a disease without a cure.

Our genetic makeup hasn't changed much since the era when we lived in caves. Our world has become a lot safer; yet our minds perceive more of what surrounds us as dangerous. As we hunt for jobs, social media likes, material possessions, or a suitable mate instead of hunting for the calories that support our daily diets. As we commute through airports or busy streets to find coffee and movie theaters instead of warmth and shelter. As we plan for retirement, redundancy, and the weekend party instead of storing food for the upcoming winter, the stress keeps mounting until it all becomes too much. So how do we respond? We learn to become . . .

COMFORTABLY NUMB

Stress is pervasive in our lives, spreading exponentially as we stress *one another* out, and yet, we rarely even acknowledge it as such. Many of us hide it, and many even wear it as a badge of honor. To say how stressed out one is has become the shorthand way of saying, "I'm needed. I'm wanted. I'm invited. I'm important." We stay alive while it slowly kills our ability to feel joy. We learn to disguise our stress. We try to ignore it, to brush it off and carry on. With time, it grows into a monster, which makes us even more afraid to face it. So we hide our heads even deeper in the sand and pretend that nothing is wrong at all. We learn to accept feeling stressed as normal. We learn to accept feeling tired, even exhausted. We learn to settle for a life lacking in passion and excitement. Somehow we believe that if we've managed to live with it so far, then we can live with it a bit longer.

If it's not *fully* broken, don't fix it, we reason.

It's ridiculous, if you think about it. It's like being at the top of a high-rise building during a serious earthquake but refusing to leave until you see the concrete cracking.

Remember ! Society's collective stress is vigorously spreading, but our acknowledgment of its magnitude is steadily dimming.

Pink Floyd, in what I—Mo here—consider the best song ever written (and surely one of the best guitar solos of all time), brilliantly described how we numb our emotions and constantly try to ease the pain just to get on our feet again and keep walking through the show of life. Despite the pain, the song imagines a doctor's visit where an injection is prescribed to remove all the stresses of life. *Can you stand up? I do believe it's working, good. That'll keep you going through the show. Come on, it's time to go,* the doctor says.

It's all a scam. It's time for you, and everyone, to sing it out to the top of our lungs. This stressed-wreck version of me is not how I am.

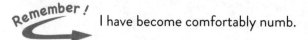 **Remember!**   I have become comfortably numb.

Alice and I decided to write this book because we firmly believe that the damage stress causes is preventable. One reason we believe is because we've both experienced it ourselves, and as we found our paths to a calmer life, we felt the urge to share and benefit others.

Our stress responses are so predictable, they can fit into mathematical equations. Anxiety is a programmed response. The point at which we reach burnout and fatigue can be predicted with as much accuracy as the physics that help us build resilient machines. I use those equations, in a simplified form, to help you redesign yourself as that resilient machine that you have the potential to become.

The equations will show that stress is not just the result of the circumstances of your life, at least not entirely. The stress you experience has a lot to do with the abilities, skills, and resources you have at your disposal to handle the challenges you face. It's something like the way an obstacle course of many challenges feels easy to a trained athlete who practices regularly, while a walk in the park might feel hard for someone who is not in shape.

Worry, fear, panic, and anxiety too can be studied algorithmically. When we understand the parameters that magnify them, we learn how to address them.

To understand burnout, we will explore a concept known in physics as *fatigue*—the reason why most objects eventually break not when subjected to a powerful force but to an insignificant one repeatedly. It may sound odd, but there is a lot to be gained from looking at stress in humans similarly to how we study it in physics.

Stress, biologically, too can be described as a predictable machine. It can be viewed as a factory process. Our biological machines control us by pumping chemicals through our bodies. Those drive us to take certain actions that are beneficial for our survival and performance in critical situations. Once a challenge is addressed, the chemicals are supposed to dissipate, switching the stress machine off so that you can return to a normal, healthy life. Sometimes the machine gets clogged and requires maintenance. Like good mechanics, we intend to show you what clogs the machine and prevents it from performing as intended and introduce you to healthy habits that will keep it in good working order thereafter.

Remember!   Stress, being predictable, is also mostly preventable.

Yes, it's preventable, not just *manageable*. If you know what you're doing, you won't even need to suffer from stress in the first place. This may make you grind your teeth a little (a typical stress response), because this is a big expectation. But we will get you there with one simple model and one (rather intensive) language course.

We will call the model *the three Ls*—limit, learn, and listen. Limiting the stressors that you let into your life is easier than you think. It's a bit like driving your precious car carefully so that it stays in good shape and continues to take you where you need to go. Learning is the process of preventive maintenance. It's all about learning the habits that you need to increase your ability and resources when it comes to dealing with the stress that you cannot limit. Finally, listening is just that—to keep observing the signs so that you know when something is about to go wrong or when the signs are telling you to do something differently. You would do that with a precious car and stop to take care of it when you heard an unexpected rattle.

To listen attentively, you will need to learn four new languages that correspond to the different ways in which stress affects us. You can feel stressed **mentally, emotionally, physically, or spiritually.** Based on the gate through which stress grabs hold of you, the signs will differ, and how you need to deal with it will differ.

Mental stress is triggered by your thoughts. It happens in your brain, which speaks to you constantly but never, ever tells you the truth. Emotional stress lives in your heart, which speaks in subtle, blended ways that need your complete attention to decipher. Physical stress is felt in the body. The language it speaks is aches and pains that turn into illnesses when ignored. Finally, spiritual stress can only be sensed by your intuition and cured by the balance you need to seek between your true purpose and actual existence.

Ignore the language of stress and it will fester. It will grow to take hold of you and all that you hold dear.

BECOMING AWARE, COMMITTED, KNOWLEDGEABLE, AND SKILLED

The reason our modern world is so stressful is not because of the challenges it presents. Any which way you look at it, our lives today surely present fewer threats to any of us than the lives of our ancestors or even grandparents not too long ago. The reason we are so stressed is because we let our stress fester, accepting and even wearing it as a badge of honor to signify our importance and success in a world that only celebrates those who do, earn, and "influence."

Stress is our new addiction. One has to wonder why we are so obsessed with being "busy," instead of being obsessed with feeling amazing.

The reason is four gaps between the joyful state of being calm and the painful state of being stressed. This gap is made up of awareness of the stressors within oneself as well as the environment we inhabit, commitment to change, knowledge of what is needed to live a stress-free life, and the practice needed to build new habits and solid skills.

Let's start with the first gap: awareness. Please take a couple of minutes now to write a short list of what is currently stressing you. There must be a few reasons why you picked up this book—challenges at work, relationship issues, a pain in the back, a feeling of loss, or the constant demands of life. Whatever it is, write it down. We will call this list your Stress Inventory, and we'll use it to reflect on later in the book.

Be honest with yourself. Unless you know what's wrong, there is nothing you can do to make things better.

But awareness is not enough. There is no way you will feel better until you choose to bridge the second gap: commitment.

No one wakes up in the morning thinking, *I know how I want to feel today—STRESSED!*

The problem is, however, very few of us wake up thinking the opposite. When was the last time you woke up thinking, *It is my highest priority to feel calm all day today.*

It is this kind of commitment to doing what it takes to remove the stressors from your life through regular practice, to find a path to a calmer life, that changes everything. I can tell you right here and right now that making fitness your priority and working out four or five times a week will make you fit. If you're an able-bodied individual, I guarantee it. Only when you actually make fitness your priority do you choose to skip that brownie and only when you show up at the gym will you ever start to see results.

Make that promise. Right here, right now. It is worth your commitment.

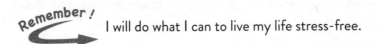 **Remember!** I will do what I can to live my life stress-free.

Living unstressable, however, takes one more ingredient beyond awareness and commitment. It takes knowledge and skill. Just look back at things that stressed you just a few years ago, that you *now* know how to handle with ease, to remind yourself of the value that your skills and experience bring to reduce your state of stress.

Knowing something is useless until you know how to apply the knowledge practically. You could read a hundred books about how to ride a bicycle, but you will not get a single step closer to learning until you put your foot on the pedals and give it a try.

This is not a five-magic-tips-to-end-stress kind of self-help book. This is a book for someone who is able to understand what needs to change and commit the time to practice making that change. If you find yourself thinking, *But I'm busy,* remind yourself of the truth. No one truly is that busy. We just like to be seen as busy because it makes us feel important. If your favorite band showed up in town tomorrow, you would make the time to go to the concert. Make the time to save your own life. You can transform yourself in as little as five to twenty minutes a day. You are likely wasting more time feeling stressed every day.

UNSTRESSABLE.COM

To help you maximize your learning from this book, we're happy to offer you a discount of fifteen dollars on the cost of the first month of subscription to our exclusive community at Unstressable.com. This discount will hopefully amount, more or less, to what you paid for this book (which varies depending on which country you bought the book in). As part of the Unstressable.com community, you will learn about the concepts of this book in video training form as we hold your hand through the practice and reflection exercises one by one. It also gives you access to our community of members, who are committed to living unstressable. There you can meet like-minded people, create a support network, and share your progress and challenges while you learn. As a member, you can also join our monthly live webinars where you can ask your questions directly to us and get inspired by the stories of other members.

Use the gift code IAMUNSTRESSABLE as you register. You can cancel anytime if you so choose, though we would love for you to stay and be part of our family.

Take a minute to do this now before you read further.

MORE CONTENT ON SOCIAL MEDIA

While you're at it, please take a moment to follow us and the official *Unstressable* accounts on social media. There we will be posting regular tips and advice to keep you on track with your lifestyle change as you become unstressable. Follow Mo @mo_gawdat on Instagram or @MoGawdat on LinkedIn. Follow Alice @alicelaw._ on Instagram or @unstressable_alice on TikTok. Unstressable itself is @unstressable.official on Instagram and www.linkedin.com/company/unstressable/ on LinkedIn. We look forward to seeing you there.

THE WAY THIS WILL WORK

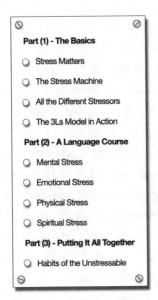

Part (1) - The Basics

○ Stress Matters

○ The Stress Machine

○ All the Different Stressors

○ The 3Ls Model in Action

Part (2) - A Language Course

○ Mental Stress

○ Emotional Stress

○ Physical Stress

○ Spiritual Stress

Part (3) - Putting It All Together

○ Habits of the Unstressable

Our intent with *Unstressable* is to give you a comprehensive model to surround the topic of stress from every relevant direction. The book will be split into three parts. This is part I—the basics, where we have already covered why this topic matters. In the next chapter, chapter 2, we will discuss the actual machinery that causes us stress—first the biology, then the physics. In chapter 3, we will cover all the different types of stressors—a concept we call a TONN (trauma, obsessions, noise, and nuisances) of stress.

In part II of this book, you will start your stress language course. We will take you through the four languages in which stress speaks. We will start with a quick survey to help you take stock of how stressed you actually are and which of the corners of your stress are leading. Then we will flow through the languages: mental stress in chapter 4, emotional stress in chapter 5, physical stress in chapter 6, and spiritual stress in chapter 7.

Finally, we will bring it all together in part III, chapter 8, with a summary of the habits of the unstressable among us.

This is not a quick read. It is the kind of handbook that is intended to give you every tool you need for the task at hand—becoming unstressable.

Before we take the stress machine apart, I think there is one more small thing to cover. I feel we may have not been properly introduced, so allow us just a few more pages to tell you about Alice and myself—our qualifications and why we chose to write this book. If you are already familiar with our work, please feel free to skip directly to chapter 2.

Otherwise, we're pleased to meet you. Here are a few lines about who we are.

THE MODERN-DAY PROFESSIONAL

I'm no stranger to stress (it's Mo here, by the way). As a matter of fact, I am the ultimate example of that naive, wild racing driver that threw himself in the race. I remember vividly how it all started with falling in love.

As a young man, though I graduated with honors as an engineer, I wanted to be a carpenter. I wanted to spend my mornings in peace, building beautiful things, and I did. I started a small workshop and made a bit of money, but then came a day when, like all the rest of us, I needed to grow up.

I wanted to start a family with my college sweetheart, Nibal. In Egypt, where we lived at the time, this meant that I needed to ask her father for her hand in marriage—a rigorous *interview* process for which a carpenter who's living for his art, surely, was not going to cut it. I needed a real job, and with a bit of luck, I got much more than just any job. I was hired at IBM, which at the time was, by far, the leading tech company in Egypt. This came with good pay, a prestigious title, and a lot of work and stress. But it was all worth it. I got the prize. Her dad approved.

Nibal is a very, very wise woman. She instinctively understood that my hard work enabled us to build a life for ourselves and our future family, and yet she not only encouraged me to slow down to limit my stress, she also did what she could to wipe my stress away. She flooded me with love, created wonderful experiences on the weekends, kept us close to our friends, and planned fun times and vacation. Because of her, we lived a wonderful life with barely any noticeable stress until that all changed.

It was the first time I laid eyes on the face of my wonderful son, Ali. I was in the delivery room when Nibal gave birth, holding her hand when the doctor held up this crumpled little pruny thing, and my heart skipped a beat. I was overwhelmed with love, and like many other responsible fathers, I instantly committed to dedicating the rest of my life to providing for his every need.

I'm sure you can guess where the story went from there. I worked harder and harder to make more money, but still attempted to stay sane until the day when it was time to send my wonderful daughter, Aya, who joined us the following year, to kindergarten. I could afford to send Ali to one of the best in town, but my income then was not enough to send them both there. That was when I willingly agreed to sacrifice myself for them. I stopped taking care of myself and worked every possible hour to earn more. I gained fifty pounds, stopped working out, felt aches and pains all over my body, and suffered persistent headaches that often lasted for weeks on end. I had moved away from being the happy artist that I once was to become the typical example of a stressed modern-day professional.

Things were not any easier for Nibal either. She, now a mother of two, was navigating a new environment where everything was alien and more expensive, with no friends and no family to rely on and with a husband who was stressed, unavailable, and unhealthy, let alone grumpy. She had given up her career to focus on the kids and had to be a true superwoman to keep the complex project we call family on track, and keep the children shielded and happy while everything around them was becoming tense and difficult. As I look back at my life then and how frequently I snapped, I can surely say that this was the most stressed I have ever been. I was a disaster waiting to happen.

Sound familiar?

I will never forget that day. Aya must have been five. It was a Saturday, and Nibal had planned a fun day for us as a family. When Aya woke up, she could not contain her excitement. She was literally jumping up and down as she described the day ahead—"Papa, we're going to the yummy pancake place, and then we will go to the kids' park and then to Toys 'R' Us. Can we please buy Coke and popcorn before we go to the movies?" I, on the other hand, was anxiously reading a work email, feeling more and more irritated with her interruption until I responded in an angry voice and said, "Can we *please* be serious for a minute here?"

Serious? What serious? She was *five*!

And, of course, she reacted as a five-year-old would. Tears poured from her beautiful little eyes as I witnessed with my grumpy gaze the heart of my daughter breaking. That was my wake-up call.

That day, I realized what I had become. I could no longer live with that version of me. That day, I started a journey that got me back to my old happy self until, as many of my readers know, life took me through the ultimate test.

On July 1, 2014, my wonderful son, Ali, left our world due to a medical error during the simplest of all surgical operations. It was sudden and preventable, a devastating tragedy that can break down any loving father, but my response was as unexpected as the loss.

Seventeen days after Ali left us, I started to write *Solve for Happy*— which was published in thirty-two languages, sold hundreds of thousands of copies, and became an international bestseller—and assigned myself a mission—OneBillionHappy, which aims to deliver Ali's message of happiness to a billion people and which has already reached and affected tens of millions around the globe.

I left my job as chief business officer of Google X, wrote two more books—*Scary Smart* and *That Little Voice in Your Head*, which topped charts and got international recognition—and launched my chart-topping podcast *Slo Mo* to invite listeners to slow down and disconnect from our stressful world as they listen and learn about happiness from some of the wisest teachers in the world for free. I chose to dedicate the rest of my life to the mission until I join Ali wherever he is right now.

As soon as I committed, I started to recognize the fierce warrior I had always been against unhappiness, depression, anxiety, burnout. Like most of my readers, listeners, and followers, I believed that my journey to being happier started with breaking Aya's heart and that my commitment to the mission started with Ali's departure. It wasn't until Alice asked me to write about stress that I remembered a deep, older wound. It goes back to the only person I remember to have loved as much as I did my ex-wife and kids—my father.

My dad, also named Ali, was a brilliant engineer and, unlike the typical Middle Eastern man of his generation, a bundle of love. Throughout his career, he became a very distinguished engineer in our home country, Egypt, because he led the development of the road and bridge network that became the country's main economic backbone of the time. He was straight as an arrow, and he fought corruption, which was rampant in the industry when he started, which benefited the country in very visible ways. Later in his career, however, organizational politics led by those who benefited from a corrupt environment forced him to step aside and away from his leadership role. That single moment devastated him. He felt helpless and unjustly treated, and as a result, he fell into deep depression. He spent the last few years of his life in his living room's chair with his face in his palms, obsessively thinking about what came to be.

I loved my dad dearly, and as I often sat in the chair opposite him silently, it hurt me to witness his pain. He was no longer the happy, full-of-life role model I had grown up knowing. My dad faded away, day by day, as I sat there trying, and failing, to bring him back.

On the last day of March 1991, as I was leaving home to pick up my brother from the airport, he insisted on joining me. That was very unlike him, as he didn't really like busy, crowded, messy places. I, of course, jumped on the opportunity to take him out of the darkness of that living room. I spent the whole time on the drive to the airport and as we sat waiting for my brother to arrive entertaining him with stories. He did not speak a word back. Instead, he sat there in silence as if he were waiting for something. When my brother showed up, he stood up and hugged him. Then he said, "That's it; we're done. I'm ready to go home."

Those were his very last words. I didn't know back then that he meant another home away from the pain of depression he had suffered for so long. As I drove back, my brother and I caught up and laughed about a hundred little stories, but Dad did not speak a word. When we arrived home, he went straight to his living room chair and sat down as if he were calmly waiting for something. When my eldest brother walked in with his family, Dad hugged and kissed every one of them. As they left the room to say hi to Mom, he lay on the floor with a sense of calm I had not seen on his face for so long. I didn't comment. I thought he was stretching his back, but then a minute later, he suffered a heart attack. He looked into my eyes while I held him in my arms, and he quietly left our world.

I spent the whole night in his room reflecting. I didn't know if I should feel sad to lose him or happy to see him free of the stress and depression that consumed him. In the following weeks, I went back to my usual routine, not knowing the gravity that his departure had had on my life. Recently, I realized that over the years I'd spent next to him in his depressed state, I had subconsciously made up my mind who the real enemy of humanity was. I marked the enemy as the stress that cost my dad his happiness and the depression that took him away from me.

Stress is the enemy. If I had the means, I promised myself, I would do what I could to make sure no one ever suffered what my dad had to suffer. My mission, OneBillionHappy, was set in motion then—the day my dad left our world. I put in the work to qualify for it when I broke Aya's heart and was triggered, more than twenty years later by my son's departure, to leave everything else behind and make the mission real.

Now, let me hand the keyboard over to another fierce warrior against stress—Alice.

NO PARTIES IN MY TWENTIES

I was lucky to be brought up in a family where my parents were together and happy. My dad was an entrepreneur who had built successful businesses in property development and renewable energy. He worked hard but always made sure he was also around to give us the proper attention and love a child deserves. My mum is as kind and caring as a mum could possibly be. She dedicated her time to us fully, and as such, growing up, I felt safe, cared for, and very loved. Even when my dad got diagnosed with kidney cancer—I was three then—my parents covered it up so well that neither I nor my sister, Georgina, had a clue what was going on.

Life until nineteen years old was easygoing and trouble-free, mostly, but then it was time for another plan.

After the credit crunch of 2008, my father, like many with money tied up in investments, grew concerned about his business and his family's financial future. Typical of my amazing dad, he felt he needed to solve it all by himself and carry the burden alone, so we rarely felt any issues at all. But I could sense a different energy. It was the first time I had encountered real worry and stress, even suffering, despite him changing the topic when we asked. We were slowly losing our security, the first of a long line of stressors that flooded my way.

He gradually became unlike the dad I was used to. He started drinking more, and he was laughing less. He was losing his lightness and joy of life.

Not long after, my dad was forced to put the company he had spent years building up into receivership or face bankruptcy.

On top of the work pressure that the company administration process demanded, my dad's mental health was suffering—the irrational shame, grief, and worry that came into play were eating at him from the inside. Having been brought up in a time where "men provide," his very identity was shattered, and I was starting to lose the dad I knew.

Heartbreakingly, he was forced to sell personal assets, including our family home, which I had known my whole life. Life was tense, but it was about to get a lot worse.

One evening out of nowhere, we got the worrying news that Suzanne, my eldest half sister, whom I loved very much, was diagnosed with cancer. An amazing woman, a loving mother, and an entrepreneur herself, Suzanne found her life instantly changed and, with it, my dad's deepest trauma was triggered. It wasn't just that he feared losing his eldest child; my dad knew cancer all too well, having lost his own twin sister to cancer at the exact same age as Suzanne was then, and coincidentally a mother to children of the same age too. Having struggled with cancer himself, it seemed all too real. We could see this deep worry for his daughter, as well as the stress of his company and financial concerns, was all starting to wear him down. As it was to us all.

Suzanne recovered, giving us some hope that the tide would turn, but the cancer returned and we watched her suffer bravely through different treatments. Her relentless strength overrode her cancer once again, and she was back in the first stages of being all clear. Relief had flooded over us all until, out of nowhere, what was meant to be a weekend of family celebration at her home turned into a new nightmare.

I was driving to her house from London when she rang me and asked if I could pick up our dad from the village pub on the way in. I merrily walked in to find my dad sitting quietly, having a drink with a family friend. I smiled and walked to hug him, but something was clearly off. I sat down in my blissful ignorance as my dad looked down momentarily when I asked merrily, "How's Suzanne?," while our friend Nick replied to me, "Oh God! Has no one told you?"

My body froze, and I was instantly filled with that feeling of nausea, looking at my dad's face for an answer as he quietly replied, looking down at the floor, "Suzanne wants to tell you herself."

I later listened to Suzanne in disbelief as she told me her cancer had not only come back but that the doctors had now said it was terminal. *This must be a joke*, I thought. *How can someone be clear one moment and terminal the next?* We were not only losing her, but by now, I was starting to lose faith in life itself.

Then, in my early twenties, I dreaded looking at my phone because I feared more bad news from my family. I was consumed by hidden anxiety. At work, I would spend my days distracted, worrying about my father's mounting depression and his escape to drinking, worrying about my sister's pain, sensing the suffering of my mum trying to hold everything together for my dad, worrying about finances and the sale of our home. Worrying about my entire family. I was clearly not doing the best I could at my job, but I still did okay. As the double assistant for the MDs, it was quite literally my job to remember things for someone else, and my suffering memory and focus surely added more stress.

Then there was the social pressure. When I met friends, I was smiling on the outside, while dying on the inside. I would be totally in my mind as they chatted about normal, silly, twentysomething post-university concerns. Which made me feel totally disconnected and alone. Just one more weight to add to my mounting stress.

To make the suffering complete, my then long-term boyfriend had moved to Singapore. Because I couldn't deal with having to process anything else at the time, I hadn't ended the relationship before he left. Even though I knew in my heart that we were no longer meant to be together, I held on to the relationship at this point out of fear and desperation to keep just *one* thing in my life feeling comfortable and familiar. I attempted a long-distance relationship that was, clearly, not working, gradually dwindling away, and causing me even more stress from the unknown date of his return. My efforts went unrewarded and eventually ended in a broken relationship, only a few months after we devastatingly lost Suzanne. Shattering her own family, her husband and two children, and the extended one of our own.

It was in the height of my dad's pain of knowing he was about to lose his eldest child that a lawsuit was filed against him by people we had once considered family, for a loss on investment from years and years before. They wrongfully went after him at the most horrific time of his whole life, breaking what was left of his already crushed spirit.

He didn't have the mind, or the financial ability now, to hire the best lawyers, or the piece of evidence he needed at the time to prove his innocence (which was only found in his final hour), and the looming legal battle dragged on and on, draining his finances while the mounting depression drowned him deep into more drinking to try to numb his pain.

I was devastated to watch my dad disappear in front of me. I felt so alone. I was worried, grieving, and in a constant state of anxiety. I had lost faith in the life I once knew, and then came the final straw.

We had returned home just a few days after Suzanne's funeral when we had to call an ambulance to rush my dad to the hospital, where they found a blood clot in his leg. The blood clot was resolved, but having taken a full scan of his body, the doctors also found that his cancer had returned, this time in both his pancreas and his lung.

By this point, it was clear that he had given up. He refused to treat his cancer and had no interest in spending any more time in hospitals. So, there I was again, now watching my father, my hero and best friend, not even wanting to fight as he faded away. I, on the other hand, refused to surrender.

I tried to demand answers and a decisive plan, but he would simply brush off my questions, changing the topic. He had made up his own mind already. He had decided he wanted out.

Loss, in all its varieties, by this point was becoming more prevalent in my life than life itself, and then there was my loss of control. I was trying to design an outcome that wasn't mine to create and imagining the worst, because blow after blow, I was now conditioned to believe that life will keep failing you. I had lost all sense of faith. With no more hope, my stress and anxiety had reached their peak.

Soon, my body started to wear down and add its own physical stress to my long list. I developed a severe case of irritable bowel syndrome with symptoms so bad that doctors feared that I too might have colon cancer. The pending unknown for my own health naturally reinforced the cycle, causing me even more stress. And to add a *few* more things, my latest romantic relationship had suddenly ended, leaving me heartbroken at the same time my company needed to leave the UK market, so I was made redundant and lost the last bit of stability and routine my job and the people I worked with every day, whom I loved, provided.

It was my rock bottom. All my old emotions that I hadn't dealt with from all this loss and stress were trying desperately to come to the surface. So what did my twenty-some-year-old self do? Numbed the pain with as much distraction as I could find. Went to as many parties as my friendship group were having. Numbed it out with alcohol and drugs. While so many people I knew at the time were doing it for fun, I was doing it out of fear. The fear of feeling.

I was sliding down the playbook of stress, not skipping a single detail. Loss of loved ones, loss of control, financial challenges, heartbreak, losing my home, being jobless, incomeless, worrying, anxiety, insomnia, physical pains, illness, fatigue, unable to focus, distractions, alcohol, and drugs. You name it, I was there. My whole world felt like it was crashing down around me, while on the outside, I appeared "fine."

I don't blame you if you're thinking, *What can someone so lost teach me today?* Well, I can surely tell you what stress is like, in almost every one of its different variants, but I can also tell you how to leave it all behind.

It didn't take a genius to realize that something needed to change and that life was not going to help—at least that didn't seem like its intention at the time. It was time for me to revert to reality, painful as it was. I couldn't bring Suzanne back, I couldn't help my family's financial situation, I didn't have the resources to stop the sale of our home, I couldn't make my dad's lawsuit go away, I couldn't make him happy or get him to accept treatment or even to stop drinking, no matter how hard I tried. I couldn't wish my most recent relationship back, bring my job back, or magically wish my dad's cancer away.

I couldn't do anything about the outside stressors in my life—but what I could do something about was me. The one thing I could change was how I dealt with the stress life threw my way. The one thing I could choose was my response. So I had made it my mission gradually over this period of time to learn how to do just that.

I was reading everything I could find about stress. I watched and listened to every documentary, podcast, or YouTube video. I went to talks. I submerged myself in research from the moment I woke up until I was in my bed at night. Every time my bosses were out for lunch, I hit the computer or read under my desk.

There must be hundreds of different approaches to attacking stress and anxiety, from the spiritual to the scientific, from the mind to the soul, the physical body to our energetic forms, from the logical to the holistic, from our thoughts to our emotions. I researched them all.

I practiced what I was told, trying out different things and testing what worked for me. Slowly, I moved from being constantly anxious, fearful, overwhelmed, and sad to becoming more like the calm, happy person I had been growing up. The person I naturally am came back to life.

Just by putting in the effort, doing the work, I began to recover. Nothing was changing in my external environment, and yet, what I was learning was allowing me to not just stay afloat above the stress but to start to enjoy living again.

Being redundant became a gift in disguise. I was being guided by life, the life I thought was against me, to my next step—the work I now do. With the support of my former employers, I set up my business.

Noticing the paradox of how I felt, despite the lingering challenges in my life, I made the commitment to help others feel the same. I started to move to formal learning and trained in some of the different modalities of stress management that I knew from my own experience worked. Mindfulness, EFT, Reiki, meditation, and eventually Akashic healing. I studied spirituality, read the traditional texts and more modern books. I went to study kabbalah and chatted about Buddhism, Sufism, and other faiths with everyone that offered to teach me. I took keen interest in learning about psychology, coaching, neuroscience, and worked with a great coach myself. And yes, I even read books written by an engineer about the topic of happiness—I mean Mo.

When I felt I was ready, I allowed myself to learn by teaching. From this combination of a deep life experience, training, and an ever-evolving learning, I designed programs for my expanding client base that were focused specifically around stress and anxiety, which allowed me to consult for some of the most stressed-out executives and speak to groups at large corporations. The variety of our human experience expanded my horizons even more.

I guess I was being trained for the ultimate test. This test came when out of the blue, my mum messaged my sister and me to say, "On the way to hospital with Dad, ambulance here. But don't panic, I will call you later. Love you lots. Mum."

Despite what she was saying, something inside me said, *You need to go up to see him right now.* So, I got on a train and went straight to the hospital. My dad looked every bit as exhausted and frail as I had feared. I knew it was probably time, but somehow I remained calm.

I did what I could to make sure the doctors and nurses were fighting for him as much as we were in the weeks he was hospitalized. Bad medical mistakes were made, and my mother, sister Georgina, and I spent all our energy on just trying to make sure the right things were being done for him at the right time, while staying positive for him. Still, nothing had been solved, and he continued to deteriorate. It was only after he had a sudden cardiac arrest in the hospital that doctors eventually found the answer, while he was now fighting for his life in the ICU: a large stomach ulcer had burst, causing severe complications. His sudden departure a week or so later, after finally spending one night at home under palliative care, was the result of this ulcer and the cardiac arrest it had caused—the result of stress, the silent killer that took him from us in the end.

Like Mo's dad, my father had suffered a health complication due to stress. Mo suffered the stress of surprise and confusion that results from sudden loss, while I suffered the prolonged exposure to adversity. We came to the same conclusion, the same mission, through different paths.

At that moment, I made my choice, consciously, for what my life was going to be about as I stood next to my father's body in the funeral chapel. He looked more peaceful than I had seen him in over eight years. In that moment, I knew my mission was to try to help as many people as I could find that peace while fully alive.

I promised to make the chronic stress that took my father away, both mentally and physically, my nemesis. I committed to sharing all that I learned through my harsher experiences with illness, love, loss, grief, and need, and how I found my own path back to being calm. This book is part of my effort to fulfill this promise.

While all the work I do will not give me back the years I lost with my dad, it makes me feel that I'm helping others that are suffering like he did. As he struggled with his own stress, grief, and gradual depression, no matter how much I tried, I was not able to help. Now, when someone comes to me, I feel that I am helping to guide someone else's dad or loved one to saving themselves. It fills me with happiness to know the effect this has not just on an individual but on their family, even if I couldn't pull my own father back to being his true self.

As I look back at that time of suffering now, I feel grateful. Yes, grateful that I embarked on learning what I now teach—that not only did it bring me back to myself, it also saved my relationship with my dad in the last couple of years of his life. As I became more aware, I stopped trying to control his health decisions, and I tried to enjoy the time I had left with him in the best ways I could, as he was. I feel grateful that what I experienced, not just what I know, is what gives me the right to tell those that struggle that there is another way.

If I could renew my own life in my twenties, then no matter what you are going through right now, you absolutely can do it too. You just simply need to understand how.

So, let's begin the work to make you unstressable. Back to you, Mo.

Part I

The Basics

To fix a machine, you have to understand how it works, what makes it break, what you input into it, and what the resulting outputs are likely going to be for every mode of its operation. To make it unbreakable, you need to learn every detail of its preventative maintenance and service process.

Stress is a highly predictable machine that is intended for a purpose.

Run it well and it will serve you. Let it run wild and it will break you down.

1

Welcome to the Machine

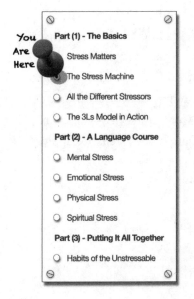

You Are Here

Have you ever imagined an easy-flowing and stress-free life? Can you remember a time when you lived that way? When things were not too complicated? There were not too many commitments to clutter your day, and when things became a little challenging, you rose to the occasion and handled them with ease? Is it even possible to live predominantly stress-free?

Well, this book claims that it is—that it is easy to achieve and that it is your absolute duty to make that a reality. Stress, as a cycle, is not difficult to understand, and when you get how it works, it's not difficult to avoid and suspend. A bit of stress is needed to keep us safe and help us reach peak performance, but to be stressed all the time is not how things are supposed to be.

Our machines seem to be broken. We need to get them into the workshop and fix them. But before we do, like any good engineer would, we need to grasp the very details of how the machines work in the first place.

BIOLOGY, CHEMISTRY, AND NEUROSCIENCE

Feeling stressed is the product of a very complex process that happens across the nervous and endocrine systems of your body. Complex but highly predictable, as in it happens exactly the same way every single time you or I have ever felt stressed. That feeling we've become accustomed to in the modern world requires a highly synchronized interaction between biology, chemistry, and neuroscience for you to feel it. Several parts of your brain and nervous system work in tandem with your glands to get you there. Like with the turbocharger on a sports car engine, when mixing the fuel with oxygen in different ratios, a normal engine turns into a beast of a machine. Similarly, when you're stressed, you're a totally reconfigured machine, different from your normal self.

There's been a bit of a debate across the scientific establishment for years around where stress originates. While the traditional view seems to imply that thoughts in your rational brain trigger your stress, lots of recent research points to the opposite—that your stress is triggered first, and then the emotions and physical sensations resulting from stress prompt your rational brain to think. Those thoughts would then help you calm down or boost you to become more stressed. I guess both scenarios apply depending on what stresses you. Let me explain.

FEELING STRESSED

Stress is an automatic response. Your stress starts with a trigger. An event that seems like a possible threat takes place.

The event stressing you is not even recognized by your thinking brain. For example, when that friend you never really liked sneaks up behind you and shouts, "Boo!" As he stands there laughing, you jump out of your skin, your heart beating fast, and you feel a version of the stress that you would feel if you were up against a saber-toothed tiger. In a fraction of a second, you feel the stress first, and then you think about it later. What engages instantly, in those cases, is one side of your *autonomic nervous system* (which, as the name implies, is responsible for automatic functionalities of your body, such as keeping your heart beating without you thinking about it). The side of this system that engages is normally referred to as the *sympathetic nervous system*, which is activated upon recognizing threatening events that demand a fight, flight, or freeze response. Your survival instinct does not have time to analyze what that apparent threat is all about. It reacts first to sound the alarm.

The security guard in charge of sounding the alarm is the amygdala. Located at the very bottom of your brain right before your brain stem, thus in the best possible position to communicate with the rest of your body, the amygdala truly can be considered the paranoid part of you. It's constantly on the lookout for things it needs to protect you against (it also is responsible for feelings of pleasure when life is good, but we're not going to discuss those today—just stress for now).

When the amygdala is engaged, emotion is in full swing, and that's when the electrical signals passing through your nervous system hand over to the chemical side of your body. A highly synchronized trio, normally referred to as the *HPA axis*, takes over. The HPA includes a group of hormone-secreting glands—namely, the hypothalamus, pituitary gland, and adrenal glands.

Stressful emotions, felt by the amygdala, trigger the hypothalamus to release a hormone called *CRH*—or corticotropin-releasing hormone—which, in turn, signals the pituitary gland to secrete a hormone called *ACTH*—adrenocorticotropic hormone—into the bloodstream. The news carried by ACTH travels fast across the bloodstream to prompt the adrenal gland to release the infamous hormone called *cortisol*. Now it's official. You are stressed.

Cortisol is a crucial hormone that protects overall health and well-being. Because most cells have cortisol receptors, it affects many different functions in the body. Cortisol helps control blood sugar levels, regulate metabolism, reduce inflammation, and assist with memory formulation. It balances the ratios of salt and water and helps regulates blood pressure. Cortisol also supports the developing fetus during pregnancy.

That's in normal, easy times. During moments of stress, however, cortisol serves one primary function—to get you out of trouble. To do this, it needs to direct energy to your brain, so you can think of a way out, and to your muscles, so you're ready to run or fight if needed. The food your brain prefers to burn for energy is glucose. Cortisol's clear instructions in moments of stress are for the fat cells to release fat into the bloodstream, and for the liver to release glucose. It tells the muscles to burn only fat so that all the sugar remaining in the bloodstream is available for the brain to burn. The result? A turbocharger that leads superpowered feats—all the energy and focus you need to get things done, save your life as you need to, then come back to your normal self.

This kind of reaction to the stress you felt is good (we call this *eustress*). It keeps you safe and enhances your abilities. It gives you what you need to overcome the challenge.

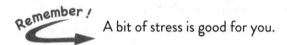 A bit of stress is good for you.

Now we understand the biological cycle that triggers stress. A perceived threat. The amygdala panics. The hypothalamus orders the pituitary gland to sound the alarm. The signal is carried by the bloodstream to the adrenal glands, which release the booster that you need: cortisol, along with other stress hormones, such as adrenaline and norepinephrine. This enables you to perform the superhuman miracles you need to survive or overcome adversity. But this is not where the cycle ends.

Once the stress has served its purpose, your body actively regulates so that you get back to normal. What ends the stress? Well, that's another cycle that is normally referred to as the . . .

NEGATIVE FEEDBACK LOOP

Your human machine is designed to deal with stress as a disruption to its normal chill self. It understands that stress is not supposed to last indefinitely. When cortisol levels in the blood are high, the receptors back in the hypothalamus and the hippocampus sense cortisol's presence, so they keep looking for threats. If they find any, they reinforce the cycle so you stay at your peak abilities, then scan the environment again. Eventually, when they don't find any threats, in the absence of a lasting reason for concern, they recognize the discrepancy between the state of your body— stressed—and the reality of the situation—safe—and shut off the stress response to bring you back to normal. The booster is removed from your bloodstream, and you're back to the calm version of you. Simple, really.

Put together, the stress cycle and the negative feedback cycle form a full trip down the stress lane that looks something like this:

WHAT IS STRESS?

The term *stress* has had many negative connotations attached to it in our modern culture. This is a natural response to stories like mine and Alice's as we each watched our fathers being consumed by stress, then dying from illnesses that resulted from it. Everyone knows at least one person who has gone down that path. Stress does not have to be negative. It can be good for you.

At the very top level, stress in humans is just another survival mechanism. It's the turbocharger, the high-octane fuel, that provides you with

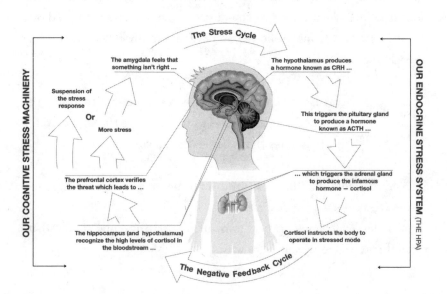

the boost you need to survive challenging situations. When it works well, it's awesome to be stressed. Like those days before a big proposal when you got together with your team at work and pulled an all-nighter, working hard, laughing, and feeling the camaraderie, or that day when you intended to ask her to marry you. Stressful? Yes! But enjoyable and rewarding still.

NONSTANDARD OPERATING PROCEDURES

So what turns those pleasant, though stressful, experiences into burnout, depression, and even suicidal thoughts?

As an engineer, I learned that in order to understand a machine fully, I needed to observe its performance in all possible scenarios. I call that a *full-cycle simulation*. A well-designed machine—say, your mobile phone—will perform as expected as long as it's operating within the environment in which it was intended to operate. Put it in extreme heat or extreme cold, or fill its memory with garbage data, and it will end up behaving very differently. It will be our task to identify those odd situations that get our stress machine to malfunction and observe how we behave as a result.

Let's start with an accurate description of the normal working conditions that we have discussed so far—a stress-response cycle triggered by a threat to elicit a response, followed by a negative feedback loop that brings us back to calm.

 Stress is a biological survival response that reconfigures our bodies and enables us to react to situations with the best abilities those bodies are capable of.

Nothing more. Nothing less. In this normal-operating-procedure scenario, stress truly is your best ally.

Now let's talk about other, unnatural operating conditions. That's when things can go wrong. Very wrong!

STARTING WITH A THOUGHT

Our normal stress cycle starts with detecting the possibility of a threat. In the early days of humanity, no one really cared if they had acne on their forehead; that did not count as a threat then. Accordingly, what your stress response system scanned the world for then were physical threats, such as a tiger or a fire. We still experience similar stresses, such as being surprised by an approaching car when crossing the street, or when there is air turbulence during an otherwise comfortable flight. But generally, civilization has managed to reduce physical threats to our survival to a minimum. The way things more often go today is that our . . .

 Modern-day stress often starts with a thought.

This takes place at the very top of what makes our brains human, in the thinking bit of the brain known as the *cortex*. The cortex is where we analyze our life events. For example, the news networks start to cover a violent conflict in a country you have never even heard of before. They discuss the resulting casualties and the expected adverse impact on the economy over there. You listen to all this coverage while in the comfort of your home, no conflict anywhere near you, just around the time your salary hits your bank account. You're not starving, not without shelter, and not in any real threat. You're basically okay, and yet, you start to feel that things are wrong. Not because they are for you specifically but because your thinking plots out all the possible scenarios and recognizes that things could change for you too. You may not be in any immediate danger, but you sure are expecting challenges ahead. Your thinking brain—specifically, the prefrontal cortex—analyzes the situation, but it does not assign an emotion to it. It doesn't tell you how to feel about it. At least not yet.

Feeling stressed about events that have not yet happened or events that are completely outside our domain of influence and control is not part of the standard operating procedure of our stress machine. The biological stress machine is capable of only one form of engagement: boosting your human physical abilities to deal with a physical threat. And while this same machine proved useful when it enabled you to boost your ability to concentrate during the short time available for an exam, it fails when a physical response won't improve the situation. When your stress response is unable to fix the situation that is generated, not by a real event but by a thought, the negative feedback loop detects the continued presence of the cognitively generated threat and keeps you in a hyper-tuned mode of physical performance for hours, days, or sometimes years. When mentally stressed, there is no real danger to take on.

Remember !   The stress lingers for as long as the thought remains.

In a world where floods of negativity that are floating around in mainstream and social media, when we allow our thoughts to stress us . . .

Remember !   Our capacity for stress is limited only to our capacity to think negatively.

Which, sadly, unless actively kept in check, is infinite, with no solution in sight for most of the negative thoughts we generate. The volume of thoughts that can trigger stress in any of our typical days today far exceeds the number of actual physical threats our ancestors experienced, even in the wildest of all jungles.

Our stress machine was not designed to deal with an endless stream of negativity. We need to intervene *before* those thoughts are generated in the first place if we are to keep our stress response confined to its standard operating environment. Your high-octane stress response is not saving you. It is destroying your misguided biological machine.

STRESSED BY AN EMOTION

Another unfamiliar territory that our ancestors likely did not experience is the stress we suffer as a result of our emotions. Our thoughts trigger our emotions, and then those emotions trigger even more emotions. Think about it. When we are single, we may feel lonely, which—to the human psyche, because we are social animals—feels like a threat. That makes us feel down and inadequate. It makes us worry that we will never find love, and that too feels like a threat. Then when in love, we feel elated at first but then may feel jealous. Our need to protect what we have makes us feel possessive and obsessive. We feel worried and threatened that the relationship might end. No specific event triggers any of those feelings. Those feelings seem to take us over and overwhelm us as if coming out of nowhere. They stress us, triggering our survival response while we are not even aware what we are fighting against or running away from. You feel stressed as long as the emotion is felt, without even being aware, cognitively, of what happened—because nothing actually happened.

Remember !   Often, you are not even aware of the reason behind your stress.

My friend, and one of my true heroes, the neuroscientist Jill Bolte Taylor, says:

Remember !   We are feeling creatures who think, not thinking creatures who feel.

Not only are we capable of endlessly feeling emotions, but our internal mechanisms let emotions create *more* thoughts and more emotions. The feelings that we feel often precede cycles of consecutive remuneration that lead to more emotions, which in turn lead to more negative thoughts—an endless cycle that is in no way comparable to the kind of stress humans felt when threats were simply physical. The number of times some of us are likely to feel stress in a typical day of watching the news or roaming the modern dating scene far exceeds the number of actual physical dangers our typical ancestors faced in a lifetime. The magnitude of modern stress we deal with is way beyond the capability of our stress machine. Like our mental stress, emotional stress is not dealing with any specific present danger to take on. It is just raging in our hearts. It too lingers for as long as its trigger—the emotion—lasts.

DEALING WITH A GHOST

The move to mental and emotional stressors has enabled humanity to create massive volumes of stress out of thin air. The irony is that none of what we stress about ever actually exists in the present moment. How do I know that?

The very fact that you have the time and space to stress about a thought or an emotion inside of you is in itself evidence that there is no nearby physical danger outside of you at this very moment.

Please think about this for a minute. If a tiger were about to pounce on you, you would not have the time to think about what might happen if you lose your job. Get it?

We are dealing with ghosts created by our thoughts and emotions when they don't really exist in the present moment.

As a matter of fact, we are dealing with a whole army of them. They're generated inside of us like pixels on a screen, and no fight-or-flight stress response can erase them. And they linger and multiply.

Our modern world is not more stressful than the past. It is much safer in every possible way. Why, then, has stress turned from being humanity's savior in the wild to being a killer today?

If we were to narrow it all down to one reason, it would be the . . .

REINFORCING FEEDBACK LOOPS

In the typical operating environment of the stress machine, the physical symptoms of stress are picked up by your thinking brain. You jump out of your seat first because of your friend's cheap practical joke, *then* you start to think things through. Your cortex engages in analyzing the situation, and in cases where it deems that the circumstance that triggered your stress is not yet concluded, it acts to stress you more. Obviously, if that tiger were still trying its best to munch on you, increased levels of cortisol are not supposed to trigger the negative feedback loop to its termination, leaving you without the energy you need to handle the situation where the stressor is still present; stress is supposed to continue till you see the situation through. That's, well, stressful, but necessary. The real issue is when the cortex keeps you stressed when there is no genuine reason for you to be. This whole cycle, however, is much, much shorter than we typically think.

When I interviewed Jill Bolte Taylor on my podcast *Slo Mo*, she discussed a concept from her book *Whole Brain Living*, which she calls the 90-Second Rule. She said,

> From the moment I think a thought that stimulates my emotional circuit—making me feel anger, for example—to the time that my physiological response runs out—the time it takes to dump adrenaline into my bloodstream, and it flushes through me and flushes out of me, from the beginning of the thought, to the time where my blood is clean of that chemistry—takes less than ninety seconds. But many of us have the ability to stay angry for longer than ninety seconds. This is not the result of the original trigger. What you're doing then is you are rethinking a thought that is stimulating the anger circuit over and over. That way, we can stay mad for days.

When that happens, the feedback loop—the cycle that works perfectly from trigger to stress to victory over your stressor, to suspension of the stress—works in reverse. Sometimes, often even in the modern world, the feedback cycle doesn't shut off your stress response. Instead, it increases it.

This is the worst part of stressors that are triggered by thoughts or emotions. They last for as long as the emotion or thought that triggered them persists, and they multiply because thoughts trigger emotions and emotions trigger thoughts. As a result, the negative feedback loop, the mechanism that is supposed to bring you back to calm, breaks. Cognition, in that case, does not lead to a realization that there is no need to be stressed; instead, it reinstates the same virtual danger it created in the first place and reinforces the need for *more* stress.

No real danger, only thoughts and emotions, and then it gets even worse. Stress in itself leads you to become more susceptible to more triggers that stress you. That's when you get caught up in . . .

THE SWIRL POOL

When you are scared, everything seems to be a demon. Awareness of the presence of a stressor of any kind leads us to obsess about it. The primary task of your brain is to keep you safe. Influenced by its own fear and worry, your brain starts to search for threats everywhere. And what you search for, you are more likely to find. Try it yourself. Search for VW Beetles tomorrow, and I guarantee you, you will encounter more of them than you did today. This is not because more of them are on the streets but because you now notice more of them as they cross your path.

Search for a reason to be afraid, and, like VW Beetles, reasons will present themselves. Life will feel like a haunted house, though nothing has

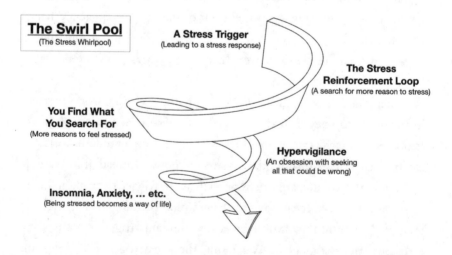

changed in real life. Finding more reasons to be stressed in itself stresses you even more, so you search even harder and find more things to stress about in an endless spiral that we call the *self-generated stress whirlpool*. Let's just call it the swirl pool.

Hypervigilance, then, takes over our lives completely. Being constantly on the lookout for what's wrong becomes our brains' top priority. We become irritable and jumpy, constantly anxious, and never calm. We suffer long nights of insomnia, even in the absence of stressors in the quietness of our bedrooms, as we obsessively think about and analyze every possible thing that can go wrong. We imagine scenarios that never happened and could never happen. We lose trust in those around us and in life itself. All for no fault of life or anyone but our hyperactive imaginations. Deeper and deeper we swirl in a whirlpool of our own making as we drown in our own dense illusions.

A *little* bit of stress never kills anyone, but repeated stressors can kill. Anything from a long commute, to an annoying neighbor, an intrusive friend, a difficult teenage child, job-related issues, the loss of a loved one, economic livelihood challenges, or health issues, and the list goes on and on and on. Those are manageable for short periods. Keep one or many of them in your life long enough, and you're heading down the swirl pool. Often we are affected by many of those at the same time, which simply means one thing. The negative feedback loop does not perform its intended function. Instead of recognizing our physical safety, it triggers it again and again.

Remember !   We frequently remain stressed for days, weeks, maybe even years, and sometimes even a lifetime.

Stress is supposed to be acute, sudden, and temporary in nature. Humans are designed to stay busy surviving, not worrying about likes on Instagram. When a threat shows up, we're supposed to handle it head-on and either survive it or, well, get eaten.

Remember !   Too much of anything is bad. Too much cortisol for too long is simply fatal.

THE SILENT KILLER

Our biological machinery, which has not caught up with the changes in our lifestyle since the cave-people days, treats every stress exactly the same: it floods us with cortisol. With so much of that steroid in our systems, I feel compelled to share with you a few facts that you need to be aware of.

Remember, you want high blood sugar to feed your brain and fat to feed your muscle tissues to give you the energy you need to get you out of a stressful situation. High cortisol over prolonged periods of time in cases of chronic stress, however, can lead to many things going wrong.

First, it will break down your muscle tissue. Muscles are made of proteins, and one way to synthesize sugar is to liberate stored glucose in the form of glycogen by breaking down proteins into amino acids, which can then be converted into blood sugar. High cortisol also breaks down fatty acids and either turns those into glucose or blood sugar as well, feeding them to the muscle tissues in case you need to run or fight. As a result, chronic stress decreases the amount of muscle in the patient's body.

It burns fat as well, so beware, my little belly. *Bring on the stress so I look skinny in my next Instagram photo,* you may think. Well, don't celebrate too fast. The opposite is actually true.

Muscles burn as much as twelve times more calories than any other tissue in your body, even at rest. With less muscle, your metabolism, the ability to burn the calories you eat, goes down. This, during stress, is typically combined with increased cravings and appetite so you eat more and provide sugar to fuel your brain. The quicker you get those, the better, and so you eat more and more of the wrong—sugary—stuff. Every side of high cortisol levels points you in the same direction, increasing the likelihood that you might gain fat.

Even the fat that you burn when you are in fight-or-flight mode is not the stuff that you want burned. Stress burns your peripheral fat, but it increases visceral fat, which is well known to be a contributor to things like insulin resistance. This leads to more retention of stubborn fat in your body and more food cravings.

While the shape of your body doesn't matter, your health surely does, and the kind of fat resulting from prolonged periods of stress is one of the most unwelcome. Visceral abdominal fat disposition, otherwise known as *belly fat*, is known to increase inflammation. Inflammation, in turn, is associated with heart disease, diabetes, cancer, arthritis, stomach ulcers, and various bowel diseases. In fact, inflammation itself is a form of stress to our bodies, and as a result, it leads to even higher levels of cortisol, and the cycle continues.

High cortisol damages the immune protective mucus layer of your gastrointestinal tract. This layer is there to protect you from infections and food sensitivities. Without it, you suffer what is called a *leaky gut*, which allows food that hasn't been completely broken down, bacteria, and toxins into your bloodstream. Symptoms of leaky gut syndrome include bloating, food sensitivities, fatigue, digestive issues, skin problems, and, of course, even more stress.

Similar to how cortisol metabolizes muscle tissue, it also breaks down bones in search of energy. This leads to diminished bone density and increases the risk for osteoporosis.

Cortisol also stimulates your antibody-producing immune system. This suppresses the part of your immune system that actually acts against things like cancer and infections.

Now, let's go to your brain. High cortisol decreases frontal lobe activity, which is associated with your working memory and your ability to concentrate. Decreased frontal lobe activity is linked to depression and decreased intelligence. High cortisol over extended periods of time can cause damage to your hippocampus, the part of the brain that is crucial for detecting cortisol levels to shut down the stress as part of the negative feedback cycle, which makes you no longer able to detect the stress that caused the shutdown in the first place.

Your hippocampus is responsible for converting short-term memory to long-term memory. Accordingly, it is suspected that a sustained decrease in hippocampus function can lead to Alzheimer's disease.

Long-lasting high cortisol also suppresses the pituitary gland, which, beyond releasing ACTH—the hormone that leads to the release of cortisol in the first place—also produces many other hormones that tell other glands in your body which essential hormones to produce. Suppressing the pituitary gland triggers the release of the thyroid hormone, which affects every cell and all the organs of the body as it regulates the rate at which calories are burned. In women, it tells the ovaries to make estrogen and progesterone. In men, it tells the testicles to make testosterone. Those are the hormones that tend to be supplemented in cases of gender transition. The way stress affects them can directly impact our alignment within our gender identity.

The pituitary gland also produces growth hormones, without which your ability to regenerate cells comes to a halt.

The point I'm making is simple: cortisol, in a nutshell, is like a nitro booster in a racing car. When injected into the engine, it breaks down into oxygen and nitrogen upon heat application. The extra oxygen burns the fuels hotter, and that generates more power to enable this temporary boost that gives a driver lightning speed for a very short time. Keep injecting nitro and the whole engine would melt down from the excessive heat, which would lose you the race, let alone all the accidents that would result on the path to that inevitable meltdown.

Sustained chronic stress does the same to our bodies. In extreme long-lasting stress such as in cases of PTSD (post-traumatic stress disorder) or chronic stress leading to burnout, for example, all of the above symptoms become very clear in patients. Chronic pain, cardiovascular diseases, hypertension, autoimmune diseases, depression, anxiety, addiction, social isolation and withdrawal, obesity, diabetes, chronic fatigue, and irritable bowel syndrome—you name it. Stress caused by trauma almost without fail predisposes people to developing chronic illnesses, psychiatric problems, and addiction problems. The rates of psychiatric, medical, and addiction comorbidity with PTSD exceed 80 percent, which makes it very unusual to find someone with PTSD who does not suffer a comorbid condition, often several at the same time. It's all the result of sustained chronic stress.

Very Important! Too much stress over long periods of time will literally kill you.

Sorry for all the negativity up there. It's important that you realize how far down the impact of constantly being stressed can go. But let me make things better now. It doesn't have to be this way.

Take any negative impacts from the above—for example, depression—and you will find the following statement to be true: most episodes of depression spring from a negative life event. The opposite, however, is not true. Not all stress leads to depression. As a matter of fact, most episodes of stress don't lead to depression. This is obvious from the numbers above. If most of us are constantly feeling stressed while only one in every four of us suffers from depression, then the other three manage to find a way out of most episodes of stress. So why don't all negative life events lead to depression?

This is also true in the case of extreme stress, as in PTSD. It is reported that 75 percent of Americans, for example, are exposed to the type of trauma that could trigger PTSD at least once in their lives. The rate of lifetime PTSD, however, stands only at 6.8 percent (10 percent in women and 4 percent in men). Regardless of the gravity of the trauma, most recover. In the case of 9/11, for example, the number of those who were first diagnosed with PTSD dropped by close to 20 percent within four months and by 90 percent within six months. Most PTSD patients, in general, recover within three months or less, leaving only 3.5 percent to end up stuck in post-traumatic stress disorder after one year.[1] Why, then, do some recover and others don't?

Understanding why most of us manage to pull out of states of extreme stress while others remain stuck, sometimes for a lifetime, could hand us the key to plotting a path to recovery out of all kinds of stress, not just the extreme cases.

Some people crumble under stress while others zoom through it with flying colors. The difference between them is not the nature of the life event they're exposed to. The person who doesn't become overly stressed has simply rightsized a reaction, where the stress canary has a negative one. It's in the way they deal with it. Sometimes those who are unstressable see the events differently to start. They see the positive in what others see as negative. What makes me feel unsafe may make you feel free. As I, for example, face a challenge, I remind myself of the potential growth I will experience when I've learned to overcome it. That way, it's not all bad in my mind. The level to which life stresses each of us individually all comes down to methods and thresholds.

In seeking a deeper understanding of how all of this works, I decided to borrow from the concept of stress through the lens of a different science from the above mix of biology, chemistry, and neuroscience. You see? Stress does not only affect humans. It affects everything, including inanimate objects. With that in mind, let's spend a little time understanding how stress works in physics.

STRESS AN OBJECT

In physics, a force applied to an object leads to stress, strain, and eventually fatigue—until the object breaks.

It was the Swiss mathematician and mechanician Jacob Bernoulli who observed, in 1705, that the deformation of an object when a force is applied to it can be described mathematically. He was the first to teach us about stress and strain.[2]

Stress is what an object experiences when subjected to a force. It is measured as the force divided by the area of the cross section of the object carrying that force.

The force applied is distributed across the area. Every tiny bit of the area carries a tiny little bit of the force. The larger the area, the more the object can carry and, accordingly, the lower the stress it experiences when subjected to an external load. Force divided by area is measured in pascals, which, ironically, is a unit of pressure. I think we can say the same for humans too.

Visually, you can imagine this concept of stress as a way for the object to carry the force applied to it. If an object has a small cross-sectional area of, say, one square centimeter that has to carry the whole force, it will be a lot more stressed than if it is made of a hundred square centimeters. In this latter case, each square centimeter will be stressed only with a hundredth of what the first object had to suffer.

It's not just external forces that lead to stress.

Remember !   With fewer inner resources to handle an external force, more stress is felt.

If you apply a force—say, the force of a fast-moving hammer hitting a nail over a small area the size of the tapered head of a nail—all that force would be transmitted to that tiny area, allowing the nail to penetrate a solid piece of wood. If, however, you change the area of contact, even if slightly by turning the nail upside down so that its wider head is in contact with the wood, the force of the hammer would then be distributed across the wider area, making it almost impossible for the nail to create more than a little dent. To reduce stress, you can either reduce the force applied or increase the area on which the force is applied.

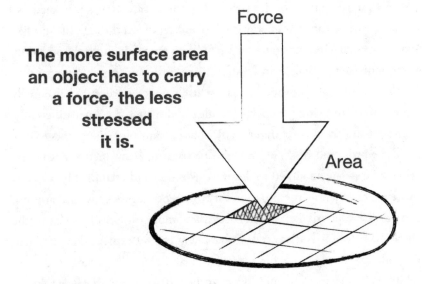

The more surface area an object has to carry a force, the less stressed it is.

Force

Area

This is very similar to the way we humans experience stress too. Forces, challenges, and pressures are applied to us all the time, from the hurtful comment of a friend, all the way to late nights at work or even illnesses and financial struggles that we are all bound to face at one moment or another in our lives. Those forces are dealt with through our ability to handle stress.

There rarely is a time when only one thing is stressing us. With the way the modern pace of life is, we are often subjected to multiple stressors simultaneously and surely tens of stressors every day. The greater the number of stressors, the greater the resulting force and the higher the intensity, or at least our perception of it, and, accordingly, the higher the load we need to carry. We get out of bed in the morning, we face triggers that cause us stress. From the days when our partner wakes up grumpy, to the annoying message we get on social media, to the negativity of the news. From the days when money is tight to the days when we find ourselves in an actual argument or a fight. From the days we don't accept our body shapes to the days when we complain about a colleague who's been bugging us at work. The resultant force applied to each of us on a daily basis is the sum of all those different triggers for as long as we let them last.

The force, however, is not what causes us stress. If we have enough resources to carry that force, we would not feel stressed at all. Instead, we would use those forces as energy that drives us forward through life just like the energy of a hammer drives the tip of a nail with ease through soft wood.

If your partner speaks in frustration because you forgot, yet again, to buy milk on your way home, that in itself is not an event that equally stresses us as individuals. Each of us deals with such a trigger differently. Some get drawn into the fight, start to argue and blame, say and receive hurtful words, and in doing so turn one stressful event into a massive arsenal of stressors, all aimed to destroy our mood and relationship. Others, however, may handle the situation very differently. Some may turn around, rush to the supermarket, adding just a few more minutes of stress to the situation before it is dissolved. Others may calmly explain that they had a rough day at work, ask for a bit of a break before they go get the milk, while the unstressable would listen to their partner attentively, apologize lovingly for having forgotten, offer to take her or him out to dinner, stop for a minute to buy the milk on the way back, and, because they used the energy of the event as a trigger to give their partner the attention they were craving when they felt upset, end up making passionate love as soon as they get back home.

It's the same trigger, and yet, the resulting stress differs. It's not just the triggers that make us feel stressed. Similar to how a bigger area, in physics, would lead to a lower measure of stress within the object for any given force applied, our ability, skills to deal with what stresses us, the skills that we possess, and the resources we can rely on to handle the situation are the game changers in how we experience the resulting stress.

Those who seem less stressed face similar challenges the rest of us face. They just know how to deal with them better.

Very Important! Life is full of stressors. We feel less stressed when we learn the skills we need to handle the pressure.

Those among us that have the skills and abilities needed to handle stress not only feel better, but they certainly also enjoy a better shot at success. One of those skills, for example, is our perception of reality. When a force, stressor, or trigger is applied to us, it gets to some but not all of us. Our perception of those forces affect us as much as their reality. Back in 2008 when I worked at Google, a major economic crisis hit our world. By all means, those times were tough. The younger members of my team felt stressed, even panicked. They claimed that it was going to be a major struggle to achieve their targets, and in that impulsive reaction, they may have been correct. At the height of the crisis, it felt like the world of business was going to end. Clients were taking drastic measures to cut costs starting with what is the core of how Google made money—marketing and advertising. Well, you know what they say: half of your marketing budget goes to waste, you just don't know which half.

Being older than the average Googler, however, I had seen many economic downturns before. I was not as stressed as many of them were. Years of experience gave me the skill needed to recognize that every challenge also presents some form of an opportunity. We just needed to calm down and find it. In physics terms, that skill offered me more cross-sectional area to carry the newly applied forces. Every experienced person in business knows that economic cycles lead to a major downturn every seven to ten years or so and that life always comes back to normal. It was wise for a smart client to start cutting that half of their marketing costs that they knew in their hearts was ineffective. Those included the fancy billboards, the expensive sponsorships, and the painfully expensive TV ads. It was clear, though, that clients would still need to sell to survive, so they would still have to keep advertising somehow, just in a more effective way. What was the most effective method of advertising then? Pay per click—the bread and butter of Google's business. Instead of feeling the stress, we started to approach our clients with a program that we called *speeding up in a slowdown*. We showed them how they could effectively reach more clients with a much smaller overall ad budget if they redirected more of their spend to measurable, effective pay-per-click ads.

I remember vividly how the faces of my clients changed when we had that conversation. Our data-driven perspective gave them hope, and the ones who got it realized that the crisis was more of an opportunity, for the clever ones, than a challenge. When they learned the new perspective, put it to good use, and could see results, they too felt excited instead of feeling stressed. We got more revenue and happier clients. No stress!

If you look at the challenges ahead through a grim lens, you will feel stressed by them and collapse under their pressure. Develop the skill to deal with life's twists and turns, and you will view them as easier, lighter, more manageable, or even, dare I say, enjoy them as a fun roller-coaster ride, throw your hands up in the air, and have the time of your life . . . feeling alive.

This is not only true in business—a passionate romantic partner can be viewed as a burden or a joy. A long commute to work can be viewed as a reason for frustration or an opportunity to listen to a good podcast. A long walk to a supermarket can be viewed as a chore or an opportunity to add to your daily step count and to unwind.

Remember !   It's not the events of your life that stress you. It's the way you deal with them that does.

How can you best deal with any situation? By summoning up the skills, abilities, and resources that best position you to make the best out of the situation.

Stress in that case is nothing more than the distribution of the challenges we face and our ability to perceive them accurately and deal with them.

This can be summarized in a very simple mathematical equation:

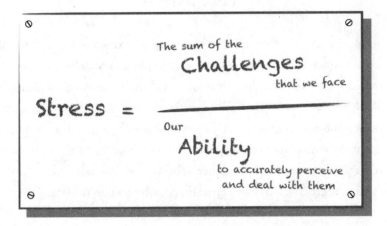

$$\text{Stress} = \frac{\text{The sum of the } \textbf{Challenges} \text{ that we face}}{\text{Our } \textbf{Ability} \text{ to accurately perceive and deal with them}}$$

Elementary school understanding of mathematics then says that if you want to minimize the outcome of this equation—in this case, minimize stress—you need to minimize the numerator (the number on top of the fraction bar) and maximize the denominator (the number at the bottom).

This puts you squarely in charge of managing your own stress. Even more interesting, though many would like to blame life for the stressors it sends their way, you can even control the stress you are subjected to. The majority of the stressors we struggle with are avoidable if we develop the right habits. Beyond the difficult events of life, I would daresay that often the stress we feel is not even the result of what life gives us but rather the thoughts and emotions we develop about it. Those too, I assure you, are within your control.

Hold this thought. We will come back to discuss it in detail in part III of this book.

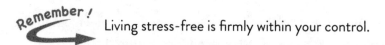 Living stress-free is firmly within your control.

Let's stick a little longer with math and logic to see what else an understanding of physics can teach us.

ROLL WITH IT

Observe the shape of an object when subjected to an external force and you will notice that it changes a little. Stretch a rubber band and it becomes longer. Throw a rubber ball on a hard surface and, upon hitting the ground, the ball gets temporarily deformed into a flatter elliptical shape.

Once you remove the stress, however, those objects, being elastic, will attempt to return to their original unstressed shape. The rubber band shrinks and holds things together. The ball exerts some force on the ground as it gets back to its original shape, which gives the ball an upward acceleration, causing it to bounce.

The deformation in the shape of an object is known as *strain*, and it is measured as the change in an object's dimensions as compared to its original size. This change leads to three important physical phenomena that are worthy of your understanding. The first, which I've just mentioned above, depends on the object's elasticity. If the object's deformation does not cause it to break, an internal force generated within it tends to oppose the stress and bring things back to normal.

This kind of inner strength, however, is true only for objects and humans that demonstrate a sense of elasticity and flexibility.

Objects that are elastic can sustain more strain and, accordingly, withstand larger forces before they break. If you jump up and down on a trampoline, its elasticity will carry your weight and stretch to dissipate it, then use its internal strength to push you back up. If you jump the same way on a sheet of glass, however, you're an accident waiting to happen. It's not your weight that makes the difference. It is the willingness and flexibility of the surface to cope with the weight applied that saves the day.

Remember ! When subjected to stress, your internal strength and flexibility can help you bounce to new heights.

This internal force that results from stress, when positively directed, can be seen as a good thing. In humans, when we feel a bit of stress and gain the superpowers that result from the boosting hormones, we tend to achieve a lot more than we would in our normal state. This counts as a positive.

The second phenomenon worthy of your attention is how stress sometimes leaves the object with a tiny bit of a permanent change in its shape. You know that because if you left a balloon full of air for a while, then emptied it, you would notice that its natural state makes it a bit bigger than it used to be before the pressure was applied. Interestingly, if you choose to blow it full of air again, you will notice that its overall capacity has become bigger. You can pump more air without the risk of it popping as it would have if it hadn't been stretched before. This too happens to us humans. You know that to be true because things that may have freaked you out earlier in life don't seem to faze you that much anymore. Previous stresses, when they pass, lead to more resilience.

In humans, this, at its extreme, is normally referred to as *post-traumatic growth*. The growth that follows a difficult, even traumatic experience is a form of positive psychological change that some of us experience after a life crisis or traumatic event. Post-traumatic growth is not a denial of the deep distress but rather that adversity can be the reason that yields change in understanding oneself, others, and the world. Stretching the elastic band for a long time almost reprograms the molecules into a design that can better deal with future forces of tension. This replaces the original configuration that assumes the luxury for a rubber band to live without being stretched.

The most resilient of us are those with a sense of open-mindedness and willingness to roll where life takes them. They don't hold on firmly to a certain view of life and stress when that view is absent from their reality. Instead, they accept—even embrace—change and deal with every situation as it comes. Just like that trampoline, the most resilient of all of us . . .

Remember ! Take the stress and quickly bounce back to release the tension

. . . as they learn and get ready to deal with the next jump.

Sadly, however, when stressed too much or for too long, some of us suffer a permanent kind of strain. You see those broken humans walking around scarred as if they have lost and life has won, not knowing that life was never really out to get them in the first place. This is the third stress phenomenon to observe about objects and humans when subjected to stress and strain. Like a rubber band that's been stretched for weeks and then looks saggy when let loose, or like a glass that ruptures when the sudden introduction of an extra-hot liquid expands it beyond its molecular ability to hold together, there are conditions where humans also reach a point when they can no longer take the stress. When we do, we give up and break.

WHY WE BREAK

In physics, there are two main reasons why an object subjected to stress would break. The first is because an excessive force, which exceeds the object's capability to carry, is applied over a very short period of time. The intensity of the force jeopardizes the structural integrity of the object, propagating cracks through it and leading it to collapse, and the second is when stress is applied to an object repeatedly over and over until micro cracks start to develop and over time bring the structural integrity of the object down. This is known as *failure by fatigue.*

KO

If you position a twig between two stones and push it with your finger, it will bend a little as you push then get back to its normal state when the pressure is removed. If, however, you jump on it with your full body weight, it will break instantly. We too break when subjected to heavy-weight, rapidly applied stressors.

We call those kinds of excessive, rapid stressors *trauma*. Serious accidents, physical or sexual assault, abuse, serious health problems, the loss of a loved one, war, conflict, the perception of an existential threat, or witnessing excessive suffering of another are all examples of stressors beyond our human ability to withstand. When the pressure applied to us far exceeds what we are capable of dealing with, our psychological integrity collapses as we sustain deep scars and struggle to make sense of the world around us. One punch of this kind of stress and it's a knockout. We fall to the ground. We break down, stop functioning, and start looking for ways to collect the broken pieces.

This can be explained algorithmically in what I refer to as the *trauma equation*.

Trauma breaks us when ...

This book is not about how to deal with trauma. When subjected to a traumatic event, we strongly recommend that you consult a trauma expert. Our chief topic here is the relentless daily stress that statistics show is the bigger driver of the modern world's stress pandemic.

Trauma can reshape us in profound ways. It leaves us deformed and scarred even after the tragedy is long gone. Yet our deformation as a result of trauma often makes us better, made beautiful by the scars, trained to be stronger. If you look back at your life, you will often realize that it was the toughest times that made you the person that you are today. When we deal with a difficult situation, we change. We become empowered to handle the same situation, if it ever arises again, with ease.

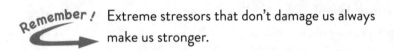

Remember ! Extreme stressors that don't damage us always make us stronger.

What, then, is the biggest reason for the widespread stress in our modern world? It's the repetition of stress, no matter how small.

HIT ME ONE MORE TIME

How often do you see people break down when it seems that their lives, at least in comparison to those who have a much tougher life, seem to be okay?

In the absence of major losses or traumas, the modern world tends to drive us into the ground. Too many stressors, some insignificant and some demanding, compounded over a prolonged period of time can truly break our backs. While none of the stressors we suffer on their own amount to anything at all, a large number of stressors or the repeated cycles of any one or a few of them, regardless of how small, can add up to be too much for us to deal with. That's when we burn out.

The first side of this concept is easy to understand. If the twig I described above represents you or I and how we deal with the pressures of life, the weaker twigs would break as a result of a tiny challenge such as, say, the harsh comment of a friend on social media. The stronger twigs, however, would be able to sustain much bigger challenges with ease. Each and every one of us, though, regardless of how strong we can be, would eventually reach a breaking point if we continue to increase the weight. If, say, many of your friends added harsh comments and kept doing it for several weeks, each comment would add to the weight until, eventually, it became a bit too much. We all feel that some days, don't we? Your boss is annoying, the traffic is slow, you have a bit of a headache, and your date hasn't called. None of those in isolation would get to you, but add them all together and you find yourself on the brink. Then, finally, add the silliest little thing to that existing load—say, your coffee spills a little bit on the countertop—and you burst out of control.

Remember ! A lot of little stressors, regardless of how small, eventually add up to an unbearable weight.

But that, believe it or not, is not the biggest reason for the stress our modern society suffers today. Even when faced with lots of challenges on any given day, we still manage to take the load and look forward to an easy day. No one burns out after a single tough day. Burnout breaks us when we allow the repetition of the same kinds of, often little, stressors over and over again. Small, even insignificant stressors often go unacknowledged, sometimes unnoticed, and so they last for longer periods of time. Day after day after day, our internal cracks and scars expand until we are no longer able to get out of bed, not even able to comprehend what went wrong in the first place. To understand this process a bit better, let's go back to physics for a minute.

Earlier we discussed the physics phenomenon of failure by fatigue— when objects that are subjected to a repeated force over time eventually break under stress levels well below their ultimate strength. Fatigue, interestingly, accounts for the vast majority of mechanical engineering failures worldwide—just like burnout accounts for the majority of human breakdown under stress. When you design a machine well, you expect it to carry the loads it will be subjected to with ease. Keep applying the same bearable force repeatedly, however, and eventually the machine still breaks. If you've ever been to an IKEA store, you may remember those glass displays where a chair is pushed repeatedly with a robotic arm to simulate someone sitting on it. A digital counter displays how many stress cycles the chair has been subjected to as a way for IKEA to brag about how resilient those chairs are as you could sit on them thousands of times while they still remained intact. The physical phenomena IKEA was demonstrating when they showed you this, notice, is not that the chair will withstand a massive force. For that, they would have had an elephant sit on it (nice marketing idea). Instead, it is a confirmation that their chair will not break as a result of repeated use—not abuse—even if you stress it hundreds of thousands of times as you sit on it, then get up, then stress it again.

What those displays at IKEA don't show you, however, is that there is *always* a limit to the number of stress cycles anything or anyone can endure. There is *always* a point, even if it is after a million cycles, when this chair, your bicycle's middle rod, a door hinge, or you as a human will eventually break.

Fatigue failure occurs due to the formation of the same structural cracks that excessive force creates within an object, but the difference is that small stresses create micro cracks that we often don't notice and, accordingly, don't acknowledge as a reason for concern that they can lead to failure. The force applied to us is usually within bearable limits, so we learn to cope with it.

First, a few tiny cracks form, usually at the surface of the object, but they go ignored. With no perceived threat of failure, we continue to stress the object, and further stress gets concentrated around the weaker cracks. With time, some of those cracks grow in size, still ignored because the forces causing them seem to still be manageable, until eventually a crack propagates to a critical size, and that's when the fracture occurs.

This is true, not just in physics. You can see it in all of us. You know when your day is stressful, but when the pain is bearable, you keep going. We don't usually break when we face a few challenges. Most people will withstand some pressure. First, the stress taints us, tires us, but we ignore it and keep going until our feeling of fatigue becomes noticeable. We give the stressors that attack us our time and think about them as they keep us awake late at night, but we still don't act to end them. When unattended, they exhaust us and stress us further, and yet, we keep the cycles of stress coming as we try to distract ourselves with a drink at the bar or switch off by binge-watching a series on Netflix. We plow through life thinking it's supposed to be stressful. "I can handle it," we say. The distraction gives us a false sense of temporary recharge, but the stream of stress keeps adding to the weight. Sooner or later, it all becomes too much, and we eventually break. We end up in burnout, depression, and despair. So what's the top skill of being unstressable?

Very Important! Always keep the levels of stress in your life to a manageable, enjoyable level.

Burnout is not random. It can predictably be described with a simple algorithmic equation.

Burnout breaks us when ...

To avoid burnout, as per this equation, you need to reduce the compounding of stressors on the left-hand side of the equation and increase your ability on the right-hand side. If you assume responsibility, you will realize that both sides are much more within your control than you think. I'll come back to this notion of accountability shortly. But before I do, I'd like to discuss the other big killer, other than burnout, in the modern world—a killer that attacks you even before the challenges appear.

FEAR AND ALL ITS DERIVATIVES

There is no doubt in my mind that burnout is the painful ending to a long road littered with stress. As much, if not more, collective pain in our modern world is the result of our frequent feelings of fear and anxiety along that path.

 Remember! We often stress ourselves not about something happening in our lives but rather about something that we fear might happen in the future.

In order to fully understand what triggers those future-centric modalities of stress, we need to spend a bit of time studying fear and its main derivatives—worry, panic, and anxiety. Let me first sum those up in a simple graph and then expand a bit on each of them.

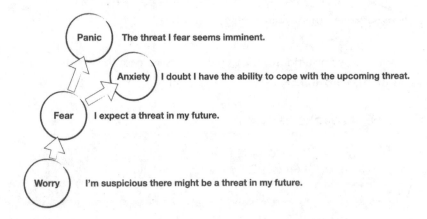

Panic — The threat I fear seems imminent.

Anxiety — I doubt I have the ability to cope with the upcoming threat.

Fear — I expect a threat in my future.

Worry — I'm suspicious there might be a threat in my future.

Among all the variants of fear, the lowest in its intensity is the feeling of worry, which is nothing more than a sense of unconfirmed suspicion. Your worry, in crude terms, is how your brain signals to you that it suspects that something might happen in the future that could threaten your safety. Your brain, then, is still unable to provide enough evidence that this future scenario is probable. It just thinks it's possible, and so it brings it up to your attention so that you can plan for it early enough. An economic slowdown where companies all over the news are laying people off is enough for your brain to worry, even if your own company is doing well and you happen to be one of the top performers in your division. Worry, then, is focused on the probability of the threat happening, not on the intensity of the threat itself, which can be summed up in a simple math equation.

Worry = The probability (a threat to your well-being in the future)

The higher the probability, the more you worry. This means that if you feel worried about something, the best question to ask yourself is not how bad it could be but rather how likely it is to happen.

helps to see it for what it truly is, so you can dedicate your brain cycles to dealing with it instead of fearing it.

Panic, then, is neither concerned with the intensity of the threat nor its probability. Panic is felt when the threat expected by your brain seems to be imminent. The closer you get to the point of impact, the more you panic. In math, here's how we could write a simple equation that describes panic:

$$Panic = F\left(1 / T_1 - T_0\right)$$

Obviously, dwelling in panic mode does not help you deal with the threat approaching. As a matter of fact, it hinders your ability to do what you need to do. So when you feel panic, the questions to ask yourself should mainly be focused on verifying the imminence of the approaching threat, to validate if there is a credible reason to panic, and if there is, your focus should be to use the precious time you have to evade or minimize the impact of that possible threat.

To reduce panic, focus on the element of time. Verify if you have enough time to deal with what concerns you, and if not, focus on how you can speed up the thing you need to do to fit within the time available to you.

Which leaves us with anxiety. Many of us in the modern world seem to be spending more of our time feeling anxious than we do feeling fearful, worried, or panicked. It seems, and I could be wrong, that those who are constantly anxious have convinced themselves that the world is a dangerous place, and so instead of spending time worrying about the possibility, intensity, or imminence of a threat, they choose to believe instead that the threat is certain and that it will be bad, and so they choose, unconsciously, to question their ability to deal with it. Anxiety, believe it or not, is not even directing your thinking to the threat itself at all. Instead, it is totally focused on your capability, or lack of, to deal with it in a way that keeps you safe. Mathematically, it is presented thus:

Instead of wasting your brain cycles, try to find solutions to
your safety.

Remember ! To ease your worry, gather the facts you need to
if what concerns you is even real.

You'll be surprised how often you will discover that there really is r
to worry about and that you are already safe.

If your brain manages to gather enough evidence that what it is v
about is likely to happen—for example, your company itself start:
off people—your worry turns into fear. When afraid, your brair
longer concerned with probabilities. It assumes, though no future-l
statement is ever certain, that what it is afraid of will certainly l
and, as such, starts to focus on bad things. Fear in that case is your
way of signaling to you that there is a danger threatening you at a m
in the future, call it T_1, which it feels will be less safe for your well
than your current state right now at T_0. The intensity of your fear
rectly proportional to how dangerous that future moment is as con
to your present, which too can be summed up in a simple equation

$$Fear = Your\ sense\ of\ safety\ @\ T_1 - Your\ sense\ of\ safety\ @\ T_0$$

Hence when you are afraid, one of the most important things
fine, so you can objectively address your fear, is how bad it could be
you can handle the worst-case scenario, because most of the time, tl
inconvenient or painful, you probably can.

Remember ! To deal with fear, gather the facts you need to veri
the true intensity of damage you may sustain if wh
you fear becomes a reality.

If something scares you, don't let your brain exaggerate it out of
portion. Question if what scares you is really as bad as you think it

Anxiety = F (1 / one's capability to deal with an expected threat)

The more confident you feel that you can handle the threat, the less anxious you are, and vice versa. For that, dealing with anxiety is not a question of assessing the threat itself. Rather, it is a practice of questioning your brain's claim that you won't be able to handle it when you have handled every other threat that came your way so far (as evidenced by the fact that you are still here, safely reading this book). It is also a practice of focusing on developing your skills and capabilities so that dealing with the threat becomes easier. Instead of spending your days and nights feeling anxious, spend them working on your plans and acquiring the needed skills for a softer landing. Even when the threat of losing your job is real, anxiety doesn't help diminish the risk. What it does is develop your financial management, job hunting, and interviewing skills so you prolong your runway and increase your chances of finding a new job. Got it?

 To remove your anxiety, focus not on what concerns you but on assessing and developing your ability to deal with it.

I hope you too are noticing that we always seem to come back to objectivity, skills and capabilities, and action when it comes to dealing with stressful emotions. This is the basis of the model we will use in this book, which assumes that you have three accountabilities that you can fulfill by committing to three practices.

YOUR THREE ACCOUNTABILITIES

As I mentioned earlier, breaking down due to a traumatic event is not something within our control, but with the right intervention, most of us recover. Suffering from anxiety is a question of increasing our ability to deal with stressful situations, and ability is a parameter that is in common with avoiding burnout too. So for the sake of the bigger picture here, I will focus on avoiding burnout. The accountabilities you need to achieve will also help you reduce anxiety.

Now, back to elementary mathematics. One look at the burnout equation and you recognize that if you want to avoid breaking down under stress, you need to minimize what's on the left-hand side and maximize what's on the right.

On the left, you can minimize the sum by taking active steps to reduce the number of stressors that you let into your daily life, reduce the intensity of each, reduce the frequency of their occurrence, or reduce the time of their application to your every day. To maximize the right, you need to invest in developing your knowledge, resources, and skills so you increase your abilities to better handle the stress that will inevitably show up in your life one way or another.

It may seem, at first glance, that we don't have control over the challenges and pressures we face in life, but that is not true. If we're honest, we would have to acknowledge that this is more the result of our resignation from taking charge of our own stress situations than it is because of the way life naturally is. Many of the pressures we are subjected to in our modern life are, in fact, the results of our own choices and actions. Very few are entirely outside our scope of control. Many are completely avoidable. If a commute, for example, is stressing you, you certainly have countless choices to reduce the stress. You could look for a different job, rent a different home, or ask to work from home more frequently. You change the time when you commute or the transportation method you use, even if it costs a bit more. If none of that works, you surely can develop the ability to enjoy the commute instead of resenting it. You could take your favorite music playlist, podcast, or drink along the journey. You could use the time to meditate or catch up with friends, or you could—and should—use the time as an exercise to feel gratitude that your commute is surely much easier than it is for those who are less privileged in poorer countries or war zones, as well as those who have to put up with a longer or more challenging commute than yours in your own city.

When at Google, I worked from the New York office for a short while.

Then I stayed in a place on Forty-Second Street, while Google's office was, then, on Fourteenth. First, I took a taxi to work. I don't even need to tell you about New York taxis—a nightmare to hail, the speed of a turtle when driving in Manhattan, and the driver is always angry. I could not handle the pressure for more than two days, so I attempted to take the underground. Well, that was worse. Never on time, dirty like the sewers, and crowded like a sardine can. The next day, I started walking—like a New Yorker. I paced through the streets like a maniac, dodging people pacing in the opposite direction and frequently rushing a little more to catch the green wave of traffic lights as I crossed the streets. This was a better experience, but it still stressed me, so one day, I decided to time my crazy morning race. It came to thirty-six minutes when I did my best. The following morning, I left home fifteen minutes earlier, stopped to buy coffee, walked like I had nothing to do, and listened to music as I sipped my warm coffee in the crisp autumn of New York. I even allowed myself to observe the madness of the pace of everyone rushing around me and, honestly, had a blast. My commute took forty-two minutes. Now ask yourself, what's six minutes more if it is going to change your day from being a stressed wreck to being so chill and joyful? We always have a choice. I'm just saying.

Choosing not to exercise the options that can make our lives easier is, in itself, a choice that we make, perhaps because we have other priorities. This preference does not deny the fact that there are options nonetheless. And even when the stressors are completely forced on us, such as the case of a global pandemic, we still can choose to examine our perception and choose to see the opportunities and silver linings, not just the downsides.

Learning to recognize the stress and to change course to remove it, as I did in the example above, is a skill. The more you learn to do this, the more it enhances your ability to handle stress and reduces your likelihood of breaking down due to burnout over the long term.

Often we invest our time and effort to learn a new language, stay fit, or learn a skill that can help us earn more money. We spend time learning a new video game or how to cook a tasty recipe, but we rarely invest the time learning the skills that help us deal with our stressful life. This needs to change. Keeping the good side of stress is about accepting three accountabilities that are as easy as one, two, three.

Your Three Accountabilities

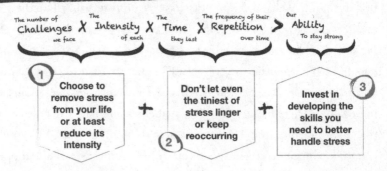

Reduce the repeated exposure you have to stressors, especially the unnecessary or irrelevant ones. If you can't fully avoid a stressor, try your best to reduce its intensity. Don't let even the tiniest of stressors linger or repeat, and actively work on developing the skills you need to cope with stressors as they affect your life.

Well, I stand corrected. It is one, two, three, but it's not that easy. It will take this full book to reverse some of the habits that allow stress to become our way of life. Time is of the essence and discipline is key, so let's discuss the habits that you need to adhere to repeatedly in order to deliver on those accountabilities. We've summarized those habits in a simple model.

THE THREE LS

All the knowledge in the world, anything we can put on the pages of this book, is not sufficient for you to lead an unstressable life unless you put what you learn into habits that you practice daily.

Those who are unstressable live true to three practices: they limit, they learn, and they listen.

Limit

The modern world is full of stressors. Unless you are living on a farm with an abundance of safety, food, and nature, with the one that you love and no access to the modern world in any possible way, you are bound to be stressed. Even if you are, the odd storm or the occasional argument . . . even your own thoughts will stress you sooner or later.

To live an unstressable life, we have to learn to observe what stresses us and actively play our parts in limiting it. Most of what stresses us—and of that, there is a lot—are things that we can limit our exposure to by changing our lifestyle choices. Even if you can't evade a stressor altogether, you can surely learn to limit its impact on you, even if ever so slightly. As the stressors add up, every little bit counts.

We will walk you through all the possible stressors shortly, and then we will show you how to deal with them in a way that makes you calm and at ease. If you want to live unstressable . . .

Remember ! Do what you need to limit the stressors you face every day.

Only a small fraction of all the things that stress you are significant enough to weigh on you while they also fall totally outside your zone of control. For those more than anything, but for every stressful situation in general as well, it pays to stick to the second lifetime habit.

Learn

Because stress is not only the result of the challenges we face but is equally the result of our inability to deal with them, a hunger to learn is surely one of the top qualities possessed by those who live unstressable.

Like when objects respond when strained, we develop the knowledge, skills, and resources we need to cope with stress every time we are subjected to a manageable amount of it. It's not the words on a page that develop our skills. It's practice that makes us stronger, more agile, and more capable. Practice does make perfect, and to practice, we don't necessarily need to be subjected to a real-life stressful situation. You can hone your skills long before the stress even arrives.

As we share the knowledge that you need to grasp the inner workings of the machine called stress and how to manage it, we will also share many practices and exercises that can help you change the way you do things to reduce the impact unavoidable stress can have on you. Don't just skim through those exercises, please. Commit to practicing them and making them part of your daily life. You see, I can tell you right now that eating healthfully and working out a few times a week will make you fit, but *knowing* that will not make you fit. You actually have to eat healthfully and work out for this valuable advice to have any impact whatsoever on your extra pounds and backaches. If you want to become unstressable . . .

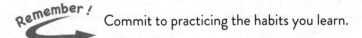 Commit to practicing the habits you learn.

You can see it as clear as day. Those who practice, either by having endured a reasonable share of stress in their lives or by developing the right habits, tend to face challenges with calm and composure almost as if they are unaffected by them. The same challenge, however, would make those who don't invest in learning cry, blame the world, and curse their luck.

But how can you use the skills you develop if you're not aware of the magnitude of stress you endure? To develop that sense of awareness, you need to adopt a third habit, a third *L*.

Listen

Odd as it may sound, a big part of this book is nothing more than a language course.

The first two *L*s will help you remove stressors from your life proactively and develop the knowledge, skills, and resources you need to cope with stressful events that remain. All that is left for you to do, then, is to tune in and listen to your mind, heart, body, and soul as they either stress you, or alert you, inform you, and ask you to change so that you don't let stress burn you out.

Your mind speaks to you all the time, but it tends to exaggerate and morph the truth. If you learn the language of the mind, you can learn to suspend the unnecessary stress it causes you.

Your heart speaks to you all the time, but its language is subtle and blended. When you ignore or misinterpret your emotions, you miss the signs that you need to change direction and heal—to choose love over fear.

Your body speaks in the language of sensations. It could tell you that all is okay through feelings of calm and comfort, or it can scream to alert you in the language of aches and pains. The physical pain we feel when under stress is an alarm that needs to be acknowledged, but it is also an additional reason for your stress. Ignore the language of your body for too long and the unheard screams break you; they could literally even kill you. When you listen to and care for your body, however, the trend reverses and you learn to live stress-free.

Finally, whether you are spiritual or not, there is more to you than your physical form. There is a nonphysical element that simply knows. Call it intuition, a gut feeling, consciousness, or call it your spirit or your soul. When you disconnect from the part of you that is not physical, it doesn't feel heard and feels stressed too, but when you listen, you get priceless personalized insights on how to live stress-free. Your soul, your intuition, doesn't speak a language of words or logic. To understand what it's telling you, you may need to redefine the very concept of what a language actually is in the first place.

Learn the language your stress speaks, through your mind, heart, body, and soul, and you'll be able to navigate stressful territories like a confident local who knows how to avoid the unpleasantness and harm of the dodgy side of this town we call *modern life*.

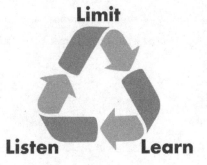

In the early days when we were first alerted to the adverse impact humanity has on our environment, we were taught to reduce, reuse, and recycle. I hope this has become an integral part of your daily life as you play your part in saving our world.

To play your part in saving yourself from stress, remember the three *L*s: limit, learn, listen.

Repeat those behaviors every day until they become second nature, and they will guide you to a life of ease.

IT'S NOT THE EVENTS OF YOUR LIFE

You should not spend another minute of your life feeling needlessly stressed. Becoming unstressable, truly, is your very own accountability. This means that if you choose to ignore your role, the mighty wheels of life are bound to try to stress you. When that happens, don't blame life. Life is just doing what it always does. It is you who needs to do what you should do to live a life that's stress-free.

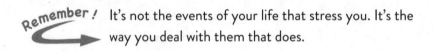 It's not the events of your life that stress you. It's the way you deal with them that does.

This chapter explained how your human machine actually works. I titled it "Welcome to the Machine," which was also the title of a Pink Floyd song, only they did not relate it to the human body but rather to the machine that grinds it—the modern world with all its stressors.

This machine will be our next stop: to recognize all the stressors that it throws at you so you can reduce their intensity and the time and frequency of their occurrences and then remove them altogether.

It's time to learn to exit the machine.

2

Trigger (Un)Happy

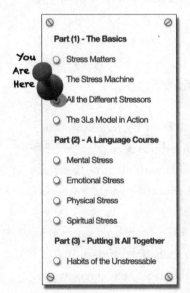

Welcome, my son. Welcome to the machine. *The machine* is the term Pink Floyd used to describe how the modern world shapes us. How it molds us and how it forces us into corners that stress us. The machine of the modern world is a place where we follow aimlessly what we are told to follow.

Our thoughts, beliefs, acts, and desires are sold to us, and we accept them. We spend a lifetime chasing them, never stopping to notice as our lives slip away. Every day, we are worn down a little more, we get stressed a bit more, day after day after day.

Often, the reason we don't take a stand is because we don't recognize all the things that cause us stress. We get used to feeling stressed, and so we let the stress slip into our lives unnoticed, starting with the very first stressor, when our aggressive morning alarm jump-starts the day in a hostile fashion. Instead of taking a stop to prevent that the next morning, we simply roll over, snooze it, so it attacks again a few minutes later, and we accept the repeated hostility as our normal unpleasant start to the day.

One minute into the day, we eagerly rush to look at the morning head-lines for our assured daily injection of negativity and fear, setting the day up with the perfect start for the stress to continue every step of the way until we are back home, exhausted, to argue with our partner or plug our minds into the violence, deception, and horror of a long series to binge-watch before we go to sleep.

Remember !   A lot of what's causing you stress is preventable if you choose to reject its presence in your life.

But the first step you need to take to prevent it is to recognize it when it pops up in your life. The stressors we suffer every day are plenty. There are so many, as a matter of fact, that we have coined a term to describe them. We call them . . .

A TONN OF STRESS

Unless you are smugly reading this off the grid from a white-sand beach somewhere, sitting underneath your very own palm tree that drops fresh dates on demand, while you sip your piña colada with no annoying peo-ple, noise, deadlines, and distractions around you, then you're likely sur-rounded by reasons to be stressed.

There's no escaping stress in today's world. Stressors are everywhere. Some are large, and some are small. Some are predictable, and some come totally out of the blue when you least expect them. Some happen to you, and some you generate to torture your own self.

Instead of counting every single possible stress, it helps to recognize four über-categories of it. That way, they become easier to deal with, either removed or minimized.

Some stress can be *external*—life events that are applied to you from outside. Other stressors are *internal*—caused by your own thoughts, emo-tions, physical pains, and misalignments.

Wherever they originate, externally or internally, stressors can be

The Stress Quadrants Diagram

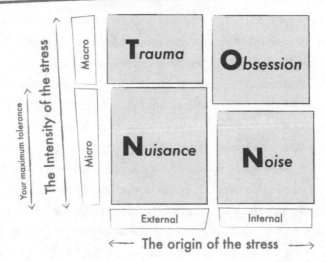

high in their intensity—we will call those *macro* stressors—or small and bearable—we will call those *micro* stressors.

With those four varieties in mind, you can visualize that all the different types of stress can fit neatly into four quadrants shown here in the stress quadrants diagram.

One dimension to observe is the intensity of the trigger that stresses you. One major event that exceeds your ability to handle is known here as **T**rauma.

One or a few internal thoughts or emotions can take you down and can linger. We will call them **O**bsessions.

Any other external stressor that does not break you on its own because it resides within your tolerance level fits within what we call **N**uisances, and all other internal thoughts and emotions that pass within you but are not big enough for you to obsess about will be called **N**oise. Put those all together and they become a TONN.

Let's discuss each in detail with the aim of helping you notice them first. Then, as of the next chapter, we will discuss how you can reduce them or even eliminate them altogether and put the right measures in place so they don't come up again, which leaves you . . . unstressable.

TRAUMA—EXTERNAL MACRO STRESSORS

Trauma-triggering stressors are the type of major external events that blindside us on a quiet Sunday and flip our lives upside down. No matter how prepared we think we are, we have no control over what might hit us. A loved one's cancer diagnosis, the death of someone dear, an accident that keeps you bedbound, a lover who cheats, or the end of a marriage that you thought would last forever. Those traumas not only stress us, they shake our faith in life itself.

It's the kind of stress that seems far out of our own orbit until it comes crashing in and takes over our entire world.

Everyone, sooner or later, faces a trauma-triggering event. It is just part of the process of being alive. There is nothing you can do to ensure they never happen, but you can surely learn how to deal with them when they hit you.

To experience the trauma, the trigger does not necessarily have to affect you. Those who observe the struggle of a loved one with an incurable disease may become health fanatics or germaphobes in the hope they never suffer the same fate. Those who live the story of a loved one's struggles with money always fear not having enough to live, even after becoming millionaires, and at the very extreme, those who find themselves in a war zone or an intensive care unit, witnessing the pain and death of others, end up struggling with post-traumatic stress and panic attacks even as they return to safety.

In the first few weeks after my wonderful son, Ali, left our world, I went to visit his grave almost every day. I felt a sense of peace there and spent the time telling him all the things I hadn't taken the time to share when he was alive. Graveyards in Dubai are simple—a massive plot of desert land where graves are dug every day by dedicated workers who don't know who will visit and book a space that day.

The evening I carried Ali to his final destination here on earth, his was the very last grave to be occupied that day. His spot was right next to the dirt road. I would park my car a few meters away from him, sit on the warm sand, and cry.

A couple of weeks after he left us, as my crying slowed down a bit, I started to observe the space around me. It was different. The dirt road was no longer there. In its place, there was a new row of graves. More visitors showed up to occupy them on a daily basis. The newer ones would be visited by grieving loved ones who cried constantly like I did at first, while my fellows who visited the older graves seemed to be a little calmer.

Not all graves, I started to observe, were equal in size. Some were smaller, clearly to welcome an infant. There were so many of those. I was not the only one that lost a child, although my child was taller than six feet. It hit me that everyone lying there was someone's child. There must have been many whose parents were still alive and struggling, as I was.

When I go to visit Ali now, years later, I need to walk a long distance, passing thousands of visitors. As I do, I remember that the departure of each of them has been marked as a big trauma in someone's life just like Ali's has been in mine.

Remember!   Hardship, even trauma, is a fate we all share.

As much as I pray that you never feel the pain of losing someone so close, at some point in time most of us will. **Accept that life, sooner or later, is bound to send a trauma-triggering event your way.** That acceptance should not be a reason for sorrow or despair. Instead, it should remind you that . . .

Remember!   There is comfort to be found in knowing that billions share your trauma. If they can survive and recover, you will too.

This is another life pattern that we often fail to notice when subjected to difficulty. When you do the math, you will recognize that harshness is just a snapshot, just a few frames, in the long movie that is your life.

Hardship is a fact of life but, surely, not the only fact, and not even a prominent fact. When we peek under the surface of our fears, we quickly recognize that the baseline of our lives is ease. Harshness is the anomaly that disrupts the norm. This is undeniable. For most of us, health is the norm we go through the majority of our lives enjoying. Sickness is the anomaly that occasionally interrupts health. Most of us walk our entire lives on solid ground. An earthquake or a natural calamity is the interruption that disturbs that norm. Being subjected to violence, suffering an accident, and facing life-threatening disasters are the kinds of challenges faced only by a small number of us for a limited number of their days. This is why those events make the news headlines . . . because they are the exceptions to the norm. It is, perhaps, the reason we freeze in the face of trauma-triggering events when they so unexpectedly cross our paths.

While traumas—even PTSD-inducing traumas, which are the most extreme—disrupt our lives to the very core, an astounding 91 percent of all who suffer a PTSD-triggering event bounce back.[1]

It's not the time when we are struggling with a traumatic event that gets us.

Remember ! The biggest negative impact the harshness of life brings is found in the years we spend fearing it and the years we spend allowing it to linger.

With the right mindset and practice, you can save yourself those years. We will discuss how in a bit. For now, let's continue to explore the other quadrants of the TONN.

OBSESSIONS—INTERNAL MACRO STRESSORS

Obsessions are as intense and damaging as the traumatic events that sometimes obstruct our paths, but they are not acts of life. They are acts of our minds and emotions. While traumas break us down instantly, leaving us shattered, confused, and trying to collect the pieces, obsessions wear us down over time. They eat us up from the inside. They may sometimes be triggered by an external event, like a friend saying, "Look at the girls on Instagram. We can never compete with their beauty"—a simple comment that morphs, within you, into a thought such as, *I will never find love.*

That thought then takes hold of you—day in, day out. It grows and grows, despite its invalidity, starting from nothing but our insecurities and vivid imaginations. With no real threat in front of us and instead of directing our efforts to deal with our imaginary demon, we sit in a corner and bring up the thought over and over again. Over time, we become sad. We become weaker. We become depressed. We become desperate, hopeless because as we live inside our heads, nothing in the real world changes, which confirms our obsessions, so we sink deeper—one thought that takes over our minds till it takes our lives away. The thought *They never appreciated me* took my dad, even as everyone around him appreciated him in every way.

In the opening scene of one of my favorite movies of all time, *Inception*, a question is asked—"What is the most resilient parasite? A bacteria? A virus? An intestinal worm? . . . An idea!"

Remember ! Once a thought has taken hold of the brain, it's almost impossible to eradicate.

Well, that's if you let it live—if you take hold of your brain instead, no idea will find the space to fester.

Obsessions live because of a deluded understanding of the intricacies of our minds and how they work. Our thoughts are not something that occur in our world; they come from within us, and even if they sometimes seem to be a reasonable reaction to the external events that triggered them, they get exaggerated till they are way bigger than the true magnitude of the event.

There are very few people that have not lost a job at least once in their lives, and yet when my dad was asked to leave his position, the event shattered his view of life and fairness. There are very few love stories that don't end in a breakup, and yet when we reach the point of a breakup, we think that life is out to get us. We think that life with all its might singles us out to annoy us—only us and no one else.

Let me share a personal experience that clearly demonstrates this level of exaggeration and the difference between traumas and obsessions. Once, I was in a relationship with a Buddhist woman who kept herself to the highest standards of calm and compassion. We had already been together longer than a year when we invited a bunch of our best friends over. We were having a wonderful evening together. My best friend's girlfriend, who was also a good friend, asked if she could ask my advice about something. We sat on the sofa in the other corner of the room, where she started to share with me how she had a heated argument with her boyfriend before they came over and that she loved him very much and did not want to lose him. She became very emotional, so I hugged her as I explained that all would be fine. At that moment, my girlfriend rushed—raged, really—toward us and screamed, "Take your hands off my man, you bit**!" Note once again that this couple were our best friends, whom we met frequently, and recall the Buddhist peacefulness my girlfriend normally embodied and you will understand how exaggerated this reaction was.

After the awkwardness dissipated, we sat down to talk. First, she acknowledged that she overreacted, and she apologized to our friend. Then she vulnerably shared that her last two boyfriends had cheated on her with a friend and that since we'd been together, her biggest fear that she obsessed about every day was that I would do the same.

I asked her if anything I did made her worry, and she answered, "Quite the opposite. Everything you do should make me feel safe, but the more you behave that way, the more my mind makes me wonder what you must be hiding. I believe that my mind, first, made its mind up and decided that you would be cheating, then it searched for confirmation for its assumption in whatever events took place." The cheating-boyfriend events—the trauma-triggering events—were long behind her. Her current life was exactly what she'd dreamed of, and yet she lived in suffering. Why? Obsession. She lived the scenario that she feared inside her head so many times that, to her, it became real.

IMAGINARY DEMONS

Alice here. Let me tell you about one of my own, combined with my dad's, as another example of the struggle we face when caught up in obsession.

When the credit crisis of 2008 hit, the successful business my dad spent years building and had poured his soul into started to struggle. Not long after, he had to shut it down. This loss later triggered a classic obsession. One thought took over him—*I can't leave my family in this mess.* That thought that he lived by since losing his business, he shared with me one evening at dinner, was what kept him up at night and was happening at first only inside his head.

The events that start a stressful obsession are real—external triggers—but they are often highly exaggerated in terms of their significance or impact in the thoughts of the obsessor. Usually, the obsession that lingers is not even about what happened. It is likely more about the thoughts that were triggered by it. Often the original event has ended and yet the stress lingers for months or, even, years.

While there is truth to some of our thoughts when we contemplate the actual facts surrounding the event, most of the made-up narrative that is let loose inside our minds should be Oscar nominated for the best screenplay of a horror movie.

My dad knew for a fact that his company was in receivership, that it needed to pay off the company debts, and that he needed to sell his own personal assets. These were all the hard facts that deserved his attention and caused externally triggered stress, worry, and pain.

His suffering, however, resulted from thoughts that were not part of that factual truth. He would spend hours thinking about our future over and over. Instead of thinking about how to wrap up the situation, fears about the future, guilt about what he really could never have controlled, and self-blame took him over completely. Though all we really cared about was not to lose him, he worried about the lack of money he would leave for us after he was gone. I could see the cogs turning in his head while he was looking into the distance in a trance. We wanted him to stay, but his obsession painfully took him in the opposite direction. He was worried about us as we worried about him. His obsession *every* single day was to keep us safe and that we wouldn't be okay, while his decline was throwing us off our tracks. The worst part was he needn't have obsessed over this, as the worst-case scenarios he imagined didn't happen and we—myself, my sister, and our mum—were fine, just sadly without him.

Despite the financial stress our family endured, my sister is successful in her career and managed to buy her own property. I am an independent, published author and speaker, happily building a company with one of the business wizards of the world (yes, Mo). If my dad had thought about the situation realistically, he would have remembered that so many successful people start from humble beginnings; that perhaps our financial loss as a family, although very stressful, would somehow end up being a good thing that would propel us to take charge and do the best we could.

Remember ! We obsess, triggered by what happened, about events that likely will never happen.

Thoughts running on continual repeat every single day, for years, grow in their own capacity to create as much stress, fear, and worry as external trauma. External traumatic events are limited to the harshness of the event itself. However, there is something even worse.

Remember ! Obsession-triggered stress is limited only by our own imagination.

It can grow into imaginary monsters that are much scarier than the truth.

Without intervention, obsession will only grow stronger until it becomes an ingrained part of our every thought, blurring our awareness of which part of the monster is fact and which is pure fiction.

Talk to a friend that you know is obsessed with something that is not real. Present them with the facts. How do they react? They resist. They get angry. They tell you about the few stories they heard in the media or watched in the movies that support their obsession, discounting the countless other realities of stories that contradict their fictional views.

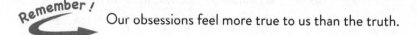

Remember ! Our obsessions feel more true to us than the truth.

Furthermore, obsessions sometimes create our new reality. Think of Mo's ex-girlfriend's temper, for example. Her constant fear led to jealousy and possessiveness, and those, not another woman, were what led to the end of their relationship.

 Remember !   Our obsessions eventually become the real monster that consumes us.

We create them from nothing. We give them life and the power to take our lives.

 Reflection Time   Take a moment to reflect on those realities and perhaps reflect on some of your own obsessions, deep negative thoughts that you firmly believe are true, and consider how true they really are and how they affect your own life.

Please do take the time instead of continuing to read. Mo and I will be here when you come back.

THE BIGGEST DEMON OF THEM ALL

Any deep understanding of how stress works leads to the realization that the bigger monster, the true pandemic threatening humanity, is not the result of traumatic events.

The true damage we suffer is the obsession that results from our own obsessions.

Depression and suicide never result from an external trauma. Read this again. Not directly, they don't. One would have to start the obsession cycle, turning the trauma into thoughts that eventually become the pillars of this further, deeper diagnosis.

 Remember !   We don't get depressed because of what the world gives us. We get depressed because of the way we think about what the world gives us.

Depression within patients that have not even experienced an external trauma is on the rise, with estimates that one of every four adults in the modern world are now diagnosed with depression. Episodes of depression frequently last for years and can be highly recurrent, with at least half the people who experience one episode having one or more additional episodes in their lifetimes.[2]

Obsessions follow from our own inability to keep our minds from going into the darkest of all places to contemplate every stressful concern after a trauma, or even without a trigger at all. They last for way too long and surely need to be kept in check. One thought held on for too long can destroy a life.

Let's keep going to explore the rest of the TONN before we discuss solutions. Time to move to the smaller stressors. Those are also found on the internal side—negative thoughts that are continually running inside our heads, resulting from our lack of understanding of our emotions and minds at their very basic level—and external events that we come to accept as part of life.

Those types of smaller stressors get their power from their numbers. Together, tens, sometimes hundreds, of them on a daily basis. Regardless of how strong we are, every one of us is bound to break if the load is high enough. Let's start with the external side of micro stressors.

NUISANCES—EXTERNAL MICRO STRESSORS

It is common to think that it's only the big stressors that break us, that we are resilient enough to withstand the smaller pressures. We run around our busy lives thinking that if we don't have any traumatic events disrupting those lives, then we surely can't complain. Surely all else is manageable. Suck it up. You're fine. Or are you?

"I'm doing fine" must be the biggest daily lie humanity tells in modern society. Surely the most frequently told lie. It's become our cliché answer when asked how we are. "I'm fine," we answer in a vibrant, upbeat tone, which really means: *I think I feel like crap, but I'm not sure, because I can't be bothered to connect to my emotional state right now, let alone explain it. So unless you ask me twice like you actually care, I'll answer "I'm fine" so we can move on. Answering "I'm terrible" will shock you into awkward silence, and "I'm great" feels like too far-fetched an internal lie for me to master today.*

Fine is a state of . . . meh! Able to cope with life. Not broken yet but not really doing well. Okay to run for another day but not happy. Smiling but . . . well . . . not fine. Think about it. Is this really the life you deserve? Why are you letting it be your life, then? We let these days drift by because we just can't be bothered to stop and genuinely check in with ourselves. When we eventually do, we start to think that maybe something is wrong with us. Why are we feeling down, anxious, or stressed, when nothing *that* stressful or traumatic is in play?

Mo here. I'll tell you why. Let me take it back to physics for a second.

Lots of smaller forces can add up ...

... to be bigger than one large force.

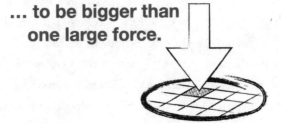

When we analyzed stress, we calculated it to be the force applied divided by the skills and resources available to carry it. The term *force* is usually measured in newtons, which is a bit of a funny unit in that it is the force needed to accelerate one kilogram of mass at the rate of one meter per second squared. Simply put, if your car broke down and you needed to jump-start it, you would need to push it with a force of so many newtons to move it and accelerate its speed until it is fast enough to jump-start. Here's the catch. It doesn't matter if you push the car alone or call a few of your friends to push it. What matters is that enough force is applied to achieve the desired effect—or, in the case of stress, we're talking about enough force to achieve the undesired effect. The net force is the sum of all the forces, large or small. When several small challenges are applied to your life, while each feels insignificant in isolation, the total net effect you need to deal with is the sum of all the forces affecting you.

It's important to note that those forces are not always tiny, as the name *nuisances* may indicate. In this group of external micro stressors, we group all the stressors that are short of a trauma and, accordingly, all the stressors that individually would not break your back. Some of those are sizable and quite demanding to deal with, and though they may not individually break you, add a few more smaller ones and things become challenging indeed.

We normally ignore the smaller forces, as each of them individually feels light and easy to handle. Add them all up, however, and you're in for a load that far exceeds your tolerance limit, though it may feel that it was that one last additional stress that broke you. An unwarranted comment from a friend or another email that calls you for a meeting at the time when you were supposed to go on a date, and you explode or collapse.

Picture the mounting smaller stresses as a house of cards. One by one, a rickety structure is erected. As it gets higher, it gets closer to its inevitable collapse. Eventually, you add just one more, practically weightless card, and it all comes crashing down. It's always that one last card that tilts everything out of balance—that last card until which everything seems to be glorious and under control. With that image in mind, perhaps, we might become less harsh on ourselves when we feel sad, stressed, or anxious for "no apparent reason." The cards have been stacking up, and often we are just a few cards away from not being able to take it anymore. Yet we keep adding cards.

Regardless of how resilient you are, there is always a point when one more insignificant stressor is bound to get you.

There is no way to fix a house of cards after it's constructed. The only way to avoid the collapse is to keep it to a manageable height by limiting the number of cards. The answer to making your house of cards stronger is to make it shorter. It really is that simple. That's why the first of your three accountabilities on the path to becoming unstressable, the three *L*s, is to limit.

 Limit the stressors you allow into your life. Remove them regardless of how insignificant they may seem.

I will also remind you, as we stick with physics for one more paragraph, of the concept of fatigue we discussed in the previous chapter, which in humans is analogous to burnout, breaking down over time as challenges stress you over and over. Your experience of a stressor is not only felt in its intensity. It is also felt in its frequency of repetitive application and the time for which it is applied to you. Poking you in the ribs lightly once is barely felt, but poking you repeatedly or keeping my finger there for a while is bound to eventually get to you. I don't intend to do that to you, so please don't let it be done to you by life. Learn to limit stressors along the four dimensions that lead to burnout.

 Limit the number of stressors, the intensity of each, as well as the time and frequency of their application.

 When we commit to this approach, no little stressor goes unnoticed. We become the masters of our own system. That's when we recognize that we, and only we, hold in our hands the key to unlocking the calmness of our lives. Close your eyes and picture for a minute a day when there is very little external stress to wear you down. Tune in to that feeling of calm and peace. Then, perhaps, commit to yourself that you will actively try to make every day as close as possible to that day. Yes, some stressors are unavoidable, but beyond limiting the number of stressors you need to endure, every stressor can be limited in its intensity, frequency, or time of its presence in your life. Think how wonderful that day will be when nuisances are limited to the absolutely unavoidable—a short commute, no annoying humans, a manageable work agenda, no unrealistic deadlines, along with the occasional break. Now smile.

Nuisances attack you from outside of you, and they may come in tens or hundreds a day. There is another type of micro stressor, however, that comes from within you and is virtually limitless in its ability to mount up on top of you. Combined, we call those types of stressors . . .

NOISE—INTERNAL MICRO STRESSORS

None of the small negative thoughts we constantly suffer from are big enough to break us or threatening enough for us to obsess about them. Instead, those sassy little mind biters—the micro internal stressors—nibble away at us like termites. They drain us, irritate us, without us even noticing that they are not real events but thoughts and emotions that we create from within us.

Noise, if you will, is like that girl at school who always found a way to tell you when your hair was looking frizzy, while smiling sweetly as if it were a compliment. It knows just how to get at your weak spot, that little place that makes you feel somehow less confident, while you go away and tell yourself internally, *I hate my frizzy hair*. (Obviously, this is Alice writing here, because Mo has no hair.)

Words and comments are *never* a threat to your survival. No one has *ever* been killed by a word. Yet in the modern world, they trigger our stress response like a tiger did ages ago, even more. They are tiny doses of internal stress that we inject ourselves with until there is enough poison in us to spoil our day.

When irritated about that one snide, critical comment a coworker volunteered, we replay the comment in our minds in an attempt to work out why they said it, if our work really was useless, what our comeback should have been to embarrass them, what we should do to protect ourselves from receiving criticism again, and if we should just quit our job altogether to rid ourselves of the pain.

 Noise is made up of all the little negative niggles we hold on to from something that, had we let go of then and there, would have caused us little to no stress at all.

Noise is highly selective and negatively biased. Remembering the one comment our partner said the day before that upset us while ignoring the twenty other comments they said that were full of love surely is not an objective way to look at our world, but we do it anyway.

We all run a narrative through our minds that aims to optimize our lives. This needs to be attended to—that needs fixing, and this needs a change. There is absolutely nothing wrong with objectively looking at life and trying to make things better. But then the narrative turns inwardly. The thoughts that we hold become noise that is self-directed to harm us when we start to veer off into berating ourselves without even noticing. We mindlessly make the unkind voice in our heads the normal one, and the caring voice becomes obsolete.

This noise hurts us when we lose objectivity and/or when we become needlessly harsh in the language we choose. Think of how many beautiful women you know who look in the mirror and see themselves as flawed or lacking in some way. This kind of internal noise is not objective. It is exaggerated by the unrealistic image of photoshopped models on the covers of magazines.

 The noise in our heads becomes harmful when it lacks objectivity.

Please take a minute now to reflect on the noise inside your own head. Try to bring it down to a simple statement that your brain is telling you, then spend some time to bring objectivity into your judgment by comparing what your brain is telling you to facts, science, or general views of others, such as your close friends, that contradict your belief. If your best friends and your partner constantly tell you that you are beautiful or handsome, it is reasonable to tell your brain that it is the one who got it wrong and it should stop the unrealistic, unobjective noise that harms you.

Mo here. I will admit that I struggled with this for a very long time. As a young man growing up, I compared myself to the bad, pretty boys that girls were interested in while they friend-zoned me because I was always a good boy—typical. I made the conclusion that I was not good-looking, and so I frequently reminded myself of that in my younger noisy brain. I have to admit, this worked well for me because it made me try to be better at things other than looks to find a place in the world, but it still stressed me every day. It wasn't until my lovely daughter, Aya, in her late teens, was browsing an album that had photos of me in my twenties, and she said, "Wooo! Hottie potatie!" (I still laugh when I remember this), which in teenage slang at the time meant she thought I looked handsome as a young man. I responded, "Thank you, darling, but I surely was not," and she said, "What are you talking about? You looked very handsome indeed!"

Years later, after my separation from my wonderful ex, Nibal, and when I started to allow other women into my life, it became clear that my perception of my looks, which caused me a lot of noise over the years, was lacking in objectivity. I resisted the compliments I received until I decided that perhaps it was my brain that made a mistake, that though I surely was not a pretty boy, I did not look too shabby, and as it turned out, my voice was reasonably attractive too. I had just managed to somehow convince myself otherwise for years on end. A few dates after my marriage ended and it became clear that the women I let into my life did not agree with my false conviction. They made it clear through their actions and words that they found me way more attractive than I cared to believe. I changed my mind, and though nothing else about me changed, with this new con- viction, the noise stopped.

Even when what our mind is telling us is true and objective, the noise can still hurt us when we speak to ourselves in a language that is needlessly too harsh. Telling yourself that you need to stick to your commitment to go to the gym three or four times a week is useful. It is very different from telling yourself that you look like a mess or that you are unreliable and irresponsible. There is no benefit to be found in putting yourself down.

The language we normally use inside our heads, you may notice, often mimics the words and tones used by the harshest critic we had when we were young. Be that a demanding parent or a harsh teacher, we tend to somehow repeat what they told us. We treat ourselves the way they treated us despite how much what they did to us hurt us and how little the criticism benefited us.

 Remember ! If you wouldn't make a comment to someone you love and respect, you shouldn't be making it to yourself.

 Please take a moment to reflect and observe the noise inside your head. Write down the words and try to recognize the tone. Ask yourself who it sounds like, then ask yourself two pivotal questions: Is the harshness serving you in any way? And would you speak to anyone you truly love and care about in that tone using those words? Think of how you can deliver the same messages to yourself in a kinder, more positive, and more constructive way.

There is a big difference that needs to be noted between a noise and a nuisance. A nuisance is something that is actually happening while the noise is just a thought in our brains. When you are stuck in traffic with your back hurting and are about to become late for a meeting, you're suffering the stress of a nuisance, but when you are sitting on your sofa at home dreading tomorrow's commute, the only thing you are suffering is the noise created inside your head by your own brain.

An even bigger difference is that the inner voice has a much profounder effect on us than the external nuisances because it is constantly running. If your life was externally full of little annoyances here and there, they still would add up to a few, maximum, tens in a day. But your ability to create little thoughts that annoy you can extend into the hundreds.

A study by Rodney J. Korba of the College of Wooster electromyographically recorded subvocalization during the silent solution of verbal tasks. Subjects reported the inner speech used to solve a problem (known as *elliptical word count*), and the researchers expanded that volume of words into a full statement of their internal problem-solving strategies (known as *extended word count*), finding that it represented an equivalent rate of speech in excess of four thousand words per minute.[3] Staggering, isn't it? This is how much inner chatter we are capable of generating within our own minds.

Like any conversation, your inner speech has an effect on you. How can it not? That continual internal dialogue can either raise us up or bring us crashing down. I know mine certainly does—Alice here. That dialogue lowers your stress levels when positive or increases them when negative. It boosts your confidence if supportive or knocks it if critical.

Which of those is more likely? Naturally, the negative. You're not alone in your negative thoughts. Our minds are wired to look for the negative. Psychologists describe this as the *negativity bias*. This served us all well back in the time of our cave ancestors. It was a way of keeping them safe, by always looking out for the threats around them. So they had a chance to notice it before it was too late and to promptly act and hopefully survive.

In ancient times, their brains were placed right in the middle of a very harsh nature. Everything was out to eat them, and so they really had no interest in admiring any of nature's beauty until they could feel safe. The slightest movement of a branch on a tree and those ancient brains immediately screamed, *Danger!* Your brain—sorry to be the bearer of bad news—has not evolved much beyond that primitive habit. If your boss is grumpy, danger. If your partner is late, danger; and if the news shows you yet another fear-based story, danger. Exactly how dangerous to you are such experiences? Not at all. Brains don't seem to feel obliged to offer an explanation. Yet they spread their negativity nonetheless.

Our negativity bias only strengthens our ability to magnify and hold on to the negative, even if in the grand scale of our day it was only a tiny portion. Neuroscientist Rick Hanson refers to this as our brains being like Velcro for negative experiences and Teflon for the positive.[4] We can so easily find ourselves slipping into a spiral of negative thoughts or un-kind inner conversations, based on the fact that our brains are wired to the negative—unless we take it within our own power to change and do something about it, he says.

Neuroscience, however, also indicates that our brains have the capacity to change, grow, and develop new pathways—a phenomenon known as *neuroplasticity*. New beliefs, new habits, with practice, are within our reach.

There is good news.

 Remember !   What we can't control in the outside world of stress, we can regulate in our inside world.

WHERE IT HURTS

Most of us would not be able to survive if we experienced all four quad-rants simultaneously. It would be too much to bear. Even dealing with trauma or obsessions alone is usually too much. Most of us, however, experience one quadrant or the other on any given day. No one is immune to the effects of those stressors. On a day when life does not give you nuisances, you look in the mirror and kill yourself with noise. Other days when there is no trauma breaking you, you put your guard down and let more nuisances into your day unchecked.

When in each of the quadrants, we experience its effects differently. Trauma breaks us almost instantly. It leaves us in shock, breaks our trust in life and others, depletes our energy, and takes away our passion for living. When untended to, it persists in the form of post-traumatic stress or morphs and hides so it lingers for weeks, months, or years, often trig-gering our obsessions.

Obsessions, on the other hand, don't break us down as fast as trauma does. They wear us out from the inside, lead us to despair and hopelessness, and leave us there. If trauma were a large block of concrete falling on you unexpectedly, obsessions feel more like dragging that block with you everywhere you go, every minute of your day. For as long as we allow the obsessions to linger, we feel anxiety, and if we let them linger long enough, we end up in depression.

We learn to cope with the nuisances and accept them as part of daily life; they irritate us, take the joy out of our lives, and exhaust us by the end of every day.

The noise generated inside us, on the other hand, mounts up more subtly. We think that it's good for us to tell ourselves negative things, and we even give those thoughts attention. With every passing comment, we feel more worthless and more insecure, worried about our future and regretful about our past. With no real external stresses affecting us, we end up being more effective than life itself in stressing ourselves out with our very own thoughts and emotions.

Add the *N*s—nuisances and noise—up over time and one day we find ourselves burned out. Not knowing what hit us, we end up unable to get out of bed or engage with life in any way.

Symptoms of the Stress Quadrants

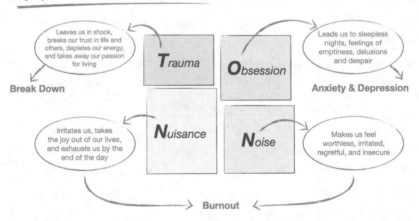

This does not need to be our reality. Perhaps with the exception of trauma, which is triggered by events that show up uninvited, all the other quadrants are firmly within our span of control. With the right focus, attention, and skills, we can reduce or even eliminate the negativity and stress they bring into our lives. Even the impact of trauma itself can be reduced and healed, though the events that trigger it reside outside our area of control.

Let's continue this line of thought and discover how the limit, learn, and listen model can help make the TONN feel manageable and easy.

3

Carrying That TONN

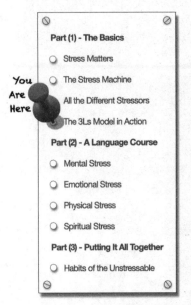

You Are Here

As the acronym indicates, stress that mounts to affect us in all four quadrants would crush us. Luckily for most of us, we seldom struggle with all four quadrants of stress at the same time, though for many of us, whenever we feel relieved of the macro stressors, we tend to slack and allow the nuisances and noise to get the best of us.

Because each quadrant is triggered differently and because each affects us differently, we need to deal with each of them differently. There is no one-size-fits-all approach to dealing with stress. Let's walk together once again through each of the quadrants, only this time with an eye for solutions and a focus on what you need to do, at the top level, in order to de-stress and create the habits you need thereafter to live a life that's stress-free.

SURVIVING THE T

Just so that we are not in the tiniest bit misunderstood, let us make this clear up front. Most trauma work requires the assistance of a professional. The next few pages will only discuss what success looks like after a trauma, but when traumatized, one is often too fragile and disoriented to achieve that success alone. When your share of trauma arrives, seek professional assistance.

Trauma is an overwhelming challenge, bigger than the tolerance capability of an individual. Because of trauma's overpowering nature, the only place from which healing begins is not found in fighting or correcting the situation. It is found in . . .

COMMITTED ACCEPTANCE

When asked for only one strategy for a happier life, my answer has always been *committed acceptance.*

When life hits you with harshness that you don't have the means to alleviate—and life will hit you every now and again—accept the new reality of your life, then commit to the actions you can take to make your life and the lives of those around you better despite the presence of that harshness.

Anything from being stuck in traffic with no clear option to move faster, all the way to losing someone you love, life is bound to challenge you with experiences that no one could change. Unless you have the power to have a few thousand cars magically disappear, you are bound to inch forward slowly until the traffic clears up. Your annoying boss will remain annoying, relationships are bound to represent differences, falling sick will require you to slow down and rest, and death will not be reversed. Those, among many others, are just facts of life. You can reject them, complain about them, or be stressed by them until you're blue in the face; they will still persist. Your resistance will not change a thing, and the only thing it will bring you is suffering.

The truth about the way life chooses to help you develop and grow contains a bit of harshness. Nothing we could ever do, you see, would have brought my wonderful Ali back. The finality of death is the untold secret behind its cruelty. As humans, especially engineers like myself, we are taught to fix things, to twist life so that it conforms to our wishes. At least we are taught to try. But just as a reminder of our arrogance, life consistently sends uncontrollable events our way, and just like with all the other forms of trauma-inducing stressors we face, there is no fixing death or any of life's other finalities.

 When life twists your arm, acceptance, which really doesn't count as doing anything at all, is the only thing you can do on the path to recovery.

It saves you the pain that results from questioning why, saves you the energy wasted in resistance, and gives your mind a seed of peace that prepares you to address the situation objectively.

You see, it doesn't really matter how much you resist. Everyone eventually learns to accept. Nibal and I could have resisted the new reality of our lives for years, and then, eventually, on my deathbed, Ali would still not be back. So what's the point?

When life is harsh beyond your control, accept. The sooner the better, so that you can start to rebuild your life after the event that shook it is done.

Accept, but don't just stay there. There is also no point in resigning and surrendering, in lying down at the low point of your life and just giving in. Acceptance prepares you for the actual work you need to do—commit.

Understand that while there is nothing to do to erase or fix what you just faced, there is a lot you can do to move away from the low point where it left you. While you may not be able to bring a loved one back, you surely can honor their memory and let it give you joy instead of sorrow. While you may not be able to heal a grieving loved one, you can hug them and be there for them. While you may not be able to save a business that made mistakes and shut down, you surely are able to take what you learned and start again. While you may not be able to mend a broken heart after a tough breakup, you surely can look forward, celebrate life, and find love again.

Only if you commit to making your life better despite—or even because of—your loss will you ever find a path to a happy life in a world that is bound to be harsh every now and again.

It's simple. Once you hit rock bottom and accept, commit to one small action that makes your life better today than it was yesterday and another action that will make your life tomorrow better than it is today.

When Ali left our world, I committed to sharing what he taught me with the world. I wrote *Solve for Happy*, founded OneBillionHappy .org, and left my job at Google to dedicate more of my life to my new mission—spreading happiness. I then wrote more books, partnered with incredible thinkers—such as Alice—to think deeper and reach further. I established my presence online, started a chart-topping global podcast, and started the Unstressable.com community. I recorded thousands of hours of content and was interviewed, in long form, by leading TV and podcast hosts. Today, millions of people are happier, or at least committed to doing the work that leads to happiness, as a result. Thousands message me regularly on social media to say, "Thank you, Ali. We love Ali," and when they do, I know that my life, with all the pain I've experienced, has always been building up to this point—a point when, believe it or not, I had never been happier despite the fact that Ali is not with me anymore.

Nothing I could ever do would bring Ali back, notice, and the pain of missing him still lingers in my heart. Yet my committed acceptance since he left surely makes my life, and the lives of those that cross my path, much better than the day he said goodbye to this world.

Remember ! Committed acceptance turns the stones life throws at you to solid gold.

And then things get even better.

POST-TRAUMATIC GROWTH

The other positive side of trauma is found in the common saying: "What doesn't kill you makes you stronger." When it comes to macro external stressors, this is totally true.

Post-traumatic growth (PTG) is a theory, developed by psychologists Richard Tedeschi and Lawrence Calhoun in the mid-1990s, that explains this kind of transformation that follows trauma. The work of Tedeschi and Calhoun describes how people who endure psychological struggle following adversity often experience positive growth as they proceed to heal.

"People develop new understandings of themselves, the world they live in, how to relate to other people, the kind of future they might have and a better understanding of how to live life," says Tedeschi.[1]

After the rush has gone and the dust of the harshness of life has settled, those who make it through one or many traumas find that they have grown. Several sides in the way they perceive and deal with life get upgraded—their appreciation and optimism for new possibilities, their personal strength and resilience when facing future stresses large or small, and they often become more spiritual as they grasp the bigger picture of how life actually operates. Smaller stressors start to show as they truly are in their eyes—insignificant—and they develop a depth of empathy toward others that far exceeds who they were before the trauma.

A *Harvard Business Review* article by Tedeschi[2] highlights that there are certain things that one can do to maximize such growth. Although post-traumatic growth often happens naturally, it can be facilitated in five ways: through education, emotional regulation, disclosure, narrative development, and service. Those interventions are often better practiced with the aid of a professional trauma therapist, but they generally could help you post–challenging times, and your awareness of them already starts you down the path of PTG.

Education, as in taking the time to learn about trauma and post-traumatic growth, helps us see the value that trauma and the disruption of core belief systems brings. A realization that the world is not always what we had hoped it would be makes us more agile. This makes it easier to accept when life contradicts one's belief system again. Education leads to a faster path to committed acceptance, which is, perhaps, the most crucial part of our growth.

Passing through serious trauma also gives us the necessary training in terms of **emotional regulation**. We learn to keep the right frame of mind, which starts with managing negative emotions, such as anxiety, guilt, and anger. Discovering the origin of those emotions in the mind's subconscious belief system is the first step to trauma recovery. Practicing this skill, while navigating a trauma, becomes paramount in terms of its importance for our future growth.

Disclosure, then, helps accelerate the process. Talking to others openly about the trauma in an objective way allows you to widen your perspective to see the truth of it and learn different ways to overcome it. Those learnings stay with you post-trauma to continue to facilitate your growth.

The next step is to produce an **authentic narrative** about the trauma and our lives afterward. This helps us accept the chapters already written and imagine a meaningful way forward. This process helps with our ability to appreciate life as it is in comparison to how hard it has been during the tough times. This opens our minds to see the opportunities hidden within every challenge. Those are transferable skills that one can use to deal with future challenges with calm and optimism. This leads to solid growth.

Finally, there are acts of **service**. People do better in the aftermath of trauma if they find work that benefits others. The ability to help others navigate events similar to the ones they have endured solidifies the learning and leads to a wider understanding of the challenge, thus furthering growth.

 Trauma feels like the end of the world when you're in it, but when you look back at it, it feels like the beginning of a new world of growth.

If you are struggling right now, when it feels like you are losing an up-hill battle, remember that you are actually far closer to your own recovery and growth than you know. Keep the faith. Your own personal expansion is waiting for you just around the corner, in ways you had no idea you were capable of.

WHEN TRAUMA COMES FULL CIRCLE

The full cycle of experiencing trauma does not end with the harsh external event that hits us. It only begins there. The difference between those who crumble under the pressure and those who fly through and thrive is simple. The latter group lives the full cycle of trauma recovery all the way to growth while others take the hit, start a cycle of obsessive thoughts, and lie down and blame the world for their calamity.

Let's put the full cycle together, then, for your reference so that you don't stop before you become a member of the thriving group.

Understand that trauma is just part of life, that we all face it, both large and small, and most of us recover. It's not the end of your life, rather a new beginning, so accept it. But don't just stay there at the lower point of your life; instead, commit. Do whatever you can to make your life better despite the challenge, even if there is nothing to do to fix it.

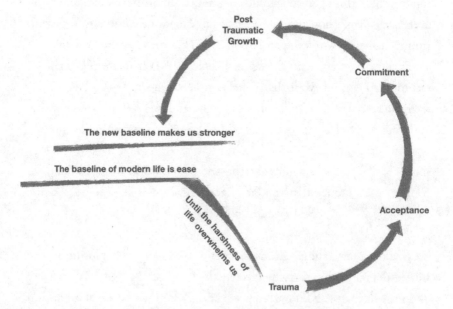

Just do what it takes to make life a little bit better today than yesterday and a little bit better tomorrow than today. Finally, allow the trauma to help you grow. Invest in your education about the topic, seek out a professional who can help you uncover limiting subconscious beliefs that your mind has created as a response to your trauma, and reprogram them. Our minds only ever want to keep us "safe," so they create subconscious limiting beliefs in response to our traumas, thinking they are helping, when in fact this can keep us stuck in our unhealthy patterns and keep us from moving forward. Uncover yours and replace them with beliefs that serve you. Learn to observe and embrace but also regulate your negative emotions, replacing them with positive optimism about what's possible. Share and talk about the challenges you face, develop an authentic, comprehensive narrative that extends beyond the negative past into the possible positive future, and engage in acts of service that help others who are experiencing what you have gone through.

This is a predictable cycle that has been lived by millions. You can experience the full extent of it too.

Often the most effective way to navigate the difficulty in times of struggle is to be willing to ask for help, to know that we are all human and those who have the experience and knowledge might save us countless unnecessary mistakes and suffering. The tools in this book will support you and help you keep yourself on track on a day-to-day basis. But whenever you feel you're swimming beyond your depth, don't shun the idea of seeking the support of a therapist, coach, or other professional if that is what you need.

While trauma is the ultimate form of stress in terms of its intensity, it is the rarest form of stress in terms of its frequency. The real reason behind this world's global epidemic of stress is not the macro, external, and uncontrollable events but the sneaky everyday stressors of the outside world combined with the internal stress we create in our own minds.

Often, the small stressors are so small that, individually, they don't warrant our attention. They are so conveniently woven into our lives that we often don't even notice them.

We need to notice them, and we surely need to learn to do something to remove them. A big part of living unstressable is about . . .

DEALING WITH THE LITTLE THINGS

Remember that rickety house of cards? We invite you to hold those cards (the nuisances and noise) in your hand to investigate them thoroughly so you can recognize them, understand their properties and how they behave, and learn how to weed them out of your life.

A MORNING OF *NS*

Alice here. I don't know about you, but if I don't take control of it, my day begins to fill up with nuisances before I even have my morning shower. Do you feel the same too? Let's take a modern human's typical morning and see if it sounds at all familiar.

Harry, a fictional committed modern human, wakes up and exhaustedly fumbles to switch off the alarm clock on his smartphone. The alarm sound, which he hasn't bothered to change from its aggressive factory setting, jolts his eyes open like a fire alarm, jarring him from his sleep. That's the first hit of stress for the day.

Sleepily, he snoozes the alarm two or three times in a desperate attempt to gather enough rest to be able to get out of bed. He finally turns it off and gets up to start an already tiring day. This counts as the second stressful hit.

Once he opens his eyes, he sits up in bed to check his phone for anything urgent, instead of checking in with himself to see how he actually feels. This is the third hit.

He reads the disturbing morning headlines and is filled with concern of what is going on in the world around him—the fourth hit. He then moves on to check his emails and finds that he has an agitated midnight email from his boss, who is complaining and letting off tension from his own stress complaining that Harry has done something wrong the day before. He then allows his mind to tell him that his boss is surely going to either shout at him that day or fire him in front of his coworkers. He reads another email from a coworker who has forgotten to do something that Harry specifically asked them to do weeks before, now putting his own work behind (hit number six). This only increases the worry in his mind about his own work and his boss's blame falling on him as the team leader. We've added up to seven hits so far.

Frustrated, he then glances at the many WhatsApp and social media notifications bidding for his attention and reads the previews of messages from friends trying to make plans for the week ahead and the many questions he hasn't yet replied to.

Although he doesn't yet feel awake enough to look at his diary and respond to them, he does of course automatically have time to mindlessly scroll through social media for five minutes.

Scrolling through the perfectly curated daily highlights reels of friends and celebrities, he stumbles across something that causes him to compare himself, which makes him feel like a loser, then feel disheartened when he sees a post of somewhere sunny where he would rather be as he looks up to see the day outside is gray and raining.

He then reminds himself of the busy day ahead, cuts himself while shaving, tells himself he looks tired and older as he glances at himself in the mirror, and realizes that he ran out of coffee and feels he's really in need of one this morning. In case you're not counting, we are now up to fifteen hits of stress only forty-five minutes into the day. By this point, Harry has already clocked up on a full load of little stressors before he has even left his home.

Can you imagine where he will get to by noon?

Can you imagine where *you*, usually, get to by the evening?

Those little hits in Harry's morning are all examples of how nuisances and noise easily slide into our day-to-day lives, right under our noses. Each on its own holds very little power over making us stressed. Cutting himself while shaving is very unlikely to drive Harry to a nervous break-down on its own. As the stressors pile in continually every day, though, they eventually build up to a sizable load as he inches closer and closer to his stress tolerance level. That's when his house of cards falls.

But Harry's morning doesn't lead him to stop and reflect on the load he's carrying. He rushes out of the door to encounter more. He brushes it off and pretends that he's "fine."

He skips his lunchtime walk to get more work done and gets into an argument with a coworker that irritates him right around the time when his partner calls to tell him that he needs to find a way to go pick the kids up from school. Then he gets stuck in traffic on the way, which makes him late for a meeting, and stays late at work to meet a looming deadline that had to be met that day. When he finally comes home, instead of giving his mind a break, he holds his phone and continues to be bombarded with messages and notifications, scrolling one last time on social media with the light from the device glaring into his face.

The phone finally runs out of battery long before Harry can wind down his thoughts enough to fall asleep. I say *Harry*, but could I have said the above about you?

Please put the book down now and reflect. Don't keep going like Harry did. A few minutes of your time may become the epiphany that you need to change direction. List all the nui-sances currently present in your life. Capture them on paper, regardless of how small.

Take as much time as you need to finish this simple reflection. We will be waiting for you here when you're done.

Unaware of the importance of the stressors that build up, we tend to do nothing to bring our system back down to a calm state. Nothing tells your mind and body that there is actually no threat and that all is well. And yet, each little stress is seen by your biological system as a reason to react. One hurts, but many can kill by a thousand cuts.

Micro stressors are like an army—alone, they are no real threat, but together, they can take anyone down.

Before you panic and think, *I have so many nuisances and micro stressors in my day, I'm screwed!* (Oh, hello, one more sneaky little stressor—noise.) Think differently. Now actually is the moment to be happy.

Be happy that you have finally recognized what's going on, and because awareness is half the battle, you can actually start to relax. Micro stressors are the easiest type of stress to deal with, once you put your mind to it, hence their names . . . nuisances and noise. Because that, truly, is what they are, nothing more, when dealt with swiftly and decisively.

YOUR FIRST ACCOUNTABILITY—LIMIT

Mo here. I can't help but remind you of the breakdown equation and the first of your three responsibilities—to limit, as in remove all unwarranted stressors, external or internal, from your life. If they can't be removed altogether, then at least reduce their intensity, the frequency of their existence, and the duration for which they apply to you when they are part of your life. Develop the skills you need to reduce them on the spot and the healthy habits you need to keep them excluded from your life thereafter.

How can we do that? It's a simple three-step approach. Remove every nuisance that is removable from your daily life, see the remaining ones for what they really are—annoying little things that should not even stress you in the first place. That way they would not trigger your internal noise and, finally, create healthy habits that make your lifestyle more stress-free.

You can't limit what you don't recognize. If an exposed pipe in your kitchen's plumbing starts to leak, it is likely you will observe it quickly and take action to fix it. If, however, the pipe is hidden inside the wall, puddles of water will build up. You will only find out that something needs your attention when serious damage has been done. Let's expose those pipes now so you are aware of the stream of stressors that you need to limit.

 Take some time now, perhaps thirty minutes, to answer the question: *What stressors am I simply allowing into my life and needlessly creating within myself that I potentially have the power to limit?*

Think of your last week as a reference and look for the external stressors first. Did you allow too many meetings into your diary? Did you spend too much time on your devices? Can you count too many mornings when you aimlessly glided straight into watching the stressful morning news? Do you still go to work during the busiest time of the morning, making your commute unbearable? What else did you let into your life to stress you? It's time to take stock.

Then shift your attention to the noise. Ask yourself what negative or critical thoughts have popped up unchecked inside your head last week. Did you make an unkind comment to yourself about the shape of your body? Did you tell yourself you were not good enough? Did you compare yourself to a social media influencer and think less of yourself? Did you talk to yourself harshly?

Limiting starts with awareness. Write down a long list of your findings. Don't stop till you run out of things to list. When you're done, take your list and let's start working.

STEP 1: DELETE THE NEEDLESS STRESS

There's no way to say it nicely, so let's say it exactly as it is. To reduce the needless stress in your life, you need to learn ruthlessly to . . .

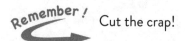 Cut the crap!

Harry's day is made up of the choices he makes. Whether it's looking at his phone before he gets out of bed or scrolling through social media in bed before he sleeps, Harry—and you—can always choose differently.

I'll take the news as an example, obviously, because I am an activist against wasting your life believing this constant stream of crap—all the negativity that we let into our lives with no agency or ability to effect any kind of change. Think about what I just said before your brain tells you that you need the news to be kept aware and make informed decisions. Think about what actually happens and ask yourself when the last time watching the news enabled you to do anything positive for yourself or others was. The government made an announcement that you don't approve of, a child is missing, a foreign nation is waging war, and Bitcoin has fallen to a new low for the year. What can you do about any of this? Did you ever write a note to your senator explaining your views and demanding a change? Did they ever respond? Did you ever put on your superhero suit and go save the child? Did you manage to find a way to save lives and stop the war? What, other than feeling frustrated, has the news brought to you? If you trade in Bitcoin, choose to search specifically for relevant news, take action, and avoid any further negativity. If you don't, why are you allowing this bit of information into your already busy brain? The stress machine of the typical human is designed to deal with its immediate surroundings, not the opinion of a foreign correspondent about currency fluctuations in Latin America and floods in the Philippines. When we expand our surroundings to include all the negativity that is happening absolutely everywhere, our stress response remains triggered—infinitely.

Even in the cases when we believe that staying informed is of paramount importance, we most often are wrong. On the second lockdown of COVID-19, I lived in Montreal for four months. Everyone was glued to their screens trying to keep up with all the updates, analysis, and predictions as they expected the world to end. The news media, playing in the small grocery shop next to my Airbnb, was bubbling with all sorts of debate. *Why did this happen? Who's responsible? Who messed up? Why is the government doing this? What will happen to our freedom? Will we all die? And how will the French language in Quebec be affected?* So much noise, so much stress. I chose not to listen to any of it. As a matter of fact, I only listened to the news for the first four days of the pandemic, and I am still here without the stress.

One evening, a friend texted me. She said, "Can you believe we're going into code red tomorrow?"

I asked what code red was.

She answered, "Restaurants and shops are closed, and we have to wear masks everywhere."

"Okay," I said. "That's all I need to know." Action taken. Months of my life saved to be lived and enjoyed. No unnecessary stress.

You can do the same too. The news networks are not interested in informing you. They are interested in keeping you glued to the screen. Cut the crap they feed you! Search for the information you need, the things you can act upon. Read the headlines and avoid the drama and the noise. Save your time and stop allowing reporters to stress your days.

What else can you take out of your life with one decision? A friend who is draining you? A partner in a dead-end relationship? A commute that can be easier if you started it a bit earlier? A debate with someone that doesn't really matter about a topic you don't really care about?

STEP 2: DON'T SWEAT THE LITTLE THINGS

We will cover this in a lot more detail when we discuss being mentally or emotionally stressed, but it is important to position it correctly in the flow of your thinking here. Cleansing your day of needless stress, however, will never truly take all the nuisances away. Some stressor will always remain—one that gets on your nerves every now and again, leading you to trigger the noise in your head. A rude person, a negative comment on your social media post, or cutting yourself while shaving all are external stresses that last a few seconds and then fade in the void of time. Only you can keep them alive in the form of noise or obsessions. *I'm an idiot. I should have said this or responded that way. Life is against me. This is not my year.*

For all those stressors that remain, your strategy is simple—don't let any of those get to you. Let them out of your mind and heart before they turn into noise.

Back at Google, I once had a meeting with a brilliant woman who was one of our heads of engineering. She came a few minutes late, and at first, she seemed furious. "The Uber driver drove me mad," she said. "He was rude, played loud music, and took the wrong route. I tried to explain to him that there is an easier way, but he just wouldn't listen, and now I am late."

As I geared up to spend some time empathizing with her situation to comfort her after such a stressful commute, she smiled and said, "Let's go have coffee."

Surprised, I asked, "What? Coffee? Don't you want to talk about this a bit more?"

She answered, "Why would I? All in all, it was a ten-minute commute. Why would I spend another ten minutes of my life feeling stressed about it?"

Now, this is wisdom. It's the answer to most of our Ns.

Remember ! Most micro stressors don't even deserve a minute of your day.

If you have to be stuck in a commute, enjoy some music or a podcast. If your partner is irritated or exhausted, enjoy hugging them rather than complain about them. If your landlord kicked you out and you have to look for another place, look forward to the novelty and new experiences this will bring.

Yes, you may not always be able to take them out of your life, but with the right attitude, you can keep them out of your thoughts and emotions, and that's what you *should* do.

STEP 3: CREATE HEALTHY HABITS

The challenge we all face with the Ns is that they are endless. They just keep flooding in. Even after you've cleaned your life of some and then removed the remaining ones from your heart and mind, in no time at all, many will return, and new ones will show up to trigger your stress again. The only way to stay nuisance-free is to create habits that ensure those stressors don't show up in your life in the first place.

Stress Hack Let's look at a few of our favorite top tips to follow. Use them all or start by picking just one to stick to, and then work your way up to two, three, or four, until you've mastered them all.

SIMPLE MORNING ROUTINE (15–20 MINUTES)

Make your morning routine your most cherished ritual. Write it down on a Post-it Note and place that on your nightstand. Try to wake up twenty minutes earlier than you need to, to fully enjoy your routine with no stress. It will likely be the best twenty minutes of your day.

- Turn your phone on airplane mode before bed, and don't turn it off until you have completed your morning ritual.
- Use a soothing alarm sound to wake you up. (I use meditation music that gets louder.)
- Think of an intentionally good thought before you get out of bed: *Today is going to be a good day.*
- Make your favorite morning drink, and then get your journal out to:
    * Mind dump for five minutes: Write, get all of your thoughts out of your head and onto paper (you can use prompts like "How do I feel today?" or just free flow).
    * 5 + 5 gratitude: Write five things down that you are grateful for in the outside world and five within yourself.
    * Set an intention for the day: Write it down, and then state it out loud, such as *I choose to feel calm today*, or *Today, I am going to create x.*
- Meditate: Use a guided meditation or simply set a timer for five minutes, close your eyes, and breathe deeply, concentrating purely on your breath.
- Center yourself for the day ahead.

EASY EVENING ROUTINE (10–15 MINUTES)

Stress Hack

Turn your phone to airplane mode at least one hour before bedtime. Let your phone sleep in another room if that's an option. Get ready for bed and make your ritual the last thing you do before you sleep.

- Use a journal to:
  - * List three things that brought you joy today, no matter how small they may seem.
  - * Write down something that you handled or did well today.
  - * Write down three things you are grateful for today.
- Connect to your breath for five minutes with your eyes closed, to relax your mind and body before you sleep. Breathe in the scent of a natural oil like lavender to relax you.
- Repeat in your mind a positive mantra—*I did well today. I am safe. I am relaxed. I am ready for a restful night of sleep and a wonderful day tomorrow.*

These routines do not count as chores. They can bring joy and calm into your life.

LIMITS IN THE DIGITAL WORLD

While the majority of us may have to accept that we need a smartphone to run our lives efficiently in this modern-day jungle, we can choose to use this device differently to make our lives a little bit easier and more convenient, but we don't. Why? As studies now show, we have become addicted to technology. One recent study shows that the average smartphone user will click, tap, or swipe their phone 2,617 times a day![3] Read that back again and take a moment to realize how insane that actually is: 2,617 times a day—and that's the average. So do you use yours more or less often?

The first step you need to do is to find out. Digital health apps will now tell you all you need to know, and I promise you, you are using your phone way more than you care to think, and the usage is not really making you happier or more efficient at all. When I started measuring my own usage, I realized that I spent upward of seven hours a day staring at that little screen. That was when I meditated less than twenty minutes a day and spent, at best, a few hours a week with my loved ones. The result? Neck pains, injury in my wrist, and a brain that is aching with all sorts of negativity and useless sixty-second clips. Please start your digital health app before you read any further, and find out what truly is happening to you with your phone.

When I figured out the disastrous use of my day, I cut that crap out of my life. I check my phone once every two hours for less than ten minutes, then switch off the data network, set a timer for another two hours, and leave my phone till the reminder tells me to check again. You can do that too.

Not too long ago, I lived in a time when there was no internet and no smartphones. I know, it's hard to believe. When I wanted to set an appointment with a client, I called them, agreed on a time, and asked for directions. As I drove to them, I had no way of predicting if there was traffic on the way, so I had to allow a bit of buffer, and if I got stuck in traffic, there was no way to inform them that I was going to be a bit late. There was no window-shopping for a mate on a dating app and no catching up with old friends with a post and a like. When you wanted to connect with people, you met them . . . as people. When you needed money, you walked to the bank, and when the bank wanted something from you, they called or sent a letter. Funny, though, without all those incredible innovations that we have today that are supposed to aid our lives, that slower life was, in many ways, easier.

Technology came into our lives with the promise of making us productive, mobile, so that we can spend more time enjoying life. Most mobile phone ads in the early years were shot at a party or on the beach. The tech was positioned as a promise to give you free time to go where you want while you can still stay in touch with the things that matter to you. That promise, of course, has never been delivered on. Humanity's greed for more utilized the technology to get you to do more, instead of giving you more time when you did what you were supposed to do more efficiently. Instead of giving us freedom, those devices became our prisons.

Raise your head whenever you are in a public place and observe how everyone is glued to their little screens. Some rush around stressed and yet still trying to get one more task in by making a call or sending a message, while others, who finally got a free minute, swipe like an addict to overcome their boredom. Both ends and everyone in between clearly getting very little joy out of the use of technology, which has now become the single biggest part of their day.

According to the latest available data, the average person globally spends six hours and fifty-eight minutes per day on screens connected to the internet. Those are averages, and so the peak examples are even worse. The average American spends seven hours and five minutes on their phone and will check it 352 times a day. Gen Z, for example, averages around nine hours of screen time per day, while South Africans spend ten hours and forty-six minutes on screens per day.[4]

With numbers that high, our engagement with tech is surely the thing we do most of in our day, perhaps, with the exception of sleep, if you sleep eight hours a day. But even sleep, for those who are on their screen a lot, seems to be the tax you pay for your digital addiction along with a whole host of other symptoms and costs. The damage of our digital addiction is not limited to wasting our time and stressing us. It also extends to affect our social connections, physical well-being, and the feelings of insecurity that result from comparing ourselves to others that we see on the screen.

Studies show that constant checkers (those who check their devices several times an hour) are 20 percent more likely to feel stressed than those who don't. Those who check for work-related emails on the weekend are 36 percent more stressed. Those who spend six hours, the global average, or more a day are twice as likely to struggle with anxiety or depression than those who spend less. Those consumers of tech are also three times more likely to feel lonely, and, of course, there is a direct correlation between the number of hours spent a day on devices and insomnia and sleeplessness, eye strain, fatigue, body aches, obesity, even diabetes and accordingly a multitude of other diseases that are its direct result.

Despite the clear damage the excessive time we spend on devices causes us, 65 percent of those surveyed in a study said that a digital detox would benefit them but only 28 percent admitted to detoxing digitally in the last year. Why? Because our modern relationship with devices closely matches the same characteristics of an addiction as in that craving for something that feels needed or joyful in the moment but ends up hurting us in the long term. This addiction is not only the result of the tricks of stickiness that the tech companies embed within their products, as much as we all want to place the blame on them as we continue browsing. It is not because of any real need to be productive either. Nir Eyal, the bestselling author of *Indistractable*, says that only 10 percent of the time we whip out the phone is to do something productive—like answer an important email. How about the remaining 90 percent? Those are the result of emotional discomfort.[5]

At the top of the list of uncomfortable emotions that we keep checking our devices to relieve are the fear of missing out (the constant need to check if there is something we are missing), loneliness (the need to connect with other humans, even if only by watching what they post), ego (the need to be noticed and the endless comparison to others), and, finally, at the top of the list, comes boredom, which is a curious emotion that I would like to focus on a bit.

Boredom existed as an emotion in our early ancestors for a reason. When you feel bored, it is a signal that you are underwhelmed with the world as it is. What should this trigger within you? In the absence of entertainment, it should create an urge to change the world and make it interesting. This emotion may have single-handedly helped us create civilization as we know it—that is, until the massive entertainment industry used this emotion to maximize their profits. When we feel bored in the modern world, we rely on the entertainment industry to help us waste our lives. We suspend the need to create a more interesting world and replace that instead with plugging our thoughts into moving images that help us pass the time—wasting the most precious resource you have ever been given: the minutes that make up your life. As you short-circuit the purpose for which boredom exists, you sink *deeper* into boredom as the need to be entertained continues to grow. The same holds true when we drown any of our discomforts into digital addictions. We don't really ease the discomfort; instead, we often end up multiplying it. When you're swiping on content because you're bored, how do you feel at the end of an hour of swiping? More bored. The more you seek validation online to satisfy your ego by posting content and waiting for those likes to come in, how do you feel? More insecure. The more you seek companionship in those little screens instead of actually being out there with real humans where you can feel the real connection, the lonelier you become. Then, of course, every time you take out your device because of your fear of missing out on something, ironically, you're actually missing out even more on the one thing that really matters. You're missing out on life itself.

The answer to all the discomfort that leads to digital addiction is to honor the original purpose for which the emotion exists or to simply go back to the old days and live with the discomfort as a yogi gets to live with an itch on her nose.

This can be done using a model I call . . .

IAAA—INTENTION, AWARENESS, ASSISTANCE, AND ALTERNATIVES

Intention is always the starting point of any form of change. Changing the intention behind how much you are going to be on your digital devices and what you are using them for changes your behavior gradually to match your intention. I am not advocating that you buy an old voice phone and drop the tech that has the potential to enhance your life altogether. What I am suggesting is that you allow yourself to benefit from technology as you leave its harm behind. Set yourself an intention that sounds something like this:

Very Important! → Every minute that I spend online will be a minute that enriches me and gives me joy.

Grab all the benefits technology has to offer, everything that makes our lives better, but drop the parts that work against you. That's the plan.

Keep this intention squarely in your mind. Place it somewhere you will see it every day to remind yourself to be mindful with your digital usage. Even better, make it your phone's home screen so that you get reminded every time you are on the edge of the cliff.

Next is **awareness**. I'm sure some of the statistics we shared above shocked you a little, and expect that if you become aware of your own statistics, you will be shocked even more. When I first prioritized my digital well-being and started measuring my consumption, which added up to seven hours a day as I previously mentioned, four of which were on WhatsApp alone. Those hours slipped by unnoticed. I was wasting a third of my life every day. How about you? Do you know how much time you spend doing what? Only when we become aware of our own digital usage and habits do we start putting the action plans in place to make the change.

 Hours are the only real asset we are given. Count how many you waste staring at a little screen.

Use a digital health app to monitor your daily screen time. Pay specific attention to the time spent on any of the addictive apps—any app that takes more than thirty minutes of your day, which I usually call "the bad apps"—like games, WhatsApp, Instagram, TikTok, and other social media apps. Also monitor the apps that you know drain or frustrate you, even if the time spent on these is just a few minutes a day, and finally observe your overall screen time per day.

We often try to find justifications for our addictions. I, for one, attempted to convince myself that four hours on WhatsApp were needed because it helped me avoid email. What that statement ignored was that I was spending long hours in chats that were conversational in nature and so were not a replacement for email but rather for a phone or a video call. Once I chose to stop using WhatsApp for chats and to instead pick up the phone and actually call the person, the number of hours on the app dropped drastically.

Awareness extends beyond how much of your time is wasted to how much of it you are *willing* to waste.

 Set a limit for the maximum screen time you think is justified.

I set myself the target of no more than ninety minutes a day. With awareness of where you are and where you want to be, it is time to take the next steps and gradually move in the right direction.

That's when seeking **assistance** works really well for you. Just as some technology is trying to trap you, other technologies are trying to set you free. They do that by alerting you when you spend more time than you set as your target on a certain app. Other techniques could be to seek the assistance of friends or by physically putting a distance between you and your phone.

Stress Hack

Think of it this way. If you are attempting to lose weight, don't keep chocolate at home, tell your partner to remind you, and, if you can, tell the store to stop you if you try to buy any sweets. Here is how to do the same in the digital world.

- Use **app time limits** from within the app. YouTube, Instagram, and others, to protect themselves from potential legal action, now allow the users to set a time limit and will alert you when you hit it.

- **Turn off all notifications.** It will not be easy to figure out how to do this. App designers know that without notifications, you will switch the phone on significantly less frequently, seldom start their apps, and spend much less time on their apps in general. This will allow you to be in command, to decide for yourself what you want to check and when. It limits your phone consumption and limits the stress that results from the endless stream of buzzing alerts. Turn notifications to silent so you are not interrupted constantly with the audible and buzzing alerts that you are not ready to part ways with yet. Check those only when you deliberately choose to switch on your phone. Think about it: the very term *alert* says it all. Your body perceives each of those as a possible warning sign that something is wrong or at least needs immediate attention, when in reality, it's likely all okay. Trust that the world will not end if you read an email when you have consciously chosen to dedicate time to read your email. You're not that important (sorry), and if it is that urgent, they'll call.

- Try **grayscale mode**, which removes the colors from your phone and turns it black and white instead. You'll be surprised how much less tempting a phone becomes without the flashy colors UX designers use to capture your attention.

- Use **airplane mode** to disconnect from the endless stream of distractions. Turn your phone to airplane mode an hour before bedtime.

- **Switch your phone off completely** as often as you can. The time it takes for the phone to switch back on is a real deterrent to our compulsive habit of reaching out to the phone to feed our discomforts.

- Let your phone **sleep in another room**. That way, it's not the first thing you reach for when you wake up in the morning.

- Put your phone away in a **phone cemetery**—a drawer or a closet where it is kept out of sight—for a few hours each evening when you're supposed to spend time with loved ones. Out of sight, out of mind.

- Set **phone-free zones**. Your phone is not welcome at the dining table, for example.

- Set **phone-free times**. Put it away at least one full hour before you go to sleep, for example.

- **Cleanse your social media**. Stop following accounts that make you feel down. On top of the list of those are those news accounts that bombard you with a constant stream of disturbing news. Unfollow those who supply news or opinions that stress you when you can do nothing to change them. If you absolutely have to be informed, take the time to customize your news feed so that you get only the news you need. Stop seeking influencers who badly influence your mood. Limit those you follow who are not actual friends to thirty people at most. Only follow those that uplift, educate, or inspire you. If you're brave enough, delete your social media app. Welcome to a simpler world.

- Seek the **human assistance** of those that you trust. Ask them to remind you if your habits plummet again and to encourage you when you spend time in their presence without using your phone.

Finally, instead of just attempting to resist your phone, perhaps indulge yourself in the joy of other **alternatives**. Dedicating more of your time and attention to interactions that enrich your life consumes the time that you would alternatively dedicate to those that stress you. What healthy alternatives can you enjoy to not be on your

Stress Hack

phone?

- Can you connect more to yourself? Meditate, journal, reflect, go out for a walk, stretch, exercise?
- Can you connect to others? Go out for dinner with a friend? Enjoy time with your kids or loved ones?
- What's a hobby that you can submerge yourself in instead of staring at your phone? Do you want to go to tango classes? Go back to cooking? Or pick up a pencil and scribble?
- Remember the good old book? Can you spend time with a paper book (that doesn't come with a notification feature to interrupt you), a cup of coffee, and some music?
- How about nature? Any chance in your neighborhood to spend more time in front of a river or near a tree?
- Have you ever tried a silent retreat? This doesn't have to be the strict type but just a day or two off the grid. Those to me are life changers.

A digital detox will benefit each and every one of us. Technology stresses us more than we realize. Make it a priority to limit the stress that tech causes you.

Remember !   Put your phone down.

Let's go back now to cover the rest of the TONN. Trauma is rare and needs the help of an expert. Most of the *N*s need you to rise up to your first accountability and **limit** first and foremost. Obsessions and the *N*s that slip through your limits can only be addressed with your other two accountabilities—**learn** and **listen**.

ABILITIES, RESOURCES, AND SKILLS

Let's go back to the basics once again. The stress equation shows that our feelings of stress are not only the result of the challenges we face but that they are equally the result of the abilities, resources, and skills we have at our disposal to deal with the challenges we face.

It is intuitive to think that abilities and skills are developed within us through learning—and that surely is partially true—but there is more. First, learning is the process of acquiring knowledge. Turning that knowledge into abilities and skills requires practice. We will spend the majority of the remainder of this book sharing information and logic with you to enable you to learn, intellectually, but we will also share lots of practical tips—marked with the Stress Hacks symbol—to apply in the real world, and numerous exercises—marked with the Reflection Time symbol—to practice in the safety of your own home.

The learning is not complete without the practice, so please don't just skim through the pages. Instead, stop, reflect, and include the hacks as part of your daily habits. Success as we discussed early in this book is that you not just de-stress but become unstressable—calm and solid in the face of future challenges. This can only be achieved when you have changed your lifestyle to face future stressors with the abilities, resources, and skills that you need to solve the issues while you remain calm. Knowledge alone is not enough.

 *Remember!* Practice makes perfect.

The other side of developing those skills is found in a language course that we are about to take you through. Imagine that you are an amazing mechanic who has all the abilities and skills to solve the most complex mechanical issues with any car. In your hometown, you are a celebrity. When the client walks in, you learn the issue from them, talk to the rest of the team at the workshop to explain your views, and then call the suppliers to get the appropriate parts. By the end of the day, the problem is solved, and you are, once again, celebrated for the star that you are. One day, though, you decide that there is more opportunity for business in a foreign land. You take all your knowledge, skills, and abilities with you but somehow struggle to secure your place of stardom there. Clients can't speak to you, you can't discuss the issues with the team, and even when you know what needs to be done, you can't explain to the suppliers what you need to get the required parts. Disaster!

 All the skills in the world are useless if you don't speak the language of the environment in which you need them.

This, surprisingly, is also true when you deal with stressful situations. Stress speaks to you, and you speak back to it in four languages. Unless you know those languages intuitively, you will not be able to respond in ways that lead you to your calm place.

SPEAKING IN TONGUES

This TONN of stress triggers affects us in four different modalities—call them MEPS. Humans, we believe, are made up of four layers of being: mental (where our thoughts and cognition exist), emotional (where our emotions live), physical (our biology and physical form), and spiritual (the term many spiritual teachings use to refer to our nonphysical self).

When stress is triggered, we suffer differently in each of those layers.

The Four Modalities of Stress (MEPS)

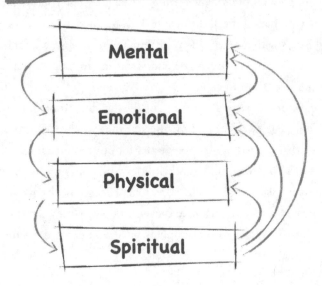

Many ancient teachings, even medical practices that work surprisingly well, though not supported by modern medicine, rely on the interactions between those layers. Reiki energy healing or acupuncture, for example, assume that invisible energy fields affect our physical well-being and even our emotions. Lots of therapy practices acknowledge that our emotions affect our physical health, and my body of work on happiness explains how our thoughts directly affect our emotions.

We live in those four layers, and so when stress is triggered within us, it manifests in one of them; that layer then affects the others as the stress propagates. To eradicate our stress once and for all, we need to work on all four layers in tandem. Leaving any of them behind leaves a residual stress that expands and grows to trigger new waves of stress in the other layers.

Each of the layers that make us human speaks to us constantly to tell us what it needs us to do to de-stress. We can also communicate back to it, only if we speak the language.

You see, those layers don't speak in plain words, perhaps other than the mind, which seems to be telling us what happened when in reality it is only telling us what it thinks happened. It exaggerates, filters, is negatively biased, and is a bit of a chatterbox. If we take its words at face value, we often misunderstand the truth.

Remember ! Your mind speaks constantly, but it rarely ever tells you the truth.

Our hearts speak not in words but in feelings and emotions that blend as drops of color dropped in whirlpools of water. You need to be a bit of an artist, attune to the subtleties of emotions, to sense what your heart is actually saying. You need to develop an appreciation for the whispers and the screams expressed emotionally. You need to break a feeling down to the basic emotions that it is made of. If you don't fully feel and acknowledge those emotions, a lot gets missed in translation.

Remember ! Our hearts speak to us constantly, but the voice is subtle, blended, and often dampened or ignored.

How about our bodies? Those magnificent physical forms speak in the vocabulary of pleasure, pain, vibrancy, depletion, and aches. They speak in unmissable sentences if we pay attention, but we don't. We notice the messages but ignore the signals and keep pushing through until our bodies start screaming to be heard.

Remember ! Our bodies speak clearly, but we ignore what they say.

Finally, our souls, which seem to know the whole truth, speak to us in connection and intuition, a language that our hyper-analytical modern world deems inaccurate and accordingly irrelevant. We ignore the words our spirits whisper, and we remain unaware as we stress them.

Remember ! Our souls speak in the language of intuition, a language that we often distrust and discredit.

The rest of this book is a **language course**. Through it, you will learn to speak in the tongues of the four elements that you are made of, to listen attentively and understand, to respond, to acknowledge your understanding, and to act upon it with the commitment it takes to make yourself feel better.

With the exception of chronic physical pain, over which we have very little control, and genuine threats to our lives, for which stress is useful, everything else starts with a thought. We generate a story inside our heads and choose to let it stress us.

For that, we might as well start there, where most of the modern-world stress is initiated—the thoughts that make us mentally stressed.

I'd suggest you take a short break now. Then come join us, feeling refreshed, for part II.

SUMMARY OF PART I
A Look Inside Our Stress Machine

- Stress is part of humanity's survival machine. It is triggered in the face of threats and challenges to enable us to perform superhuman feats, engage our fight-or-flight response, and overcome the adversities of life. In that sense, stress can be good for you.
- In our modern world, however, prolonged, intense, and chronic stress has become the norm. This is despite the fact that the physical threats for which our stress machine has been designed have diminished, even vanished altogether for most of us. In the absence of tigers roaming our cities, we learned to label every type of challenge as a stress and respond to it as if it is likely to take our lives. As our human machine remains constantly hyper-tuned for stress, many of us have started to pay the price as our mental and physical health deteriorate. Between depression, suicide, diabetes, PTSD, hypertension,

cardiac conditions, and a whole host of other debilitating and often deadly medical conditions that can all be directly attributed to stress, it is safe to assume that stress truly is the pandemic of our age.

- We start to stress even before the challenge we anticipate in the future hits us. Fear and its derivatives take control of our thoughts as they lead us into cycles of needless stress about a future that has not yet arrived. Dealing with fear requires us to look at the possible upcoming threat and attempt to tackle it or reduce its intensity. When worried, however, we are not even sure that the threat is real; we're just concerned about it. When worrying, focus on finding clarity if the reason you worry is even real. Anxiety is also not mainly concerned with the threat but rather with your ability to deal with it. When anxious, focus on your skills. Verify if you truly don't have the skills you need or if your mind is exaggerating and focusing on developing the skills you need. Panic is concerned with the element of time. We panic when a threat seems imminent. If you feel panicked, look for what you can do to grant yourself more time.

- Stress in humans is no different from how stress is measured in physics. It is not just the result of the intensity of the pressure applied to us but it is, equally, attributed to our ability to deal with those pressures. In that sense, stress is so predictable that it follows a mathematical equation:

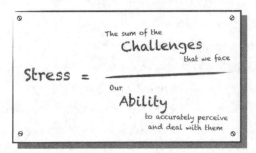

$$\text{Stress} = \frac{\text{The sum of the } \textbf{Challenges} \text{ that we face}}{\text{Our } \textbf{Ability} \text{ to accurately perceive and deal with them}}$$

- In physics, *strain* refers to the changes in the shape of an object when stressed. Objects that are stiff will rupture, while objects that are higher in elasticity will bend a bit then get back to their original shape. This can be observed the same way in humans. The more flexible we are in the way we deal with stresses, the better we are at dealing with the things that stress us. Also like objects, some of the deformation in shape post-stress remains. What doesn't break us makes us stronger. The stress that we survive eventually makes us who we are.

- It is not stress that we are up against here, though. A bit of stress can be good for you. It is burnout and breakdown that we are trying to avoid.

- We break down when the intensity or number of the different pressures we are subjected to and the time or repetition of their application exceeds our ability to carry the load. This too follows a predictable equation. We break down when:

Burnout breaks us when ...

The number of Challenges (we face) X The Intensity (of each) X The Time (they last) X The frequency of their Repetition (over time) > Our Ability (To stay strong)

- With a mathematical equation in mind, there are really three accountabilities that we have to exercise in order to avoid reaching our breakdown point:
  * Choose to remove stress from your life or at least reduce its intensity whenever possible.
  * Don't let even the tiniest of stresses linger. Don't allow the same stress to keep reoccurring.
  * Invest in developing the skills you need to handle stress.

- Stress comes from everywhere. Some of it comes from outside of us and some from within us. Some of it is major in its intensity and impact, and some is minor but large in numbers. Categorizing stress by its source and intensity leads to four quadrants that we have called TONN—trauma, obsessions, nuisances, and noise.

- While we clearly will never be able to control the trauma-triggering events of our lives, stats show that more than 90 percent of us recover from their impact within the first few months of their occurrence. This post-traumatic growth can enhance our lives through things like increased empathy, as long as we become aware of any limiting subconscious beliefs our minds may have created as a response to our trauma in order to help keep us "safe." These limiting beliefs can be reprogrammed with the help of a professional to allow us to show up and view the world away from the lens of our trauma.

- Smaller external events truly are not worth our attention. We should remove as many of them as we can and let the rest be, because they really don't matter.

- What really matters is the internal stress we cause ourselves, whether in the form of obsession over certain beliefs that sometimes lasts a lifetime or in the form of the noise that keeps building up inside our heads every day. Our self-generated stress truly is the reason for the stress pandemic the world suffers from today. This is where we need to focus so that we survive the constant attacks of stress that we are subjected to in the modern world.

- Stress manifests within us in each of the four layers that makes us human: our mental, emotional, physical, and spiritual forms. Noticing where and why and learning what needs to be fixed and how to fix it is the skill we need to learn so we can overcome stress wherever it is triggered.

Your Stress Score

Where is most of your stress coming from? Which language should you learn first?

It's only once we are aware of where our stress is coming from that we can then do something about it. Taking this quiz is optional, though highly recommended.

It will help you identify the triggers and the manifestations, as well as the intensity of your stress profile, giving you your current overall stress score, while also showing you in which of the four elements you currently have the highest and lowest stress levels: mental, emotional, physical, or spiritual.

Simply scan the QR code below to find out your score. It only takes a few minutes.

www.unstressable.com/unstressable-quiz

Now that you know your score and in which element you currently hold the most stress, it's time for you to be able to protect yourself against it, to shield yourself from the stress of both the world and the stress you create inside your head.

So let's start there, in the place where it all begins, where both the magic and often the confusion happens: inside your mind.

Part II

A Language Course in Becoming Unstressable

Complex puzzles are only solved when every piece is fully in balance with all the other pieces. Our recurring stress, despite our attempts to overcome it, is mainly due to an imbalance of our mental, emotional, physical, and spiritual stress. When one eases, the others take over, and we find ourselves in an endless loop.

4

It's in Your Head

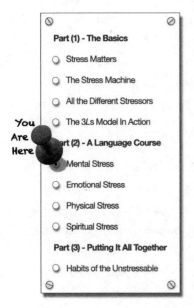

You Are Here

I'm sorry you feel this way. If it's any consolation, we *all* do. I, for one, spent years at the peak of my career sleeping four- to five-hour nights. I thought it was a good thing. It made me more productive. I'd catapult into waking up, usually between 3:00 and 4:00 A.M. I'd open my eyes, check the clock, praying that it was 7:00 and that I'd had enough sleep. The realization that I was up against another night of tossing and turning would push me into an immediate, desperate attempt to go back to sleep. But my brain would beat me to it. It's fast, that little bastard. It would generate an important thought. Or at least it would make it seem so. Something timely. *Remember to ask Alex to call Rob. Why, brain? Why?* Now I am left with a prisoner's dilemma: I can either get up, switch on the light, and write a note so I don't forget (but then the light would surely leave me wide awake), or I can leave the lights off and keep trying to doze off, but the thought, as I worry that I will forget it, would keep me awake. I'm doomed.

My brain would then go in all directions at full speed. *What will happen if you forget? Why did you not connect them last night before you went to sleep? What else needs to be done? Why did Alex say so-and-so last week? What is wrong with you? Is there something you are not aware of? Should you write an email to ask? Who else thinks this way? It must be because you wear black. You should stop wearing black. But you have a little belly, and black hides it well. Do you think they don't see the belly? Why don't you work out more? You used to be handsome. You are getting old.* And the loop continues.

I hate tossing and turning, so I would give this a try for a while, knowing that the little bastard had already won. Knowing I will fail to go back to sleep, I would get up ten to fifteen minutes later, fill up on caffeine, and start the day.

We've all sometimes found ourselves stuck in those endless loops. The examples I give above are, I'm sure you agree, on the lighter side. Some of us wake up wondering if their partner is cheating, if a nuclear attack will wipe out humanity, what they did the last time they got drunk, and why they let the wrong people into their lives. Those thoughts can be more malicious. They can be more intense, and they can last longer and hit in succession a lot faster.

The more and more intense our thoughts become, the more they stress us. The underlying events that trigger them could be the same, but the more we give those events life after they've passed—in the form of thoughts—the more it *feels* that the events are bigger. The bigger our perception, the more we think about it, and the bigger still our perception becomes. Cycle after cycle, the stress multiplies, leaving us feeling that the world is bound to end, when in reality, what we're stressing about only exists inside our heads. When you think about it, pun intended . . .

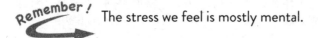 The stress we feel is mostly mental.

Thoughts happen in the brain, not in the real world. It's not life that stresses us, because even as we're lying in bed, life is actually okay. Alex will talk to Rob tomorrow, and if she doesn't, the world won't end. All the thoughts in the world won't change a thing, and the whole drama is not even worth it. It's crazy that we let that happen to us. As a matter of fact, it is totally mental.

Your thoughts, left unchecked, totally control your life, but what's obvious, though rarely discussed, is that you are in full control of your thoughts. It's not even difficult once you get the hang of it. So let's walk together down that path that helps you understand exactly how that process called *thinking* works and how you can be in control of it. Let's start where it hurts.

STRESSFUL THOUGHTS

Whether at 4:00 A.M. or as you dash out of an argument with your partner, when caught up in the kind of repetitive thinking that causes you stress and sleepless nights, you will feel a volcanic eruption of thoughts. They will feel random and erratic. You see them coming at you like rapid fire, highly charged with energy. This kind of thinking is the biggest sign of mental stress. It is usually referred to as *incessant thought*—the process of background thinking the same thoughts repeatedly without turning those thoughts into solutions, conclusions, or actions. Those repetitive thoughts mostly tend to be dark, critical, fearful, regretful, or victimizing. They tend to be full of assumptions while supported only by a tiny facet of the truth. They linger and repeat, and they make us feel sad and stressed.

If you look closely, however, you may recognize a pattern in those rapid, highly charged thoughts. The thoughts themselves will seem random, but the categories they fit in are not. Most of our stressful thoughts fit in six stages in an endless loop: a flashback to the past, an attempt to comprehend what happened, followed by loops of *I should have*, then flash-forwards to the future, waves of *I should*, followed by loops of *What if?* Then the full cycle repeats.

Our stressful thoughts are often triggered with a flashback or a flash-forward. Something that we wish didn't happen or something that we fear may happen. When a flashback attacks you, you may find yourself replaying an event that hurt you or affected you negatively. The event would by

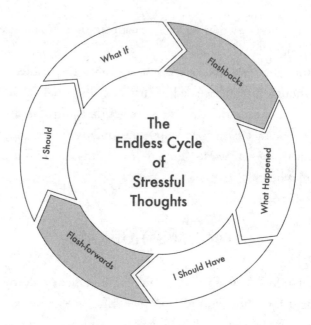

then have been far behind you, but you can give it life again and again by wrapping it into a thought and playing it back over and over inside your head. Your partner may have said something hurtful on Friday evening, then on Saturday, you think, *Remember that clip from yesterday? Let me play that again and torture myself with it.* On Sunday, you add a bit of your own fictional drama—*He or she said that because they don't love me anymore.* By Monday, you add fictional justifications. You think, *It's because they're cheating on me. It's because I'm getting old.*

I call this the *Netflix of unhappiness*—unhappiness on demand. You choose the most dramatic horror stories of your life and click to play them again and again—the never-ending loop or multi-season, multi-episode viewing inside your head.

When the flashback sets in, your brain attempts to recall the event, but this is never easy. All it can recall is its memory of the event, mixed up with some assumptions, some of its past traumas, and many of its fears and misjudgments. It constructs some kind of story from the fragments it can collect and dwells on it. This, then, triggers your brain to attempt to understand the what, why, and how. In its analysis, it floods you in loops and loops of *I should have* and *I shouldn't have*. It tries to change what has already happened by fictionally changing the past. *If I had kissed her, she wouldn't have left. I should have told her that I love her.* In the absence of a time machine, the brain then shifts to the future. By Tuesday, you turn into the oracle. You predict the unfolding of the universe as a result of that cosmic event—her hurtful words. *She will leave me. I will fail to find love again. I will spend the rest of my life alone.* Your imaginative brain will set no limits. You will tell yourself that the dog will die because she can't live without both of you. You picture yourself experiencing houselessness and selling your body for food as he walks by with his two tall, blond, new girlfriends. You imagine how the police will scrape his body off the floor after you shred him with your fingernails, and then you believe those predictions regarding them as your inevitable future on Friday evening.

None of this has happened yet, it reasons, and so your brain thinks it may be able to change what will happen. As it shifts to a new stream of flash-forwards, it imagines possible futures that it fears and other futures it desires. It parses those apart and sets elaborate action plans of *I should* and *I should not* as it tries to find a path out of the current painful place to construct the future it desires.

I should go there now, but I shouldn't cry. I should cheat on him like he's cheating on me. I should stop drinking wine. A machine gun of thoughts that are all focused on what to do and what not to do. Most of them sound decisive when in reality none of them are informed by any level of intelligence that exceeds a scene from a romantic comedy you've watched the week before or the precious advice your aunt Margy gave you when you were fourteen about how to deal with the bully in school.

The shoulds and shouldn'ts are then interrupted by a wave of worry, so your brain turns to war-gaming the situation. Your brain turns into a seasoned general and engages in building highly sophisticated scenarios of what-if. Every possible scenario is analyzed with the sole purpose of poking holes in the shoulds and discouraging you from taking the wrong actions in fear that they may lead to your demise. *What if I called him now and realize he is already with her? What if they are making passionate love when my less attractive body shows up to talk to him? What if she has amnesia like in that movie and can't be reminded of our love? What if I threatened to take the dog, but then the dog spoke and chose him? What if the dog is in on this act of treason too? Every what-if is followed by an appropriate I should. What if she slaps me? I should hold her hand in midair. What if she kisses me? I should stop her and tell her I'm hurt, then ask for her commitment to make my morning coffee for the next thirteen weeks.*

Does this sound insane when you read it? It is, but it is also what happens inside our brains when we are thinking incessantly under stress.

Take a couple of minutes now to reflect on your own thought patterns when you are stressed. Reflect on a moment when your thoughts were racing and try to pinpoint the above patterns in your thought stream. Can you see it?

Now reflect on how many cycles this normally extends to. Flashbacks to the past, loops of *I shoulds*, flash-forwards to the future and loops of *what-ifs* repeat in cycles—useless thoughts that come in highly charged streams. Every thought seems to be pointedly focused on the topic at hand, but none seem to be useful. None seem to be taking you out of the trap you feel stuck in.

Those thoughts keep looping sometimes for days, weeks, or however long it takes. They most certainly loop until either the world changes to give you what you wanted—he or she shows up on a white horse to apologize—or you take charge of your rogue brain to stop the madness by texting to say, "What you said on Friday hurt me. Can we please talk about it over dinner?"

You normally are a logical thinker. You have what it takes to take on challenges in a constructive, effective way. Why is it, then, that when you are stressed, you engage in useless loops instead? To understand how we end up thinking in such different ways, maybe we should start from the very basics of what thoughts are.

WHY DO WE THINK?

Thinking is the one human trait that has placed our species firmly on top of the food chain. It helped us defend our villages from predators, helped us learn how to farm, and is still helping us invent some useful and lots of useless things today. We humans are capable of some seriously impressive stuff. We can take a complex problem, break it down to its basic components, gather the data needed, make some assumptions, analyze deeply to find an answer, then communicate that answer clearly to fellow humans.

We can even turn our thoughts into real things. Through deep understanding of the mathematics of quantum physics—talk about complex thoughts—we can invent accurate laser guns that help us create innovations your grandma would have never been able to dream of. We can put our thoughts on paper, as I'm doing here. We can read them to learn from one another without ever meeting, and we can then agree or disagree without ever communicating. Some very impressive stuff, really, and yet the same brains that do this still frequently engage in useless cycles of thoughts like the ones we obsess over when we are stressed. What's in common between thinking to invent a weapon, to learn how to farm, or to stay awake at night thinking of something a lover said?

While the patterns differ, the underlying reason for why we think is always the same.

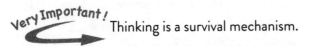 *Very Important!* Thinking is a survival mechanism.

In their very native form, our thoughts are there for one reason and one reason only—to analyze the environment that we perceive through our sensory devices—eyes, ears, and so on—to try to assess our state of safety as a result and to plot plans and take actions that improve our situation.

Our evolution as modern-day humans, obviously, makes us push that thinking all the way to inventing iPhones—a form of survival in a capitalist world where inventing products helps us make money and gain status. It makes us analyze relationships and romance—to ensure survival in our love lives. Thinking makes us build elaborate arguments to defend our ideologies, brag about our football club, or create high-quality, or just plain silly, social media posts to wow others and gain popularity to reserve an accepted place among the tribe and ensure the survival of our egos.

Every thought you think is there to advance your agenda and improve your odds at living a better life. They may seem to be a degree or two of separation detached from the kind of survival your ancestors focused on—to escape the jaws of a saber-toothed tiger—but they serve no other purpose at the very fundamental level nonetheless.

I know what I just wrote above may not be how you traditionally perceive the reason behind the process of thinking. So I invite you to take a couple of minutes to take any single thought that you think and ask yourself what the implicit benefit that comes to you from thinking it is. Then ask yourself how this advances your agenda for fitting in, gaining resources, feeling safer, and so on. Think, then, how all those needs, fundamentally, are about giving you a shot at a better, safer life or protecting the things that you deem important for your lifestyle. Yeah, none of that is strictly about staying alive, I agree. So call it an entitled form of survival in the much safer, more modern world.

The nature of our thoughts, however, tends to be different depending on the context they serve. When you are getting ready for a date with someone new, you're a bit more deliberate and organized. You recall your previous conversations and maybe list a few interesting conversation topics. If you feel the date is not going well, however, the fabric of your thoughts starts to change. You may become a bit more reactive and a bit less planned. If you've been in a relationship and things have been stressful for a while, you become even more erratic and much more defensive in your thoughts, forgetting that your new date is a totally new person. The more stressed you feel, the more panicky your thoughts become. Obviously, this is because stress clouds our judgment and makes us exaggerate the threat. By making things seem bigger than they really are, your brain is trying its best to make sure a bit more than the perceived threat is covered in its plans to keep you safe. It's just safer this way. It's a bit like when people start stockpiling food when the news announces there is going to be a blizzard. That's our panicky brains' way of ensuring that we don't end up in deep sh**, starving, when the reality is the blizzard may come and disrupt things just for one day. It's a curious response, really, but a clear illustration of how stupid our stress condition makes us when we overthink things.

 Remember! Perceived threats in a stressful mirror do appear bigger than they are.

Remember from the stress equation that the stress we feel is not just a result of a challenge we're facing. It is a result of the difference between the intensity of that challenge and our ability to handle it. Simply stated: owning a bag or two of dried pasta gives you the ability to view roads being closed to get to the shops in the snow as a nonissue. If, however, you feel stressed and your brain recognizes that you may not be qualified to deal with the issues at hand, you would find yourself up against the classic definition of anxiety. That too is predictable, even algorithmic, if you truly understand what is going on.

Hold that thought for now. I want to discuss the predictability of the other emotions that feed our stress. Those emotions that we feel when challenged—such as worry, fear, anxiety, and panic—all start from thought and can all fit into equations, but I'll do this in the next chapter where we discuss emotions and the mathematics—yes, mathematics—that drive what we feel.

For now, let's stay focused on thoughts.

WHO'S THINKING?

In everything we've discussed so far, we keep referring to your thoughts as yours. As if the one thinking is you. But here is the big shocker. It isn't.

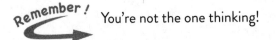 You're not the one thinking!

You see? In Western culture, that little voice in your head communicating every thought to you is thought of as "you telling you" what to do. This concept is so deeply ingrained in us that we never truly debate it. One moment of contemplation, however, would have you doubt this concept to its very core.

If that little voice were you, talking to you, why would it need to talk? Have you ever considered that? If it were you, you would instinctively know what it wants to tell you. If you were your sister, as in both of you were one and the same, you would never need to talk. The reason you *tell* her to stop taking your things is because she would not know this is what you want any other way.

If you were the voice inside your head, why is it talking? The reason is because you are not. The voice inside your head is narrated by a third party, a different entity that needs to explain itself so that you understand what it wants to say.

This subject-object relationship has been explained by science since the 1920s, when the Soviet psychologist Lev Vygotsky called that little voice the *internal dialogue*. Vygotsky observed that when someone engages in thought, their larynx moves, ever so slightly, in a way that mimics the movement associated with speaking out loud. This observation has been confirmed by endless studies that used MRI technology to show that our inner speech is produced by the same verbal-association areas of the brain— the parts of the brain that we use when we speak to others. When you are engaged in thought, that little voice in your head can only be explained by one sentence.

Remember !

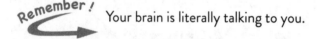 Your brain is literally talking to you.

It's not "I think, therefore I am," as our Western culture, summarized in Descartes's famous statement, tells us so confidently. It's "I am, therefore I think," and if you want to be very accurate, it's this:

Very Important!

I am, therefore my brain thinks.

Every one of our organs has a primary biological function. Your heart pumps blood around your body to keep you alive. Your kidneys take poisons out of your system in the form of urine to cleanse your biological form and keep you alive. Similarly, your brain has a biological function to observe the world around you so you can make the correct choices and avoid danger.

No one wakes up in the morning believing that they are the blood being pumped around their bodies. Nobody thinks that they are the biological product of their kidneys. Glorified as thinking has become in our modern society, you are not the biological product of your brain either.

Allow yourself the luxury of two minutes of silence to explore the implications of this simple variation on the concept of thought. If you are not your thoughts, then what does that mean to those lengthy 4:00 A.M. conversations? What does it mean to the degrading self-criticism and all the *I shoulds*, *should haves*, *shouldn'ts*, and *shouldn't haves*? What does it all mean to that relationship with the thinker?

Remember ! You no longer need to obey! You don't even have to listen.

THE GAME CHANGER

The biggest reason you get controlled by your thoughts is that false belief that you are your thoughts. If you are, then those thoughts must be correct. They deserve your attention, and you should probably do as they say. It's the biggest myth that has haunted humanity since the appearance of depression. We allow our thoughts to be the boss. Nothing will ever change your life more than reversing this game.

With your brain being, first and foremost, a survival mechanism, it tends to have a serious bias for negativity. If a tiger were about to pounce on you in the wild, your brain would have no interest in alerting you to how majestic that animal actually looks. The muscle tones, elegance, and color patterns would not be a topic of internal dialogue. Your brain would not be interested in how beautiful the flowers in the background or how relaxing the sounds of the birds chirping in the distance truly are. In stressful times, brains ignore every other thought but one: *Run!*

All the other thoughts, notice, are *also* true, but your brain's negativity bias keeps you focused on what's wrong, and that's not restricted only to tigers. It extends to every single angle of your life. Your brain—a third party, remember—will always zoom in precisely on what could be wrong.

Thank you, brain, for trying to keep me safe, but could you please try to keep me happy as well, at least when the threat is really not worth the drama?

MIND YOUR LANGUAGE

With our minds talking inside our heads day in and day out, it is easy to assume that we can understand what they are telling us. We even think that we understand nothing more than how we understand our own minds. This, however, could not be further from the truth.

Our minds, as they speak, have three major speech impediments that make them extremely inaccurate. When others speak to us, we often debate whether what they tell us is true or, at the very least, to not always take it at face value. But when our minds speak, we take what they tell us for granted. Learning to spot the errors in the way our minds communicate and calibrate them to get to the truth is the most vital language course you may ever need. Watch out for three things:

1.   Your mind communicates its beliefs before it verifies its validity.
2.   Your mind communicates what others told it without debating its credibility.
3.   Your mind exaggerates to capture your attention.

 Your brain prefers to alert you to things that may not be true but could represent a threat than to skip alerting you and end up missing a genuine threat.

This is not a defect in the way our brains operate. It's a design feature and a good one at that. When it comes to keeping you safe, there is no better ally, but when it comes to stressing you, often needlessly, you need to be in charge, pay attention, listen attentively, and fluently speak the language in which your brain speaks in order to separate what genuinely represents a threat that you need to act upon from what is nothing more than an unwarranted noisy alert that serves nothing but unnecessarily stressing you. The secret in finding that distinction resides in understanding the primary function of that genius brain of yours.

THE FIRE ALARM

The best analogy for how our brains work, especially in stressful situations, is to compare them to fire alarms. Noisy as they may be, we like fire alarms. They keep us safe. Intrusive as they may be, always picking the exact wrong moment to go off, and wrong in their assessment of the danger as they often are, we still acknowledge them and respect them. We give them the benefit of the doubt and act in accordance with their intended purpose. When the fire alarm goes off, we walk out of the building, verify if there is an actual fire, and then take appropriate action.

 Remember !   Your brain's stressful thought cycles are identical to the repetitive loud sound of the fire alarm's siren.

If you choose to stay put and listen to the noise, as in spending hours listening to our stressful thoughts screaming inside our heads, the noise will torture you, you will drive yourself crazy, and you may even get yourself burned.

This, I think you may agree, is not the smartest possible response. Ask yourself, then: Why do we let this be our response to the stressful thought cycles?

Even more insane is how we behave when the alarm actually stops. In the Netflix of unhappiness, we bring back the thought as if we are placing a lighter under the alarm sensor to torture ourselves one more time with the noise.

THE THREE ANCHORS OF SANITY

If your thoughts are not yours—but merely the biological product of your brain—and if they have one primary purpose—to keep you safe—then the shortest path to stop your mental stress is to deal with the situation exactly as you would respond to a fire alarm.

The process of doing that, which I have come to call **the three anchors of sanity**, boils down to answering three simple questions:

Stress Hack

Is it true?

What can I do to fix it?

Can I accept it and do something to make life better despite its presence?

Is it true?

In her legendary book *Loving What Is*, Byron Katie discusses what she calls "the Work"—the thinking process one should go through to arrive at a calmer, happier life. Whatever challenges you face in life, she recommends you should start addressing them first with the question: Is it true?

Let's take a look at a few examples:

The event: Your boss insisted that the report he asked for is ready on Monday.
The thought: *He/she is insensitive. I'm a free human. I can't deal with this anymore.*

The event: Traffic is slower than usual.
The thought: *I will miss my meeting.*

The event: Your broke up with a partner that was not a good match for you.
The thought: *I will never find my match. I'll spend the rest of my life alone.*

The pattern, for most of us, is quite similar: a thought is triggered by an event as seen through the lens of our very own past experiences and conditioned beliefs. Once that happens, we cease to analyze the event and focus on the only reference we have to it—our thought—and herein lies the first of our stressful thinking glitches. The thought is almost never an exact reflection of the actual event.

 Our thoughts are a cocktail of the events that trigger them, mixed with our assumptions, emotions, previous experiences, traumas, a load of fiction that we see in movies, a pile of negativity that we see in the news, and a splash of our biggest concerns, worries, and fears.

Your boss might be in serious need for that report to discuss your promotion, might have meant something different from what you understood, might be genuinely upset about you being late when he had asked for it a week earlier in an email that you missed, might be pushed herself by her boss, might have been trying to alert you to something important for your success that could be found in that report, and yet your brain chooses the worst-case scenario as the thought to present to you with no proof of that thought's validity.

I love my daughter, Aya, to bits, and I believe she loves me too. One look at our WhatsApp chats when we are not together is indisputable proof. Hearts, jokes, and the explicit *I love you* and *I miss you* are on almost every page. She is wonderful, and I have grown to be a good father over the years, so why wouldn't it be totally loving? Yet I remember vividly that one time she invited me to her place to cook me breakfast, and we had an argument about something silly, like all humans sometimes do. The conversation became heated, so I said, "Baby, let me go get a coffee, reflect on what was said, and then we can discuss this when we are both a bit calmer." As I walked out of the building, my brain, primed by the argument as brains often are, presented me with this statement: *Aya doesn't love you anymore.*

I stopped in the middle of the street and spoke out loud in an angry voice, like a lunatic, to my brain and said, "What the f*** did you just say? What proof do you have for this statement? What gives you the right to make such a claim that could jeopardize my day and my relationship with my wonderful daughter without providing adequate evidence?"

I know this kind of reaction in the middle of the street makes me look crazy, but I assure you it was much less insane than letting my brain poison me with such lies. Think about it. Halting your brain in its tracks sometimes is the wisest thing you can do.

By taking a few uncompromising stands with my brain over the last few years, it has actually learned to be responsible. To reflect on what it is about to say before it offers it. This makes the voice inside my head a lot more sensible, simply because it knows that what it will say will be scrutinized and not just taken for granted. The basis for this scrutiny is a simple question that you can repeat every single time your brain goes on a tangent and presents you with a thought that could upset or stress you. The first thing you do before you crumble and spend hours regurgitating a thought is to ask: *Is it true?*

Is it true that your boss is insensitive? Is it true that one thing the quarrelling governments of the world have finally managed to agree upon is to kill their own people? Is it true that you are such a psychic prophet that your dream actually is a message from the divine sent to you to alert you that the world is going to end?

Our entrenched beliefs and the stories we tell ourselves are often so much more powerful than reality. You can clearly observe this in an argument between any two humans when they are discussing topics of faith, politics, or ideologies. Neither side will budge or even listen to the other party's views. They will cling to their views and deeply entrenched beliefs. They will wait for the other to say something, then, without comprehending a word, bombard them with a cliché answer that fully conforms to what they believe.

When I say *they* here, of course I mean their brains.

The way our brains treat other people's views when they disagree with our convictions is identical to the way they treat us when *we* object to what they say. You can't blame them; they have to believe what they believe in order to do something about it with conviction. If in doubt, they may hesitate to drive you forward with force. Your annoying debate is not helping them, especially when they are panicking, because *they believe* that a threat of some sort is imminent.

If, of the hundreds of bad dreams you've had in your life, none of them even had a chance of coming true, where, then, does your brain get its psychic powers from?

Why is this dream any different? you ask your brain. If no evidence is presented, then I think it would be fair to tell your brain, like I did when it told me, *Aya doesn't love you*, to shut up and stop stressing you and wasting your day.

It's okay if you feel a little bit stressed about something that actually deserves your attention, but to waste your life in cycles of concern and stress about things that are not even true is a total waste of your precious time.

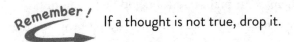 If a thought is not true, drop it.

But what if it is true?

What can I do to fix it?

It's a fire alarm, remember? All those negative emotions are only there to alert you that something needs your attention, something needs you to take action.

If there is a fire, and you could actually confirm that with the question *Is it true?* then don't just stay there. Do something about it.

When you take action, two things happen: first, you start engaging in problem-solving, which is a very useful kind of thinking that takes your mind away from the stressful thought cycle, and second, obviously, the action in itself will likely make your life better.

All your brain wants is for you to be safe, and when you ignore the alarm, what does it do? Your brain keeps sounding it, making it louder and louder, and then when you keep ignoring it, your brain tries every other possible way to get your attention. First, it tells you that something is wrong, then it starts to increase the pace, the thoughts hit you faster and faster, then, if you still don't respond, it brings up every other negative thought it can find. It wakes you up at four in the morning because it truly believes the issue you've been ignoring can no longer wait. Faster, louder, and all over the place. That is your mental stress. Answer the call. Let your brain know that you got the message, and it will relax and stop.

Let's take a simple example: Your brain brings up the thought *I am not ready for the presentation on Friday*, and that statement is actually true. Instead of spending hours imagining how scary this situation is for you, use the time to put a plan in place for how you can be prepared. Cancel other commitments to free up time to get ready. Call someone you trust and ask them to help you, or simply reach out to the person expecting the presentation and ask to move it to a later date. As you start to move in the direction of fixing the issue your brain is bringing up, you are responding to the fire alarm. This helps your brain find calm and helps you improve the situation at the same time. The minute you move to a problem-solving mindset, you start to make things better and, poof, the fire is gone.

Remember ! The shortest path to cut stress is to act upon what stresses you.

Different events may require you to take different actions. Some events may demand a full resolution. When your boss is upset because a report is late, you need to sit down and work on the report. Finish it, because wasting cycles worrying about your boss feeling upset will not write the report or make your boss feel better. If you can take the full action, just do it.

Other events may just demand an appointment with your brain. Your brain may be nagging about your weight and that you need to go on a diet, because somehow it believes this is a survival issue. You can simply acknowledge the thought and set a time to work on it. You can tell your brain, *Okay, I realize we've gained a few pounds, and I promise that we will sit down and work on a plan when we get home tonight at six o'clock. Can we please get on with the workday now?* Call me weird, but trust me. Talking to your brain, as you would a six-year-old, works. All it wants to know is that you are taking charge and that you will put in the effort to address the matter at hand. Ask yourself the question: *Is there something I can do about this?*

Remember! If there is something you can do, don't wait. Do it.

Do it even if the doing is limited to putting together a plan of action that your brain can feel confident enough about.

But what if there is nothing you can do to fix the situation at hand? Ask yourself the third question then.

Can I accept it and do something to make life better despite its presence?

Sometimes life will challenge you with a problem that you can't fix, an obstacle that you can't overcome. If learning to deal with the stresses that you face by doing something about them is the black-belt level of winning against mental stress, then dealing with those challenges that can't be overcome is the Jedi Master level. I call this approach **committed acceptance**.

Some events have a finality to them that leaves us helpless. Losing a loved one is but one example. There's no way to bring them back. The same is true if you lose your job, crash your car, or misplace the earring your grandmother gave you. You can blame yourself, others, or life itself, you can hit your head against the wall if you want to, and if there's nothing you can do to get your job back, fix the car, or find the earring, then life has already decided for you.

Remember! Learn to accept.

Learn to accept what you can't change, simply because it is stupid to waste your life and effort when you know that it is what it is. But don't just stop there.

Remember !   Learn to commit.

Learn to commit to doing whatever you can to make things better despite the challenge you face, even because of it. You may not be able to fix what was broken, but you can surely build new things around the loss.

The fifteenth-century Japanese form of art kintsugi, which literally means "to join with gold," is all about repairing what's been broken. The kintsugi artist, however, does not try to hide the cracks. Instead, the cracks are made more visible by mending them with lacquer dusted or mixed with powdered gold, silver, or platinum. This acts as a reminder to stay optimistic when things fall apart and to celebrate the flaws and missteps of life. Instead of holding on to how things were, perhaps this beautiful form of art invites you to see the potential of how beautiful something can become because it has been broken. So inspiring.

There is beauty in imperfection. As a matter of fact, there is beauty only in imperfection when you think about it because nothing is really ever perfect. This is what the Japanese philosophy of wabi-sabi, on which kintsugi is based, teaches.

Life is never perfect or at least never fully matches your expectations of what perfect is. Resist and your efforts will be futile. Accept and you will be able to focus on what you can influence and save your energy and effort. Commit and you will direct that energy to create a life that is as fulfilling as can be.

When my wonderful son, Ali, left our world, we were asked if it was okay to perform an autopsy on Ali's body and his incredibly wise mother had asked in response, *Would that bring Ali back?*

That one question defined our entire process of grief. It firmly anchored us in the truth. It made us realize, within a few hours of losing Ali, that nothing we could ever do would bring him back. It fast-tracked us through the five stages of grief to acceptance. Acceptance is not a sign of weakness; it is not a form of surrender. It is a sign of strength, an acknowledgment of the new reality of one's life that prepares us to recognize what we can no longer influence and, as a result, to focus on what we can actually change.

That is what I mean by *commitment*. Two days after Ali's departure, his sister, Aya, came to me and said, "Papa, there's something you should know. Two weeks ago, Ali called me and said that he had a dream. He dreamed that he was everywhere and part of everyone. He said it felt so amazing that, waking up, he felt he didn't want to be confined into his physical body anymore." With my blurry mind at the time and my business executive training, the only thing I heard when Aya said this was my son, who was also my coach and mentor, giving me a target. I heard Aya saying, "Ali is telling you to take his essence everywhere and make what he taught you part of everyone." I had been at Google for seven years by then. I knew very well how to reach billions, and so my brain responded as my heart was shaking by saying, "Of course, habibi [*my love* in Arabic]. Consider it done." Now, I don't know if you will choose to believe that this was truly a target set for me by my master or not, and in all honesty, it doesn't even matter. What matters is that I got up to write everything he taught me in my first book, *Solve for Happy*. I kick-started OneBillion-Happy.org to spread his message, and I quit Google to be allowed to speak openly about artificial intelligence and how humanity needs to reform in my book *Scary Smart*. I have never looked back. I am on a mission that still drives me and defines my entire life today. I have never in my life been committed to anything or anyone as I have to this mission. Perhaps through my work and through six degrees of separation in many, many years, a tiny drop of Ali's wisdom will be everywhere and part of everyone. Nobody knows for sure, but you know what I know? I know that this commitment is what saved me from breaking down and crumbling. It is what made my life what it is today. It is what brings so much love my way from hundreds of thousands of readers and followers to fill the gap in my heart that was left when Ali was no longer with us to pour his love on me.

None of it brings Ali back. But I have accepted that he's gone. It does, however, make my world and the lives of countless others better every single day. It makes it feel that it was not for nothing that he left. When life twists your arm beyond your ability to change it, and it will every now and again . . .

Very Important! Accept what you can't change, and then commit to making things better however you can.

Take a few minutes to reflect on the Jedi Master you have the potential to become. Reflect on your own behavior when faced with a challenge, perhaps one that you are facing right now. Observe your thinking and try to pinpoint if any of the thoughts attacking you have not yet been verified through the test of asking yourself, *Is it true?* Try to observe if you're stuck in loops of repetitive thoughts instead of shifting your focus to taking action. Ask yourself the question: *What can I do about it?* Try to investigate if any of the challenges facing you are beyond your control or beyond your ability to fix. Ask yourself if you can accept them as your new reality and commit to making your life better despite the presence of those challenges.

May the Force be with you.

THE DEAL

The three anchors of sanity are the checkmate move in the game of stress. They are almost certain to bring you back to calm and sanity every time your brain goes astray, lost in the cycle of stressful thought.

But why wait for the cycle to begin at all? Wouldn't it be much better if you never found yourself stuck in those painful cycles of stressful thoughts in the first place? It's possible. The technique I use for this, which I mentioned in full detail in my previous book—*That Little Voice in Your Head*—is called the deal.

The deal is a very simple agreement that you sign with your brain.

Stress Hack

It starts with the realization that every kind of insistent thought is useless. It tortures you and yet does not make any positive difference to your reality. There are only two types of thoughts that are positive. Think as many of them as your brain pleases. They are:

1.   Useful thoughts
2.   Joyful thoughts

The deal requires you to agree with your brain that those two are the only types of building blocks that are allowed in your conversations going forward. Think of your brain as an old friend—one that you spent years and years with, that you love and care about but one that is simply . . . annoying sometimes.

Picture that kind of friend who always complains. In a typical conversation, he would bring up lots of issues that are wrong with the world—and a few more that are not, but he complains about them anyway. Then he would spend a bit of time making you feel bad about yourself, poke you in the ribs a few times, and then would leave without offering any solutions or constructive ideas.

What would you do if you had a friend like that? Would you just let him blabber away, or would you take a stand? Would you stop him in the middle of the negative streak one day to say, "Hold on. Why do you have to make me feel so bad every time we're together?" Would you give him an ultimatum? Would you lay out your conditions for the friendship clearly? I would. I would say something like, "When you have genuine reasons to be concerned, I'll be there for you and listen, but when you don't, I'd like to make sure that we focus our conversation on the positive. I will no longer listen when you blabber all your negativity. If you want my attention, there are only two types of topics allowed between us. Useful conversations, ones that make a difference and leave a positive impact, or joyful conversations, ones that leave us both feeling good. No more useless agony." I would tell him to . . .

Very Important! Say something useful, joyful, or simply shut up.

This is the exact kind of deal you need to have with your brain. I learned to do this as I learned to "manage" the brains of others. No. This is not some kind of science fiction or magic. We all do it with our friends and coworkers every single day.

As a manager, early in my career, I struggled with how to deal with the emotions of my team. Managing a business was easy, I thought, but managing people . . . that was tricky. Frequently, someone would walk into my office, unsolicited, and start complaining: "Sarah from Legal is making my life miserable. The customer is waiting for the contract, and she is insisting on some nonsense that the customer will not agree to."

At first, I would get overwhelmed with the negativity, and I would join in the complaining session myself. I'd been there before, and I knew how it felt all too well. It would sometimes go on for an hour, and by the end of it, both of us would feel helpless and drained. Then, quickly, I realized that this was neither my role as a manager nor the best use of my time. So I learned to follow a set process. Once the complaining began, I looked at my clock and timed thirty minutes. For the first ten, I would listen and show empathy. I would ask for more of the negative thoughts to surface, because venting is better than keeping negativity trapped inside. "What else is wrong?" I would ask, until it was all out in the open, and then I would ask about the positive for ten minutes in an attempt to find the whole truth, not just what is going wrong. This would quickly trigger some joyful thinking. "What is good about your relationship with Sarah and the legal team? Have they helped you before? Are they committed? Are they nice people? Do you think they feel stressed too? Do you think they have the best interest of the company in mind?"

When the picture, both with its positives and negatives, was complete, I would then use the last ten minutes to focus on useful thinking. "What can we do about this? Would a meeting between them and the client help? Should I attend this meeting? Could you ask Sarah about the reasons why she is resistant and if there are alternatives that can deliver what she needs but also meet what the customer needs? Should we seek CEO approval as an arbiter?"

In no time at all, my team observed and learned the pattern. So when they walked in, they would follow it unprompted: ten minutes of acknowledging how they feel, balanced by ten minutes of joyful thinking, followed by useful thinking. They learned, and so can your brain.

Sit in a comfortable position for a few minutes where you will not be interrupted. Close your eyes for a few seconds, as long as you need, to disconnect from whatever it is you were doing before. Now open your eyes and scan the space around you. Your task is to find three things. Everything that is in the color white, every letter or digit, and every living being. Take as long as the exercise needs, and when you're finished, come back here. I will be waiting for you.

Did you do it? Or did you just ignore me and continue to read?

Go do it, please. It will take just a few minutes.

Good. Welcome back. I find this exercise fascinating because, although many ignore what I ask them to do and keep reading, no one ever ignores what *they* tell themselves to do. This means that the minute you choose to work on the exercise, you will instruct your brain to find every white thing around you, and it will obediently start searching for white. I have yet to meet anyone who tells their brains to look for white things only to have their brains tell them, "No, I don't like white. I will look for green."

You tell your brain to look for white, it looks for white. You tell it to do some research, it switches on Google. You tell it to play a game, it plays the game. Even those who decide to continue reading, they instruct their brains, and what do they do? Read. Your brain only goes astray when you leave it unchecked, but if you tell it to focus, it will—every single time.

This holds true even during tough times. How often did you get to work or to a party when you spent the entire commute obsessing about something that upset you? Then as soon as you arrive and others demand your attention, you tell your brain, *Enough of this now, we can continue complaining when we get back home. For now, let's focus and talk to those people.* You do that, and your brain will oblige. Immediately.

 You're the boss.

You can always tell your brain what you want it to think about and it will follow. Simply ask your brain gently to shift the theme of its focus. All you need to do to achieve that is to explicitly highlight to your brain that those negative thoughts are not making things any better, and then tell your brain in as little as five words . . .

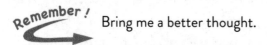

Remember ! Bring me a better thought.

USEFUL THOUGHTS

Is there something I can do about this? Or, *Can I accept and commit?* Those are positive thoughts that prioritize the tendency to take action and have a bias to a level of optimism that taking an action, regardless of how small, is bound to make things better.

Useful thinking comes in various formats—problem-solving, inquiring and researching, analyzing, reviewing and learning, planning, and performing tasks and execution of plans. The trap that we all sometimes fall into is that we assume that sitting down to incessantly ruminate on a past event is useful because it helps us learn from our mistakes. This is only true if you're disciplined in terms of seeking the facts so you can note them down and fully internalize them. This kind of thinking is directed and targeted. It makes things better. If your thoughts are just an incessant stream that delivers nothing but ignites your rampant emotions, however, there would be no learning to be gained. Those thoughts should be stopped.

When facing a challenge, you need every moment and every brain cycle to focus on making things better. If your brain strays, you need to bring it back like you would an emotional friend or a team member when they blabber streams of useless nonsense. You need to interrupt the cycle when the answer to the simple question "How is thinking this making anything any better?" yields no positive contributions to your life.

One day, while I was teaching *Solve for Happy* to a class of a few hundred people, a woman approached me during the first break. She looked battered by life and was a little bit angry at me. She said, "How can you say that happiness is a choice? You have no idea what happened to me!" She then paused for a few seconds and then began, "When I was seventeen . . ." She was sixty-seven and appeared to be ninety-five at the time. I looked into her eyes, hugged her, and said, "You've been holding on to one thought about that horrible event for the last fifty years. Did it work? Did it change anything? Could you, perhaps, have chosen to think another thought?"

We're in charge of where we let our brains take us. Don't waste your life on useless brain chatter. Tell your brain . . .

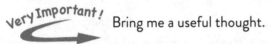 Bring me a useful thought.

For the first four days after losing Ali, my brain kept attacking with the thought: *You should have driven him to another hospital. You should have driven him to another hospital. You should have driven him to another hospital.* When I realized how useless that thought was, I shouted at my brain: *Yes! I heard you, brain! I wish I could have driven him to another hospital, but I didn't. Can you bring me a thought that I can act upon? A thought that actually makes things better?*

Just this simple instruction made my brain stutter a bit before it ever brought that thought up again, and then, after Aya told me about Ali's dream to be everywhere and part of everyone, my brain, reluctantly, presented this thought: *Let's write down what he taught us and share it with the world.* I said, "Yes! I can do that. If his essence as represented by his teachings could reach a few million people, then, through six degrees of separation in a few tens of years, part of his essence will be everywhere and part of everyone." All as a result of one useful thought.

JOYFUL THOUGHTS

My mum always used to tell me, "All work and no play makes Jack a dull boy." I don't know who Jack is and I don't know which mother asks her son to work less, but I was a serious A student, and I just enjoyed learning and studying and making things. Yes, I was such a nerd that, into my teenage and college years, I did not really play much at all. Only later did I learn that life is to be lived fully, to be enjoyed. I learned that, often, when we flow, life tends to take care of itself. Learning to let go and enjoy what is, is a skill that's rare in today's world. We're always concerned with doing better, faring higher, and our brains, naturally, are always concerned with what's missing, what's wrong, and what can be done better.

Thinking useful thoughts is, surely, the most valuable and impactful skill you can use your brain for, but sometimes, useful thoughts are not that useful. Either the problem at hand is actually not solvable or the improvements gained by solving it are not really worth the effort you need to put into it. In those situations, it actually is a much better idea to save your effort and enjoy the moment instead. When your brain realizes that there is no solution to your predicament, it usually turns to complaining. It makes you feel trapped and often victimized. As a result, you focus your thoughts on *why me, why now, how can life be so unfair,* and a whole list of other thoughts that deliver nothing but pain. Remembering that you, not your brain, are the boss, you can rise above this victimization by ordering your brain assertively . . .

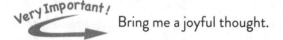 Bring me a joyful thought.

Losing a child must be the hardest thing any parent could ever suffer. It surely has been the hardest thing I've ever had to deal with. Even today, years after Ali left our world, I feel an intense pain whenever I'm reminded that he's no longer with us. My pain is so intense, I physically feel it in my heart. I can accurately point to it. It feels like the bottom-right part of my heart is missing. Despite the pain, my brain doesn't seem to want to give me a break. Several times every week, I would hear my brain repeating the same exact thought: *Ali died.*

I've learned to accept that this will be the case for a long time. I don't even blame my brain for it anymore. It still struggles to comprehend how life could take the best human I have ever met. It still can't accept that there is nothing to be done to reverse or erase what happened. Instead of feeling angry for the pain this thought causes me, I learned to deal with my brain gently. When it tells me Ali died, I reply: *Yes, brain, he did.* **But to see the full truth, before Ali left our world . . .**

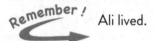 Ali lived.

Now, this tiny shift in perspective is a significant paradigm shift. *Ali died* is a true statement. Thinking about that side of his life brings me back to the time he was in the intensive care unit. It reminds me of the moments I laid his beautiful body to rest and reminds me how much I miss him. Those thoughts cause me pain.

Ali lived, however, is the brighter side of that same coin. It's a thought that reminds me of all the amazing time we spent together. All the jokes and laughs. All the video games we played, when he kicked my backside. All the deep conversations and wisdom. All that he taught me and every precious moment that we spent together. Of those moments, there is an endless archive that represents a bottomless well of joy to bask myself into. The thought *Ali died* hurts me, while *Ali lived* makes me smile. It reminds me that I've been blessed with this precious gift for years. We didn't plan to have Ali. I was making love to the woman I so deeply loved, which in itself was a gift, and then to add joy to joy, I was given the biggest gift I was ever given—a wise little Zen monk of a child who completely defined my life and the person I've become. I never signed a service-level agreement with life to be given so generously. Life, God, never owed me any of what it had given me—twenty-one and a half years of heaven given to me without expecting it.

Take a couple of minutes now to reflect on your recent thinking patterns and if they conformed to this new deal. Pinpoint the kinds of thoughts that diverted and caused you needless pain and commit yourself to changing those going forward. This exercise may take a bit more than a few minutes. Grant it the time it deserves till you master it. This may well be the most important deal you will ever sign.

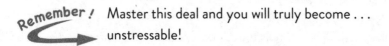 **Master this deal and you will truly become . . . unstressable!**

Please take a short break now to contemplate what we've discussed so far. I know it's been a lot to take in. Get up and stretch, play some music, and energize yourself.

When you come back, we will look at how our brains sometimes come together to stress all of us at the same time even if there is really very little to stress about. We call this phenomenon . . .

CYCLICAL STRESS

There are times in the year that are undeniably emotional and appear charged with stress. These emotional markers challenge our mental resilience and appear unforgiving toward us when they arrive. These cycles that appear stressful may differ in impact, like all stressors, from person to person, but the majority of us can relate to the understanding that we find certain dates, anniversaries, holidays, and particular times of the year more challenging than others. I know I do. (It's Alice here.)

From looking at these cycles, we have found that there are three common types of stressful times; these are what I call: collective, phantom, and personal highlighters.

Collective

Collective stress is a time where everyone around us is more stressed. This is not limited to our family but impacts our extended community and even nation. The best example of course that stands out for the collective is the festive period. Studies show that over half of Brits describe the festive season as the most stressful time of the year,[1] with another study showing that in the US rates are even higher, with a staggering 88 percent of Americans also finding it the most stressful period of the year.[2]

This seemingly stressful time stems from the combination of increased financial pressure to buy gifts, an intense workload to get things done in time for the holidays, fatigue from lack of sleep, and increased alcohol consumption due to the festive parties in the lead-up to holidays. There is also increased loneliness for those finding this time of year difficult to be without loved ones they are missing while everyone else is surrounded by family and their romantic partners; yet others find the presence of certain family members that they only see at this time of year stressful in itself. Another study shows that due to all of this, a couple will have on average seven arguments during the festive period alone.[3] As a time of collectively shared stress for the majority, it makes it even more stressful as we find others are feeling burned out and at the ends of their tethers, while we have already reached our own.

Similar to the end of the school year, where parents and children have reached the ends of their tethers—parents rushing around the manic end-of-term scheduling while trying to balance their own, and children facing the pressure of end-of-year exams. Things at home can become more fraught than usual while everyone is trying to make it to the summer holiday finish line.

These are collective times of stress with the factual reasons behind them making it seem inevitably so.

Another time of year shows the reality of what I call a *phantom* stress.

Phantom

Phantom stress is one of the most interesting cycles of them all. It's a time that is made to be more stressful or depressing only through the outside world telling us it should be so. It's a make-believe period during which we preempt stress and low mood based on certain narratives that we hear.

So in reality, it's a phantom, where the reasons for feeling stress at the time don't even exist.

Blue Monday is a well-known (or perhaps unknown) example of this. While the UK and Northern Hemisphere know it to be the most depressing date of the year (the third Monday of January), the term was actually coined by psychologist Cliff Arnall in 2004, when the company Sky Travel asked him for a "scientific formula" for the January Blues.[4] The formula itself has been debated, but it took into account a lot of factors for that time of year in the Northern Hemisphere—including the dark nights, cold weather, and back-to-work postholiday blues. This combination led Arnall to call the day *Blue Monday* in what is fictitiously believed to be the most depressing day of the year with the highest suicide rates; the creative origin was not a response to suicide and depression rates but purely as a way for Sky Travel to market holidays. Despite its true origin, the term is now widely used in the UK, with the majority of us mistaking it for the day with the highest suicide rates and fearing it when it looms around the corner. In fact, it's merely a modern myth resulting from a marketing campaign. Despite the prevalence of seasonal affective disorder at this time of year, the suicide rate does not increase in January; this particular day is no more depressing than any other, with the Centre for Suicide Prevention stating that the suicide rate is actually consistent throughout the whole year, with a slight rise in spring and early summer, not the winter, like most of us believe.[5] Which is even more conflicting, as this is a time of the year that so many people feel more upbeat and alive again as they have made it through the winter.

When we give meaning to a day due to an outside or even an internal narrative, we can convince ourselves that we either do or should be feeling a certain way, simply from the thoughts we have created around it.

Personal Highlighters

These are the dates that we give particular meaning to because they had once been a day that either caused us great pain and suffering or were once a reason to celebrate someone or something that we have lost, like the anniversary of the death of a loved one or their birthday, which now only highlights not that they are here but that they are gone. These dates, although surely not phantom in their invention, as they mark the date of a significant and real event in time, are given an emotional charge still through the thoughts that we create toward them in our minds, often with the lead-up itself being more emotional than the actual day.

These days then become personal highlighters—highlighting to us what we no longer have. Although our loss is factual, the story we give this day in the present is now make-believe. As in reality even if this day reminds us of something we have lost, what we are now experiencing on it is no different from the days before or the days after. The event did not happen at this moment in the present, and our loved one was gone the day before and they will be gone the day after. Yet somehow this day becomes more emotionally stressful for us to handle as our minds drag us into the depths of our past suffering and create a narrative for us to believe that we should be still suffering in the now. Doing all that it can to latch on to every thought to remind us that they are gone.

I'm not saying that none of us should feel *anything* on the anniversary of the death of a loved one; it's an emotional time that can slowly slide us into a spiral of sadness while we allow our minds to fixate on the void. But the truth of it is that this day itself is no different from others in *circumstance*. The day before, you were also without your loved one, and you will be the day after, yet we torture ourselves emotionally in the lead-up while our minds signal to our bodies to remember the loss we went through and start to highlight it to us as much as we can. What we are really in need of is a systemic method to deal with the cycles.

THE P3 METHOD

Perspective

First, we have to identify which cycle we are in with perspective. Once we have identified the cycle, we can use perspective to then shift our own outlook. If it's a collectively stressful time, we need to accept that we are not the only one who is going to be feeling stressed; we should be aware that others around us are finding it difficult and they too may have a shorter fuse than usual, so we need to be kind to both ourselves and them, to not take things personally and accept this, rather than victimizing ourselves when someone's stress is unleashed on us unexpectedly.

If it's a phantom time of stress, then our perspective needs to shift strongly into the reality that this cycle doesn't exist, that we should not be feeling stressed or low in mood because of something make-believe, so it's time to take back control and simply ignore the outside noise giving meaning to this particular day.

Finally, if we are in a time of a personal highlighter, then our perspective is the first thing to use at our disposal to try to change the outlook in our minds. To shift our perspective to look for the good memories and use them to be something that we laugh with, rather than wallow in. Use this day as a wonderful reminder to talk about whom you love, for example, and all the many stories you have of them that make you smile. Remember how lucky you were to have had that time with them; even if it was cut short, you had it. So, try to imagine what your life would be like if that time had never been. Remind yourself that this day is no different from yesterday or the day before, so don't allow it to swallow you up in your mind; use it as a day for remembering them, remembering them with love.

Preparation

When we know that a time of stress is coming up, be that collective or personal, take it into account and prepare. Prepare like you would for an exam you want to pass; collect the information you need in order to be able to glide through it rather than getting stuck.

When we prepare for the festive season, we can look at what it is that personally causes us the most stress around this period of time—is it the lack of sleep for you? Or the increased expenditure? Is it the time spent with difficult family members? Or the fact that you miss your own?

Identify exactly what it is that causes you to be stressed at this time of year, so you can then prepare for it. For example, in preparation for the festive period:

- Create a boundary with yourself about how much alcohol you are going to drink before the holidays and how many holiday parties you are going to say yes to, so you don't get overtired.
- Try to buy some of your gifts early to navigate the holiday rush.
- Don't engage in conversations with difficult family members on topics you know you both disagree on.
- Create a new tradition for this time of year with a friend to bring you joy, or ask them to carry on an old one that you once loved doing with those you are missing.

Prepare in ways that make your life easier and bring you more joy.

For a personal highlighter—acknowledge that you find this day difficult and prepare by making sure you are surrounded with those whom you love, even those who also cherished that person you lost, so you can all share your stories and remember them with joy. Make sure that in the lead-up to this day you are not overly tired or hungover, highlighting your misery even more, and try to do something on that day that you love. Share a lovely meal with friends, go on a beautiful walk in nature—prepare with people and activities that make you happy. Whatever you do, don't sit inside ruminating on your own. Allow yourself to process your emotions and feel what you need to and then shift into doing the things that bring you more joy. Which brings us to the final *P*.

Prioritize

If it's a phantom season, prioritize your true reality and ignore it; don't give it energy. But if your season is real and not a phantom, then you need to prioritize your own happiness and well-being during this time. Create rituals that are going to make you feel your best, not add to your strain. Exercise, meditate, journal, connect with loved ones, sleep. Prioritize your well-being so that you are better able to navigate the stress that comes.

Don't get pissed off—in your mind, go out of your way to give yourself self-love, care, and kindness. Don't be hard on yourself. Be mindful that it's a time of stress and accept this with kindness and preparation. Do this before the season starts so that you have a great foundation to work from, not acting from a place of depletion but better managing it from a place of already feeling nourished instead.

As you take command of your thoughts, they work for you, not against you. This is the answer to the biggest myth surrounding tranquility and calm which are often said to be found in the quietness of your brain. We disagree.

THINK AWAY

A myth that surrounds the concept of finding calm and happiness is that the teachings, which often see meditation as the top tool to reach those states, seem to position an active mind as the enemy and so seem to say that the path to calmness is a silent mind. This is a massive misunderstanding. To imply that the path to calmness is a silent mind is ridiculous and unattainable. Instead of futilely attempting to silence your mind, think away!

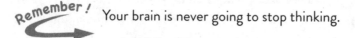 Your brain is never going to stop thinking.

Just as your heart will never stop pumping blood around your body and your respiratory system will never stop breathing until the day you leave our world. Thinking is the biological function of your brain, its life purpose, what it is made to do. When we meditate and enjoy those wonderful moments of clarity and calm, we actually don't stop thinking even then. We just learn to switch up how we think from incessant chatter to observing the world as it really is. Whether you focus on your breathing, the heart of a rose, or the itch on your nose, you are still thinking, your brain is still ticking. It never really stops. It just changes focus. Calm does not result from the absence of thoughts.

Remember ! Calm is the result of the absence of negative thoughts.

All the stress that you feel is not related to the volume of your thoughts. It is related to the polarity of those thoughts. Thoughts of awareness—such as the thoughts you generate when you are fully absorbed in the present moment observing your breathing, the flickering of a fire, the waves of the ocean, or the magnificence of nature—don't drain us. They energize us as they bring us back to reality and take us away from being stuck inside our own heads. This is the reason why we all love to spend time in nature and why we find calm through meditation. But being fully present in the moment is not the only place we should aim to be. Being present is the spiritual way. The practical equivalent for being effective in the modern world is positive thoughts.

Positive thinking is concerned with overcoming a challenge or solving a problem. Pondering a concept or seeking the truth. They do keep us inside our heads, away from full presence, analyzing past and future sometimes, and they do take effort—but they make our lives better. They fill our brains with something other than the negative thoughts that drain us, and in the process, they remove obstacles from our path so that we can find the space we need to be fully present. Even the world's top meditators confirm this concept. While they do meditate to practice how to silence the mind sometimes, more often they meditate to reflect on or cultivate a concept such as compassion or loving-kindness.

If you can't choose to be a monk or a yogi spending the majority of your days in meditation, then learn to master the art of avoiding the negative thoughts, and think away.

Remember ! There's nothing wrong with thinking. Learn to stick to positive thoughts.

Once you learn how to weed out the negative, then I would recommend a life of balance—moments that you spend with a silent mind and other moments when you fine-tune your machine to only think positively, and then you push the pedal to the metal and think away at a hundred miles an hour if you can.

Mastery of the art of controlling your mind like that is not reserved for the senior monks, gurus, and sages. It is something that is attainable for you and me with practice. Just like an athlete would work out to stay fit, the unstressables too can exercise their minds regularly.

A GYMMMMMM FOR THE BRAIN

Our brains are not static. The brain you woke up with today is different from the one you will take to sleep. Every single thought that you think is not only shaped by that magnificent brain of yours, it also shapes it. The way we use our brains shapes them literally like the way we move our muscles at the gym builds our bodies.

Your neocortex, your thinking brain, is where your conscious awareness occurs. Every time you think something new, you light up a new synaptic connection, evolving the neurons needed to create that thought. Every time you think that thought again, your brain uses the same connection and in doing so strengthens it and makes it more permanent. Learning to balance yourself on a bicycle, for example, requires incredible spatial awareness and muscle coordination. When you first try to do it, your brain scrambles to process all the things it needs to stay upright. Every time you do it right, however, your brain saves the successful pattern it used so it can access it later. If it works, keep it. The patterns that fail fade away. That's exactly why it's said you never forget how to ride a bicycle: once the successful patterns are formed, they can only be dug out with effort and via new patterns being imposed on top of them.

With every thought, your brain physically changes . . . just a little. Over time, what your brain keeps changes its very structure. With the programs it saves, its performance improves (or worsens depending on the program), just like how apps on your smart device enable it to do more. Unlike your computer or smart device, though, where new information is stored in a specific compartment, a memory chip, or a hard drive, when you read a new line in this book, your brain changes the hardware itself. It upgrades itself as if it is building a slightly different computer with everything that it learns.

This principle, in neuroscience, is often referred to as *neuroplasticity*— "neurons that fire together, wire together" is the way neuroscientist Donald Hebb describes it.[6] This concept doesn't only apply to new information or new thoughts; it also applies to maintaining and sustaining existing connections.

Every time you remember a specific memory, or discuss a topic in a specific way, your mind becomes better at it. World-renowned neuroscientist Dr. Joe Dispenza says that just like any relationship, the more you communicate, the more bonded you become. Neurons behave exactly the same way.

When neurons begin to fire and wire together, they form neural networks that are centered around an idea, a concept, a memory, an experience, a skill, or a behavior. Repeated use of those networks enables you to become better at recalling or performing the thoughts they are related to. This, in terms of the results it produces, is very similar to what happens to your muscles when you go to the gym. Hypertrophy is the process that refers to an increase in muscular size achieved through exercise. The more you exercise a certain muscle, the more you signal to your body that you need that muscle, so your body makes it stronger. The muscles you ignore, on the other hand, diminish and become weaker. So if you only work out your upper body, over time, you will look like a triangle, and if you only go to the gym to squat, you will end up looking like a pear. The same happens through neuroplasticity with your brain, though the changes are contained within your skull so not as visible. The more you use it to complain, the better it becomes at complaining, and the worse it becomes at problem-solving. The more you hate, the better you become at hating and the more difficult it becomes to love. Now we wouldn't want that, would we?

Allow me to be your personal trainer for the remaining few pages of this chapter through seven exercises that can configure your brain to stay positive: be **g**rateful, **y**ield, **m**editate, be **m**indful, **m**eet your brain, **m**ake believe, **m**ind your own business, and connect to **M**other Nature.

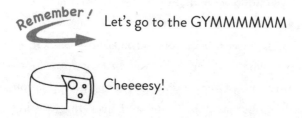

Remember! Let's go to the GYMMMMMM

Cheeeesy!

BE <u>G</u>RATEFUL

Stress Hack Most of the stressful loops and negative thoughts that take us over are not just the result of our thinking process but more the result of our selective focus, which informs the thoughts we generate only of the negative side of things. This is often referred to as the *negativity bias*—our tendency to register negative stimuli more readily than positive ones—and our positive-negative asymmetry—our tendency to dwell on the negative.

As an example, consider that a boyfriend could be kind, loving, and understanding. He buys you gifts and joins you on trips filled with long, wonderful hugs. Yet one dreadful moment when there's one french fry left on your plate, he reaches out to take it. As his hand swiftly reaches out for that precious resource, your brain launches in every direction. *How could he let himself do that? Why didn't he even ask me? Does this mean I don't matter to him? How can I live with someone so selfish?*

Taking the last fry is truly an unforgivable act that could even be considered a crime sometimes, but only when seen in isolation. When it is seen in context, without forgetting all the gifts, hugs, and trips, however, the true picture is not so bleak. Would you agree?

Remember! Remembering what is going right balances our brains' tendency to focus on what is going wrong.

Studies by the Cleveland Clinic, the National Science Foundation, Stanford University, and many others indicate that 60–80 percent of the thoughts in an adult brain are negative. Of course they are. It is the job of your brain to highlight the negative. There is nothing that threatens your safety in the positive, and your brain, first and foremost, is a survival machine.

Think about it. Is it even conceivable that 60–80 percent of the events of your life are negative? Could it be that six to eight things out of every ten things that happen to you are a threat to you? Obviously not. If that were the case, you wouldn't be with us now reading this book. You would have perished a long time ago. The truth is that most of our life is positive. The reason everyone panicked so much about the outbreak of COVID-19 is because it was the very first pandemic in your lifetime and mine. Health is the baseline for most of us. The majority of humans spend a lifetime mostly healthy interrupted only by a few time-bound episodes of sickness. Earthquakes and natural disasters don't happen every day. As a matter of fact, most of us never lived through even one.

 Remember!   Most of life is okay.

But that does not seem to be the way your brain, left to its own devices, thinks. Which means you need to train it to think differently. How? One sure way is to use an attitude of gratitude.

When you force your brain to look for what is good about life, it easily finds it, because it is always there. Only your brain wasn't looking for it. First, this incredible discovery that gratitude reminds you of surprises the negative brain—there is good in life! Then with time and practice, the miracle happens. Neuroplasticity reshapes the grateful brain so that it sees more of the positive until eventually a positivity bias becomes its second nature. The result of this kind of rewiring is that a grateful brain rarely sits stuck in negative cycles, simply because it tends to swiftly switch the mood to seek and celebrate the positive.

To nurture your grateful brain, I urge you to:

- Keep a gratitude journal if you're a beginner. In it, write down at least one thing you are grateful for every single day. Review your entire gratitude journal at least once a week to remind your brain of how blessed you really are. The key here is consistency. Make it a point to not miss a single day.
- For black belts—as in gratitude experts—whenever your brain brings up a negative thought, ask for a positive one to balance it. If your brain tells you something it doesn't like about your partner, ask it for one thing it likes before you continue the conversation. If you are a true black belt, though, you will ask for three or four, maybe even nine good things for every one thing it marks as bad. Remember, most of life is okay, and so should be most of your thoughts.

Jedi Masters of gratitude recognize that something doesn't need to be good to be grateful for it. It just has to be less bad than it could have been. They realize, if they dislike their job, that at least they have a job. They remember when they are stuck in traffic that at least they don't need to walk several miles to work in all weather. They remember that at least they are inside a vehicle sheltered from the rain and that in their country, when it rains, it rains water, not bombs, as it often does in war-ravaged countries. Jedi Masters find a way to see gratitude in everything. They do this through years of committed practice that rewires their brains. Just the fact that you are still breathing deserves your gratitude. Start practicing.

 Be grateful for every breath you take.

<u>Y</u>IELD

It's easy to be grateful for what is going well in your life, but what about the parts when life is not going great? Most of that too, if you took it for what it truly is, is not worth being mentally stressed over. To complement the practice of gratitude, you can develop a positive attitude—to not sweat the little things.

Yes, life sometimes takes us through hardship, but most of the time, that hardship is either irreparable or just not worth the attention or the sadness we dedicate to it. If you are faced with something that is irreparable, resort to committed acceptance. We already spoke about this, and when it is not worth your attention, simply try to yield.

What's the point in wishing it didn't rain today? Will your wish change anything? What good would cursing the delays on your commute do? Would it make things move faster?

Often we obsess about things that truly are not even worth thinking about. They happen, they annoy us, and they pass. We give them a life they don't deserve, and we grant them the power to annoy us by turning them into thoughts that we play over and over in our heads needlessly. Think about it. An annoying Uber driver or a few moments wasted in traffic. So what? You are here now with a life to live. So live. Don't sweat the small stuff, and when life sends some of that your way, smile at the silliness of the game, accept, and yield. Sway with life.

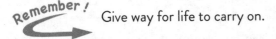 Give way for life to carry on.

To nurture your yielding brain, spend a few minutes once a week to review how your week has unfolded. Note the things that upset or irritated you in any way, and then question if they deserved the time and negative brain cycles you dedicated to them. There is no blame and no need to do anything about them. Just observe them and set your intention to not let similar events take you over the next time they occur. Laugh about them if you can and about the cute grumpiness they caused you when you could have seen them for what they really are—nothing more than life's sense of humor. Week after week, you will develop the neural networks you need to observe them, not at the end of the week but as they happen.

Black belts who master the art of yielding develop the skill to let go of things that stand to annoy them as they happen. They deprive them of the energy they need to persist and carry on with life. They don't get stuck and don't let the grumpiness linger.

Jedi Masters go one step further: they don't even get upset in the first place. They sway with life and play with it. They enjoy the ups and downs. They laugh at the grumpy Uber driver, even joke with him. They play music and prepare a nice cup of coffee when they sit down to fill out government paperwork, and they hug their partner if they attack them while feeling emotional. They realize that nuisances are just a part of life, and they insist on enjoying life with whatever it brings.

MEDITATE

Yes. Everyone's been telling you to do it. So do it. Meditation for your brain is like what practice is for a musician. It gets you deeply in tune with your instrument. One of the bigger myths out there about meditation is that to calm the mind is the target of the practice. This is the opposite of the truth.

People are often under the impression that in order to successfully meditate, they must not have a single thought and sit like Yoda on top of a mountain in total peace. This target is impossible, and so many shun meditation altogether and decide it's not for them because they fail to achieve that state. Monk, author, and meditation teacher Gelong Thubten once explained to me in a podcast conversation that a meditation with a mind that's totally silent defies the purpose. Meditation is the practice of trying to reach that state. Without a mind that gets distracted, there would be nothing to practice.

A meditation that is effortless is like going to the gym to work out with weights that are so light that they don't cause your muscles to feel fatigue. What makes your muscles grow is that moment when you struggle a bit with your exercise. That struggle acts as a signal for the body to build the muscle mass it needs to be able to perform the exercise better next time. The more you reach that state of fatigue, the more your muscles will grow. Similarly, meditation is about bringing your mind back from noisy thoughts to calm over and over again like a tense resistance band being allowed to relax and contract. It's not the calmness that trains the mind. It's the effort associated with recovery, and the more you do it, the better you become at that vital task of bringing your mind to calm on demand—the exact skill that you need in order to find calm when you find yourself feeling mentally stressed.

Meditation brings awareness. When we take the time to meditate, we start to notice what thoughts continually try to pester us. From this, we can notice the patterns of how we are really feeling, what we are thinking about that is causing us concern. It becomes harder to ignore a thought that keeps bubbling up until you notice it and bring your attention back to here and now so you calm your brain before it bubbles up again. Once we become aware of those thoughts, we can transcend them.

So meditate and love the noise. Celebrate when your mind is active. Learn to bring it back to silence in the meditation room and you'll be able to find calm on demand, when you need it most, during a rough patch of mental stress.

This is not a book about meditation, though we can't stress the value that it brings to your life more wholeheartedly. So much so that part of the unstressable membership will offer daily meditations that you can use to reduce your levels of stress.

We invite you to come join us there on Unstressable.com. Remember to use the gift code IAMUNSTRESSABLE to get $15 off your first month. Invest the time and commitment to learn.

It doesn't matter how long you meditate. Even five minutes a day is better than nothing. What matters is the reps, like in the gym, of doing that same exact move of bringing your mind back from noise to calm, over and over, every day. Every time you do it correctly, the neurons that make that happen fire together, they will wire together, and they will build a stronger network that you can rely on when thoughts start to race inside your head. I surely recommend that you try to aim for at least twenty minutes a day. Get there gradually. Start with five, then add a minute every day. It's also a good practice to do it around the same time each day. I meditate early in the morning, before the madness of the day takes me over, and then often again right before I go to sleep.

The Jedi Masters of the meditation world are those monks that dedicate their lives to the practice and often acquire tens of thousands of hours in lifetime meditation. Their brains become completely reconfigured for calm and happiness.

BE MINDFUL

Mindfulness is the art of focusing on the present moment and, in doing so, avoiding the possibility of being stuck inside your head. Back to the fitness analogy. Even after a good workout at the gym, which for your mind is analogous to meditation, you still need to move, walk, and not sit around for too long. You need to observe your food and eat healthily if you want to become truly fit. Staying focused on a healthy lifestyle for your brain would be analogous to mindfulness.

The math is simple: if you spend ten minutes of your day intensely attempting to calm your mind in meditation but then spend ten hours distracted during your day, you are simply firing the wrong neurons six hundred times more often than the right ones. Your brain will still be a lot better at being distracted than at staying focused.

We need to practice bringing our minds back to focus as often as we can. I use several exercises to do that every minute I can during the day. Here are a few ideas.

When I walk anywhere, I make it a point to take one picture of something beautiful on the way. This makes me pay attention and look for beauty all through my commute. You'll be surprised how much beauty you've been missing out on even in the busiest cities in the world. If I drive, I set six radio stations on the radio and make it a point to never hear something I don't enjoy. If the music is interrupted by an annoying presenter, I switch to the next station. If it's not playing a song I like, I switch to the next, and if that's playing an advertisement, I switch to the next. If none are playing something I like, I switch off the radio, wait a couple of minutes, and start again. I call this *mindful music*. It helps me bring the joy of music from the background of my life, where most of us usually keep it, to the front and center. Try it; you will enjoy your music a lot more, and it will teach your mind to focus.

I also play lots of games with my mind. When walking, I look for a certain number in all signs, number plates, or building numbers. When waiting for a doctor's appointment, I scan the room for colors one at a time. When sipping my coffee, I follow the wood grain on my coffee table and try to find similar patterns, and when eating, I try to leave my cutlery down between every two bites until I slowly chew, savor, and swallow. I try, with little success, to guess what herbs are added to my meal. Even as I write books for you, I set a kitchen timer to forty-four minutes and eleven seconds for every writing session and completely lose myself in writing with no distractions before I get up and stretch, then do it again. I can go on for hours, but I think you get the idea, and you can create similar games to play with your own brain too.

 Engage your brain in the here and now.

So that it focuses outside the thoughts in your head. As you start to get the hang of mindfulness, the hours that you spend exercising your brain multiply exponentially. Those hours, spent in the real world, teach you the skill you need to deal with real distractions that don't exist in the quietness of your meditation room when your eyes are closed.

My favorite of all those mindfulness exercises, however, and the one I want to single out is being with humans. Look people in the eyes, listen carefully to what they say, observe their body language, ask for clarifications, feel their energy, connect to their emotions. Pay attention and never, ever touch your phone or allow yourself to feel distracted when given the joy of connecting to another being. Those connections are what life is all about, and we are blessed with so many of them every day. If you let them pass, they never return, and their absence leaves us empty, feeling lonely even when we are surrounded by thousands all day.

Alice here. The greatest thing I tell my clients to bear in mind when practicing mindfulness is kindness, as mindfulness is about paying attention but with kind attention. There is no use being mindful of what's going on around you while criticizing and judging both yourself and others. That is only going to increase your stress. Mindfulness is about the willingness to kindly observe without judgment the simple facts of the here and now. Don't attach opinions to what's going on around you; simply learn to observe what is.

Don't even let one moment of connection pass unnoticed, unlived. Smile at the barista who's making your coffee, make him feel noticed, start some small talk, and make the cashier feel appreciated. I promise you your coffee will taste better if you do, and you will have made their day. Help the older lady behind you in the supermarket line. Give her your spot, and help her pack as you chat cheerfully with her. Even the grumpiest of all of us are not immune to a joke or two. Ask for what you need in a store, even if you know where to find it. Ask the shopkeeper what she thinks of it, even if you know that you intend to buy it. Dare to sit next to a houseless person, as my wonderful son, Ali, so often did, and ask them to tell their story. Don't judge them and just listen. Humans, when acknowledged, radiate positivity that will not only keep you mindful but will also fill you with joy. The mindfulness of being here and now with others will completely redefine your life as you know it.

MEET YOUR BRAIN

No one is worthier of your dedicated attention than you. How often do you actually spend time with yourself? Other than those times when things are tough and you need to reflect or simply stay away from the world to lick your wounds, how often do you actually spend time with you?

I don't know your answer, but I imagine it's not enough. You can and should do it more.

Without spending enough time listening to our own brains, they tend to pile up a lot of garbage. They bring thoughts up—thoughts that might not be healthy—and we ignore them, so they play them again and then build on top of them more thoughts that are even unhealthier.

Investigating those thoughts is a bit like decluttering your home. If you don't do it for a while and then you do your spring cleaning, you encounter all kinds of demons and garbage hiding there in your closet. We all need to meet, and declutter, our brains way more often.

This is hard at first, but it does become easier over time. In this practice, I hold space for a regular meeting with my brain, two to three times a week. I call this exercise *Meet Becky* (Becky is the name I call my brain). When it's time to meet, I set aside twenty-five minutes for Becky and me to engage in a conversation that has only two rules. Rule number one is that I will listen attentively and acknowledge every single thought that my brain brings up, and rule number two is that no thought should be repeated.

Although this exercise is considered an advanced type of meditation, becoming aware of what you're aware of, I don't attempt to slow my brain down or bring it back to calm. As a matter of fact, I push it in the other direction and encourage it to think of anything and everything as manically as it wants to.

The conversation between my brain and me would normally go something like this:

Remember to call Aya today.

Sure, brain. We shall call Aya when we're done. What else?

Those tacos yesterday were simply divine.

OMG, yes. Great tacos. What else?

You're not good enough.

Why, Becky? Why would you call me that? Anyway, you think I'm not good enough. What else?

The idea here is to not hold on to any thought regardless of how appealing holding on might feel. Everything's allowed. You acknowledge the thought, let it go, and ask your brain for the next one. I even allow myself a paper and a pen to write down some of the more interesting thoughts that come up. This helps me let go of the thought because I feel that I can revisit it later.

One thing you will notice is that once you start listening to your brain, it starts to slow down. It feels surprised at first that you're actually listening, and as a result, it tries to say something smart. This takes it time and forces it to filter through the stupid stuff that it realizes on its own is not worth sharing. But believe it or not, there's not much worth obsessing about in our brains anyway. They quickly run short of thoughts worthy of airtime, and that's when rule number two comes in.

Rule number two is there to make sure no single thought is repeated incessantly. What usually happens after a while—when your brain has vomited all sorts of crazy thoughts at you for ten to fifteen minutes, especially if you listen and do not ignore it, is that it runs out of things to talk about. Your brain says something like, *This report is due tomorrow. We need to work on it today.*

Sure, brain, you will say. *We need to work on the report today. What else?*

Then silence will linger this time as your brain searches for something to say, and then it will say, *You're not good enough.*

You respond, *Ha ha ha. You said that before, Becky. It's still not nice. What else?*

Now the silence really lingers, and then your brain, with a tone of shock, will say, *That's it. I have nothing more to say.*

This is when the miracle happens. Real silence sets in, and it lingers. The most joyous, amazing moment is the one when your brain finally shuts up not through the strenuous exercise of bringing it back to calm through meditation but because it actually has nothing to say.

Enjoy those moments while they last—at least until the end of your twenty-five minutes—and then start looking at your notes.

When you review those notes, which came out uncensored from thoughts inside your head, you will for the first time realize how ridiculous some of your thoughts actually are.

As you read those thoughts, scratch some of them out and say to your brain, *That was ridiculous. Please don't think that again.* If you notice some important ones that have been left unattended to for a while, this would be a good time for you to plan the actions you need to address them in order to tell your brain that you intend to work on them soon. Your brain will usually not bring either of those, pending or ridiculous, thoughts up again for a while. Once you have the clarity of having listened to your thoughts attentively, your brain tends to slow down, knowing that it has already communicated to you and that you seem to be responsible enough to listen.

MAKE BELIEVE

Also known as *mental visualization*, make-believe is one of the most effective techniques you can use to lower your stress level and pave your way to success at the same time. Recall from our conversation about neuroplasticity that firing your neurons together works the same way when you are actually doing something as it does when reliving a memory or visualizing a future scenario. To your brain cells, it doesn't really matter if what you think of is an actual event in life as long as the neurons fire.

The most common form of visualization is to practice something before it happens. If you prepare for a speech by giving it in front of the mirror, you get better at it. If you start to imagine the questions you may get and picture in your head how you will handle them, you will respond to those and other questions better.

Many years ago, I attended a talk by Debra Searle, who rowed solo across the Atlantic in a twenty-three-foot plywood boat. She started the journey with her husband, but he needed to be rescued after only two weeks. One of the audience asked her how she managed to handle her fear. Her answer as I remember it sounded something like this: "I had all day to imagine every possible scenario that could take place. I would visualize them in my mind all the way to the end. What would happen if a big wave flipped the boat over? I would picture myself holding on the rope that ties me to the boat, falling into the water, then pulling myself back and working things out to the best possible scenario. I would play the scene over and over until it feels like I've lived it before and survived.

I then would get up and check one more time that the rope was tied to me properly, then visualize the next scenario. The first time I thought of a possible threat, I would be terrified, but the more I thought about it, the more I came to realize that it is manageable and, more importantly, that I am capable of managing it." What Debra said that day changed my life. She likened this exercise to horror movies. The first time you watch a scary scene, you jump off your seat. If you watch the movie again, however, things don't scare you as much because you know what's going to happen and you are ready for it.

Our brains are visualization machines. In their attempt to keep us safe, they anticipate future threats in order to plan a safe course of action if they eventually happen. When we let them visualize only the worst possible cases of anything, they lead us to feel anxious and mentally stressed. Use the machine, as intended, all the way to conclusion.

 Remember !   Learn to visualize the answers, not the problems.

Think of the solutions, not just the challenges; your moments of victory and success, not your moments of failure and demise.

Practicing inside your mind costs you nothing. Don't stop at practicing how you will overcome challenges. Leap further and visualize the best that can happen. Practice that date with the person of your dreams even before you meet them or verify that they exist. Practice a life of ease, love, and connection. Practice money coming your way; practice how you will use it to make others happy. Visualize how cute your grandchildren will be. Visualize baking them cookies and munching on them with a full set of teeth that show when you smile in your seventies. In the Middle East, we believe in the proverb: Be optimistic that your fortune will be good, and so it will be.

Many schools of spirituality teach that visualizing a certain event makes it come true. I believe that, beyond just a spiritual belief, visualizing something prepares you for it, convinces you that it's possible, alerts you to the path to take when it shows up in your life, and develops your neural pathways in a way that makes you better at attaining it.

Very Important! → You get what you expect from life.

Start expecting the best. Start visualizing. Don't let your mind go astray. Take charge and visualize the path you will take to happiness, love, and success. Visualize your path and practice, like a pro, inside your head.

The reason why our brains, untamed, often visualize the bad side of everything is that they are trained, even beyond their negative nature, to do so by forces outside themselves, including the media. To stop this, learn to . . .

MIND YOUR OWN BUSINESS

Modern-day media, mainstream or social, operates with one target in mind—keeping you glued to the screen for as long as possible. To achieve that, they capitalize on your brain's negativity bias and tendency to filter what is familiar. They mainly play on two attention grabbers—negativity and awe (and often *awww* for cute animal videos).

If a news network broadcast that a loving couple hugged yesterday and that two more kissed, would you tune in? If a post on Instagram mentioned that someone worked out a reasonable number of times a week and had a normal healthy human body as a result, would that keep you swiping? Of course not.

You tune in to the story of a wife who killed her husband, a virus that might wipe us out, and a politician who did something appalling. Your brain's negativity bias zooms in to consume the bad news, and so what do the news networks do? They fill twenty-four hours of programming with the most negative stories they can possibly find, and they add a bit of commentary to make them seem even more negative. You swipe on the most unusual posts on social media, things you really would rarely ever see in real life. Those trigger your awe, and so they cut through your brain's filters, which tend to block the mundane. The more unexpected a story is, the more you like it. Because who wants to see what's normal? Normal is all around. So what do influencers do? They come up with the most creative ways to entertain you, by behaving in ways that you would never encounter in real life, so you follow them.

The more of your time that you spend absorbed in those mediums, the more you end up with a highly skewed version of reality—one that is much more negativity-, envy-, and confusion-inducing than the reality of your life when you put your phone down and switch your TV off. The math is clear: there are orders of magnitude more couples that don't kill each other overnight than there are murderers, many more safe places on the planet than places where there is danger. There are many more aspects of your life that are going well than there are disasters. As a matter of fact, if you switched the media off, you would probably see very little negativity and fakeness, if any at all. Don't take my word for it. Try it yourself.

I write this to you from the Dominican Republic. When I need to double down and get a book over the line, I normally choose to disappear from the fast pace of the world. A couple of days ago, I started to get messages from friends and followers asking if I was okay. An earthquake hit Haiti—the DR and Haiti share one island—and people thought I might be at risk. I don't watch the news, not ever and certainly not when on a book deadline, and so to me, there was no earthquake, and my life over the last two days had not been in any way different from the couple of days before or the two to come.

In a way, if you did not live in the strike zone, the earthquake happened mainly on the screen. In the absence of the media, the world seems to be a lot safer than news networks make us perceive it to be. In the absence of the media, you would not have known that there was an earthquake either. As a matter of fact, in the absence of media, the majority of the world's population would not even know that earthquakes existed at all, because they would not experience one ever. A lot of the stress that we feel results from news that we never need to worry about, which surely makes them things we have no control over anyway.

You may be thinking, *What are you saying, Mo? Are you saying I should not be watching the news? But I need to be aware of what's going on in the world to be able to make informed decisions.* Do you? Really?

When you need to know about a specific event, sit down and search for the exact information you need. Get the answers to the exact questions you need answered. No fluff, no heightened emotions, no opinions, no aggressive debate. Save yourself the endless hours and the resulting stress. If there is nothing I can do about an earthquake, why should I waste a minute of my life learning about it anyway?

Because there are things that matter, Mo. Because there are things, such as social justice or freedom or democracy and the coming election or the score of the football game that matter. Yes. Tune in to what really matters to you. Choose the causes you want to champion and learn about them. Master them, even. Remember, though, if you truly want to champion a cause or get in-depth knowledge about a topic, you might as well drop the other topics that waste your time and energy so you can dedicate more of yourself to what you truly care about. Because if you truly believe that you can end the wars, hold the politicians accountable, save the economy, rescue the boy that fell in a well, erase the national debt, end terrorism, prevent natural disasters, and save the next husband before the wife hits him, then I would urge you to put this book down for a few minutes to reconsider why you still mix with the rest of us mortals. If you are humble enough to know that no one can fix all that is wrong with the world, however, then you may want to ponder why we are attempting to be aware of it all. Why are you dedicating so much of your time, attention, and resulting stress to things you can watch but do nothing to influence?

In his mega-bestseller *The 7 Habits of Highly Effective People*, Dr. Stephen Covey explains that there are two types of people. There are proactive people who focus their efforts and attention on their Circles of Influence—the part of their lives they can control. They work on the things they can do something about. When you are proactive, you are able to reduce stress while you advance to more success, because you can initiate and influence change.

Reactive people, on the other hand, focus their efforts in the Circle of Concern—things that pop up on their radars over which they have little or no control. Reactive people often neglect those issues that demand their attention and are within their control and influence because their focus resides elsewhere. Their Circle of Influence shrinks as a result of their distraction. This stresses them not only because most of what they pay attention to is stressful, scary, and out of control but also because that circle of madness seems to grow and grow the more they pay attention to it. The more you look for what's wrong with the world, the more the whole world feels wrong. But is it?

It's not. The work of cognitive psychologist, linguist, and popular science author Dr. Steven Pinker proves the exact opposite. Our world has never been safer. In his analysis of data on homicide, war, poverty, and more, he teaches that the world is doing better now in every one of those dimensions than we did as little as thirty years ago. The reason why we feel that everything is worse simply is that our horizon, in terms of what we get informed about, has grown exponentially. Of course there are challenges facing humanity. Those should be looked at as problems to be solved, not apocalypses in waiting.

The media, mainstream or social, takes away far more than they give you. Their product is not the content they show you. This content is just bait. *You* are the product they sell to advertisers. They stress you to keep you watching and, in the process, they make you feel unsafe when your life is actually okay. They make you feel bad about yourself as compared to the highly filtered images of social media influencers. You view what you learn from them as the reality of the world. As a result, you end up in stress and negativity, feeling helpless and hopeless about the state of the world. And then you wonder why you're not sleeping well at night. The effort that you dedicate to your area of concern shrinks your area of influence, and then neuroplasticity makes you better and better at finding a dark perspective in everything that life sends your way. The truth is most of life is okay, and most of what's not okay is none of your business. You will never be able to influence it, let alone change it.

If you truly are unable to shake the itch of staying informed, schedule your anxiety. Plan a set time every day when you can immerse yourself in all of the tension and negativity of the modern world. Thirty minutes would be plenty to get your heart racing and your mind chasing. Once the time's up, switch off the hose of toxicity and call it a day.

 Switch off those screens.

CONNECT TO <u>M</u>OTHER NATURE

This last brain workout is one that I added to my regular routine recently. It hit me how much I was missing out on the joy of being in nature and how negatively it affected me when I had the pleasure of hosting Craig Foster, the Academy Award winner for Best Documentary with *My Octopus Teacher*.

At the beginning of the documentary, Craig tells the story of how he needed to escape from the mounting stresses of his life and that the only way he knew how to do that was to be in nature. I shared my own cravings and asked him why he believed we all needed nature so much. He answered, "Our species has been here for approximately three hundred thousand years. For most of that time, everybody has always felt they were part of wild nature. They wouldn't have understood the separation that we feel today. It's a trauma, a shock, to be separated from the Great Mother. It's the first time we feel this way since the beginning of time."

He went on to say, "What people don't realize is that the biodiversity, which is the enormous number of species of animals and plants on this planet, is allowing you and I to breathe from second to second. No matter where we are, we are literally breathing in the living system of this planet. Great Mother Nature is allowing us to stay alive. Everything you need is being provided by her. She is our life support system on every single level, and yet we think that we can live independent of nature."

I had never thought of it this way before. I thought of myself as a cosmopolitan, urban animal who viewed nature as a vacation—a break to recharge before going back to *the real world*. I was wrong. It is the opposite. My life in the mainstream is the interruption. Think of it as a long dive. I take a deep breath to dive on a mission for a few minutes. It feels that the mission is my life, but the truth is that sooner or later I need to get back to the surface to breathe. The surface is my habitat—the mission is the interruption.

Remember !   We are fish out of water when we are disconnected from Mother Nature.

And yet we remain disconnected day after day after day.

The only way to reconnect is to visit again and again and again, Craig said. Small things like going for a walk, stopping to observe a flower, a leaf on a tree, establishing a relationship with the insects in your backyard, with the bird chirping in the morning before the city takes it over. It's all about feeling curious, taking care, inquiring what they are, how they survive, and what behaviors they follow. It's all about stepping a little bit back into that other world—the world you came from.

If you can, take a trip every now and again. Visit a farm, a field, a garden, or disappear for a couple of weeks on a retreat. A lot of the stress that we feel is because, as familiar as the big cities and the fast pace have become, we are not from this place. It feels alien deep down inside, and that feels unsafe. This disconnection is stressful at a very deep level. It's in the background, and we may not even notice it, but away from nature, something in our lives is always missing.

Those who spend more time in nature are often calmer. You may think that it is more threatening out there, but it isn't. We are made for the wild, and while at first the ants may annoy us and the extreme cold or heat may cause us discomfort, our bodies remember. They adapt, and quickly, we blend back in. As we fit in, our minds become calmer. The stress fades away.

I once asked my dear friend Jimmy Nelson, artist and photographer of indigenous communities, about all the tribes that he photographs. I asked if they feel stress and depression. He laughed and said, "They don't even know the meaning of the word. They are so in tune with the flow of nature that they live every minute entirely in the present, and there is never anything wrong with the present."

I said, "But what about the wild animals and the famines? It's a tough life."

"It's a tough life out here," he said. "They are in flow, swaying with nature instead of resisting it. They understand that there are threats in the jungle, so they stick together. They know that death is part of life, so they live every day."

Connect to your origin, even if you start by stopping for a couple of extra minutes in the flower aisle in your supermarket or by watching a nature documentary. Kindle that little fire that makes you who you are. The more you connect to that side of you, the more you will remember that most of the illusions that we chase in this alien habitat we call civilization actually don't matter at all. There is peace in finding the rhythm of natural life.

Remember! We are from Mother Nature. We're not just visiting.

It's time to move to a type of stress that seems a lot more unpredictable and irrational. Time to move from the head to the heart to discuss your emotions and how they affect your stress.

5

Feel to Heal

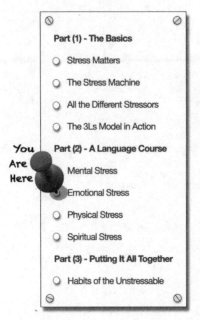

You Are Here

Oh, emotions. They are one of those great mysteries that being human asks us to navigate. We are elated by some things and become catatonic by others. We embrace the good and push away the bad. We often don't understand our own, let alone those of others around us.

We try to make sense of them, while simultaneously hiding and ignoring them. Those raw, unfiltered parts of us can connect us with the depths of our souls, the darkest sides of our fears, or the height of our capacities to love.

They seem complex and sometimes confusing, but are they? Or is their complexity just in our heads? Are we the ones that make them more confusing than we need to? Are we the ones that complicate the simplicity of our innate ability to simply feel?

Are we the ones causing ourselves to be emotionally stressed?

Emotions, even the most positive of them, can overwhelm us when we allow them to live to their extremes. Take empathy, for example. This kind of emotion allows us to tune in to what others are feeling so that we understand better, and maybe even help alleviate their struggles. Beautiful, but too much empathy can be a serious drag.

Alice here. I'm what is known as an empath, one of those highly sensitive individuals who can't stop absorbing what others feel. Put me with other humans with their raging emotions and I will feel everything fully. I mean *fully*. I will not miss a beat, even though I often pretend to if I know someone isn't ready to share their inner musings.

As an empath, when I get one sad look from a person experiencing homelessness in the street, I often have to turn back and speak to them while others may continue to walk on without noticing. If one person in a party isn't feeling like themselves, I will instantly notice, while the rest of the room is often jovial in their own celebrations.

This was once something that overwhelmed me. I remember as a child needing to just spend time alone in my room so I could have some space away from the world around me, feeling tired from all that I was feeling, being both triggered from inside me and from the outside world. Amusingly, my parents were mildly concerned about this, wondering if they were raising someone a bit "odd." Asking me why I wanted to go and spend time alone in my room before dinner instead of downstairs with everyone. At the time, I didn't have an answer. I now understand emotions at a more intimate level. I know I am emotionally sensitive, an empath, and predominantly, although outgoing, an introvert. So having a little space to emotionally recharge alone is something that I need.

With no handbook for how to handle my emotions, I felt the pain of dealing with the highs and lows, the burdens and emotional pains.

The lows were something I tried to shut off and numb for a while in the aftermath of losing Suzanne, my half sister, and watching our dad deteriorate into depression afterward. It was easier to go out partying with my friends than sit with my emotions. It was easier to keep myself distracted with loud music than face the music of my own grief or the reality that our dad had now morphed into a walking ghost.

But I missed the strong, amazing character I knew, I missed him laughing and being interested. I missed his wonderful stories, and I missed seeing him without a drink in his hand. More than anything, I missed my best friend.

I didn't feel safe and protected anymore. I felt vulnerable to the world. Like my dad who always had the answers and direction was gone. So I desperately tried to help him, hoping he would come back to us, but he was already gone.

I felt I couldn't be upset with him for giving up, as he was so broken in grief and betrayal. But I was cross with him deep down and angry with the people who were hurting him.

I suppressed it for so long, because as an empath, I was so ashamed that I could feel angry with someone when I could also feel their pain. Dad and I were always linked in this way; I could feel everything he did. During Suzanne's last moments here and after she died, Dad's pain was an excruciating thing to witness and hold. But subconsciously I wanted to, as at least then I felt like I was helping him somehow, by understanding him in some way.

I remember the day I realized I had lost him. We were all arguing in the kitchen of our old house as we yelled at the vacant human standing in front of us, "Where are you?" He shouted back that he was right here and dismissed what we were saying. I replied, "No, you're not. You're not here. You've gone."

As he grabbed his car keys and stormed out toward the door, he turned back around to us and shouted, "Don't you get it? I wish I was with her. I wish I was dead and with Suzanne."

It was that moment that any hope I had for him one day returning was gone. It was that moment that my whole world shattered again and I started to grieve my dad before he was physically gone. Stress and depression had already taken him.

But I wasn't processing this grief properly at all. I felt there was no room to. So I numbed it, suppressed it, just as I had hers.

I knew that day that no matter how hard I kept trying, and I did, I would never reach him.

He was already gone, and drinking and not seeing doctors was his hope of getting there sooner.

So he drank to numb his pain, and he got no treatment for his cancer, and I watched as he vanished in front of me. He became someone who was a quiet ghost throughout the morning until he could leave the house. Who could no longer go on walks with me or just talk and spend time together at home, play backgammon with me, or be animated about life. He couldn't really be around our family without some sense of distraction, a TV on or a busy environment outside of the house, to distract him from just being *there*.

My dad now partly saw in me what was lost. I was the only person he would ever mistakenly call *Suzanne*. A part of me represented his grief to him, and he'd become a shadow of his former self to me. Like I was being tortured by having him there but being unable to reach him and speak with the dad I once knew.

This for me was one of the most painful things I had ever gone through. I just wouldn't let it fully in. After a while, I felt I had to shut it down within myself to just function. So after two and a half years, I did. I numbed it, distracted myself from it, suppressed it.

I accepted him as he now was through spiritual surrender, knowing I could not control what was going on, but I could not accept my own pain. I knew if I did, if I felt it, then it was all really true. I also felt guilt and shame for feeling this way while he was still physically here, still, of course, holding a bit of hope that a miracle would happen and he would suddenly snap out of it and come back to us. A deal would go through that would make him a little happy, and a part of him, even if not all, would return. But it never did, just sometimes once or twice a glimmer for a day or two, which I think made it harder, as I knew again, he was somewhere inside there; he just couldn't break free.

He was the man I adored—worshipped, almost—growing up. It was like a cruel joke to see him again for a moment, only to have him be gone.

But it wasn't long after that I hit my emotional bottom. When I did, I was left with no choice but to fully face all the older and deeper negative emotions I had been trying desperately to ignore.

It's taken me till this day to truly heal from this part of his loss. Having grieved for him physically, I still hadn't looked properly at the difficult emotions from this first loss.

The reason I tell you this is because from this is why I now know that our hearts will never not be heavy until we have asked them what's *truly* weighing them down. What they need from us to be brave enough to address. What they truly want to be heard.

It doesn't matter how long we suppress it, numb it, distract from it. That ache will keep returning, keep asking for attention. It will only stop when we have finally allowed it the space.

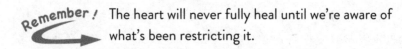 The heart will never fully heal until we're aware of what's been restricting it.

Though my path to healing was my own, the tough reality of having to learn to deal with my emotions after hitting rock bottom is something I share with every client or friend in need and now with you.

It was at this time when I realized my emotional "enemies" are the key to a power we all hold—our ability to tune in to everything and everyone around us and, more important, into our own selves—so that we access a state of emotional wisdom that, when combined with our intellect, places us firmly on a path to enlightenment that we are all meant to walk.

But leave enlightenment aside for now. Let's begin at a much more basic level—a true understanding of our emotions and why they are really there. Let us learn what triggers them, how to notice them both in the fullness of our pain and the height of our pleasure.

THE MATHEMATICS THAT DRIVE WHAT WE FEEL

Mo here. Fear and all of its derivatives—worry, anxiety, and panic—seem at first glance to be very erratic emotions. They hit us when we least expect them, then grip us and refuse to let go. But fear, like every other emotion (other than unconditional love), in my mind, is extremely predictable. So predictable, as a matter of fact, that it can be summarized in a repeatable engineering process and even a mathematical equation.

At the very bottom of the fear hierarchy comes worry. Worrying happens when you suspect, without certainty, that your future may be less safe than your present.

Your worry is measured as the probability of your state of safety at a moment in the future (T^1) less your safety now (T^0). The higher that you believe the possibility of that degradation in your sense of safety is likely to be, the more worried and the more stressed about it you become. So for the math geeks of you out there (skip the equations if you're not into math):

$$W = P\ (Safety^{T0} - Safety^{T1})$$

When you start to feel worried, that's when you start to feel stressed. You start to keep the issue that is worrying you in the back of your mind, and you become more vigilant, on the lookout, for signs that confirm or disprove your worry. Worry in itself, however, is not too concerned with the actual magnitude of that safety degradation, just the probability of it happening. Think of it this way: if you are sensing that things might go bad at work, you worry more, the more rumors that you hear that something will go wrong. It doesn't matter exactly how wrong. Fear, the next step down, is concerned with how wrong.

Fear assumes that the probability of you facing a threat is already high. You no longer are just worried; you've already made up your mind that bad things will happen. You are now concerned: *How bad is bad?* Your fear, and the corresponding stress, increases when the perceived degradation in safety is higher.

$$F = Safety^{T0} - Safety^{T1}$$

Basically, you are more afraid if you expect that you may get fired as a result of things going wrong than you are if you expect to, say, get disciplined. When you are afraid, your level of stress is surely higher than when you are just worried. Your thoughts become more cyclical. You keep thinking about the threat that lies ahead over and over to try to find a way out.

The next level down is panic, and that is not about the intensity of the threat. Panic is more concerned about time. We panic when the pending threat is imminent. That's it, really.

The closer T_1 seems to be, the more you will panic. The moment your boss calls you into her office with HR sitting there is the moment when your panic reaches its peak. Your thoughts start to race in a desperate attempt to salvage your safety in the very limited time you have left.

$$P = 1 / (T_1 - T_0)$$

Obviously, panic leads to more stress than the fear of something that may be a few months away. In your mind, you may believe that, in time, you may be able to figure things out and eradicate the threat—that is, of course, unless you don't think you can handle it. That's when the next emotion down—anxiety—sets in.

Anxiety is the mother of all stress-triggering emotions. It is the feeling we get when we have convinced ourselves that something undesirable is about to happen, have thought about a way out, and still feel that we can find a path to safety. It is the first part of the stress equation—a difference between the challenge we face and *what we believe is* our capability to overcome it.

$$A = Challenge - Ability$$

You can see here why stress and anxiety are so frequently synchronized. One is the distribution of the intensity of a challenge over the resources, our ability to handle it, and the other simply is the difference between them. Both ways, the more able you are, the less stressed you become.

Anxiety can take you over for a minute or sometimes even days as you jolt awake, filled immediately with angst. When you are in that state, the endless cycle of stressful thoughts starts to turn. The looping nature of that cycle is the result of a state of hopelessness that occurs when your thoughts attempt to figure a way out but fail, so they try again and again. The erratic nature of it is the result of your thoughts visiting the various corners of the challenge in a frantic attempt to find an answer. *What caused the situation I am in? What could I have done or not done to change it? What is my expected future as a result? And what are all the different possible variations of my future that I now need to address?* Hopelessness leads to mental stress. If we knew how to get out of the situation we're in, we would not feel that mental stress at all.

I have included this logical explanation of emotions here because many of us learned to process everything with logic, even our emotions. The problem is that this hyper-logical approach to life extends further and leads us to, frequently, ignore our emotions when they arise.

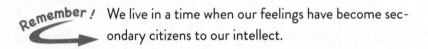

Remember ! We live in a time when our feelings have become secondary citizens to our intellect.

Come on, Mo. This is a chapter about emotion. You're still talking about thoughts and logic. Let me take it from here.

We prioritize logic over intuition, intellect over empathy, and thinking over feeling. We're constantly on the go, distracting ourselves and pushing away our emotions, hoping to avoid facing them and feeling pain.

We learn to rationalize that it's easier to dismiss these feelings than to admit them and commit to putting in the effort to resolving them. We tell the world that we are doing fine when the job that's earning us money is making us stressed, worn down, and miserable. We post happy pictures with our partner on social media instead of accepting that we are going through a rough patch. In the process, we believe our own lie. We believe what we tell others and forget that there is so much that we feel. It's easier this way, because who wants more on their plate anyway? Isn't it stressful enough as it is?

As we hide from what we feel, we also hide the keys to unlocking the path to our most fulfilled and happy selves when the obvious signals un-mistakably tell us that it's time for us to make some kind of change.

Sound familiar?

THE EMOTIONS FUELING OUR STRESS

When we are stressed, certain emotions become prominent. What was once every now and then becomes the emotional modus operandi of our days. Those emotions become far too regular for us to truly feel calm and happy, and far too regular to ignore. But what do we do? We brush them off as normal.

Let's be clear. It's not "normal" to continually be in and out of feeling anxious, stressed, overwhelmed, hazy, worried, irritable, withdrawn, unfo-cused, apathetic, or depressed. Those are some of the common emotional signatures of stress.

There is no part of our design, as humans, that suggests that feeling this way should be our normal under any circumstances. Quite the opposite.

We are born happy, calm, joyful, and at ease. In the absence of a reason to engage a short-lived hyper-tuning of our physical forms in order to deal with a stressful event, this blissful state should be our norm.

Now, I am not saying that feeling happy and calm is possible every moment. It's not. We are only human, doing the best we can with the cir-cumstances we find ourselves in. Negative emotions alert us to the things we need to change, the things we need to learn from, and the things we need to do to experience a safer, more fulfilled life.

For without bad, there can be no recognition of what's good. Without knowing sadness, how can we truly appreciate happiness?

The yin and yang of our emotions create the depth of our experience and growth. The balance between the negative and the positive, however, is the mystery we need to solve. In a balanced life, the positive sides of our emotions, excitement, peace, contentment, happiness, and joy should significantly outweigh our feelings of stress and negativity.

The problem that we find ourselves in today is that the negative emotions that we experience with stress have become so normalized that we forget we shouldn't be in them all the time. We become intertwined with them in an almost familiarized comfort.

Knowing what it is like to feel this way more than we do to feel good, we get stuck in the emotional cycle of the signatures of stress.

The first step to making this your reality is to become fully aware of your current emotional state. Let's take a moment now to check if any of the following emotions are a familiar part of your day.

- Do you wake up feeling anxious or worried, dreading or concerned about the days or weeks ahead?
- Are you sometimes alert, even at night, unable to switch off from work when you get home?
- Are you having trouble sleeping because of all the racing thoughts in your mind?
- Do you feel distracted?
- Do you find your mind wandering elsewhere when in conversation with your loved ones?
- Do you struggle to be fully present?
- Do you feel rather detached, failing to find joy in the simple pleasures?
- How about your mood? Do you feel low, deflated, or find yourself dipping in and out of highs and lows?
- Do you sometimes pour yourself a drink just so you can feel that sense of relief and calm?
- Do you binge-watch television to numb out and stop thinking about your day and the events of the world?
- Do you lose your appetite or forget to eat?
- Do you eat more than you need and find comfort in snacks and empty calories?
- Are you more forgetful than you used to be?
- Is it hard for you to focus on one thing at a time?

- Are you losing interest in sexuality? Is your libido dwindling?
- Do you find yourself easily irritated by small events or the behavior of those around you?

If any of this sounds like a normal part of your day, then you are feeling some of the strain of emotional stress. The stress that is affecting you is screaming to be noticed in the form of emotions that shouldn't be ignored.

The good news is that once you become aware and notice the emotional signatures resulting from or leading to your stress, you can start to address them. You can engage to heal the issues and to prevent them from resurfacing after they're cured. The sole reason for which those emotions exist is to alert you in such a way so you can take action, move through the negative emotions of stress, and transform them back into calm and ease. But in order to change something, we first have to become aware that it's there. This is why stress lingers. How can we become aware when we are stressed when . . .

 We're often not even aware of how we truly feel.

Emotions in the modern world are seen as a vulnerability. They are seen as something that should be hidden rather than shown, ignored rather than explored. It is the fault of a capitalist society that leads us to believe that we are not feeling creatures but thinking ones instead. That we are no longer beings but rather just doers.

But let me ask you this: If there was no use for the feelings that arise in you, then why do you have them?

Just as we are unlimited in our thoughts, we are unlimited in our ability to feel. Professor Brené Brown has counted eighty-seven human emotions and experiences. Just like with the alphabet, feeling those emotions becomes our sensory vocabulary, which we can use with the same amount of intentional intelligence as we do our thoughts. Emotions inform us of the subtleties of the world within us, just like thought helps us understand the concepts of the world around us.

Remember !   Our emotions are a form of human intelligence.

Emotional intelligence, or EQ, is the ability to understand, use, and essentially master our emotions and deal with the emotions of others. By getting to know them and relating to them intimately, we learn to see ourselves for who we truly are, informed by what we so deeply feel. EQ allows you to manage your own emotions in positive ways to relieve stress, communicate effectively, empathize with others, overcome challenges, and defuse conflict.

When the modern, target-driven world tells us that we shouldn't be driven by our emotions, it does not mean that we shouldn't feel. What it really means is we shouldn't be reactive to our raw, unfiltered emotions, screaming at people or making irrational decisions that may jeopardize our safety. The rules of the modern world, especially at work, urge us to behave intelligently so that we achieve results. What the rules of the modern world tend to ignore, however, is that mastering emotions is an invaluable form of intelligence. Surely, skillfully guiding the raw power of emotions is leaps and bounds smarter than suppressing them. Remember the last time you witnessed an explosive emotional conversation, and you will know that to be true. Emotions are a bit like having a really powerful turbo engine in your car—of course, if you're not a good driver, you shouldn't be letting the power of that engine loose on the streets of your city. You'd be causing lots of injuries to lots of innocent people, including yourself. You shouldn't even start this engine in the first place. You'd probably rev it too much and cause a lot of noise. But if you are a competent driver that knows how to turn this raw power into fun on a racing track or a beautiful memory driving along a winding country road, then rev the engine all you want.

When we master EQ, we should be allowed, even encouraged, by the modern world to be driven by our powerful engine—what our emotions are trying to tell us. We should be guided by those feelings so that we can more easily adapt and create the outcomes we truly desire in life. Mastering EQ, we would learn to observe, acknowledge, and deal with how others feel, which would lead us to deeper connections and more success.

We then would no longer need to ignore the wishes of our hearts in favor of the fears of our minds.

We would learn to recognize the powerful signal we feel when an external event stresses us, and then we should take action.

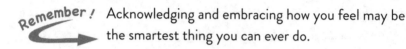 Acknowledging and embracing how you feel may be the smartest thing you can ever do.

FEEL IT TO HEAL IT

Like it or not, we all feel difficult emotions. It is part of our design as humans. Some of us learn to hide those emotions but even then, the truth is that our feelings are always there.

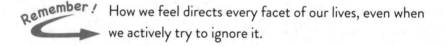 How we feel directs every facet of our lives, even when we actively try to ignore it.

When you feel negatively, your negativity distracts you, even as you try to suck it in. It slows you down as you waste brain cycles dwelling on what's upsetting you. It makes you less present as your thoughts are occupied with what led you here. It makes you doubt your loved ones even as they try to help you, keeps you on high alert, and takes away your passion and energy as you depart from the joy of living. When you feel down, you feel distracted. You become less effective at everything you need to do.

We so often fall into the pattern of trying to distract ourselves from our negative emotions. We keep ignoring emotions, keep suppressing them, successfully for a while, and then things get worse. The intensity of our brewing emotions grows beyond our ability to naturally contain them, so we try to distract ourselves in the unhealthiest ways, numbing out on alcohol, TV, food, overworking, socializing, even drugs in an attempt to push the negative feelings away. And how effective does that make us in life? The original target, remember? Those habits often take us from being ineffective to being destructive. You can keep trying to escape, but it simply doesn't work because those suppressed emotions continue to resurface for as long as they need to until we finally stop to face the music. You see, there is only one way to deal with the ever-growing power of your suppressed emotions: to feel them.

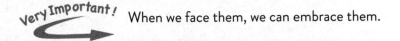 **Very Important!** When we face them, we can embrace them.

YOUR BEST FRIEND

Years ago, I attended a talk by mindfulness expert Palma Michel in London, when she told us something that changed my life. She said that it doesn't matter if I am saying something horrible to myself internally or if someone else is saying something horrible to me. Although we can physically tell the difference between who is saying what, emotionally, the effect on us is exactly the same.

Light bulb moment: this means I can create how I feel by how I speak to myself. As we discussed above, our emotions are not triggered by the events of our lives. They are triggered by the thoughts we generate about those events. It's not what someone told you that stresses you. It's what you tell yourself about what they said that does. It's not what you hear in the news that scares you. It's what you repeat to yourself, like a parrot, that does.

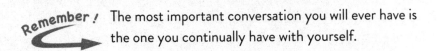 **Remember!** The most important conversation you will ever have is the one you continually have with yourself.

There is no other conversation that you will have from the start of your life right up until the very end that matters more; no one else informs you until you inform yourself. It's all you. Always you.

The true power of this was made clear when I had Nick Yarris on my podcast *Unstressable*. Nick had been wrongfully incarcerated on death row for twenty-two years for the rape and murder of a woman he had never even met. On death row, the trauma he suffered mentally, emotionally, physically, and even spiritually was beyond what the average person can even comprehend, let alone live with. Truly heartbreaking.

When he recalled his story to me, I welled up with tears. I listened with all my heart as he spoke. The kindness and compassion he had for the people that had wronged him left me in awe. I had to ask him how. How did he get through that experience for all those years of being tortured, in solitary confinement for something he didn't even do, and still come out with this level of grace? This level of unaltered kindness?

He responded that no matter what was going on around him, no matter what was being done or said to him, he made sure that he spoke to himself internally like his greatest champion, his truest friend, so that he always had some kindness with him every day.

This, he said, was the reason he is still here today, while so many others committed suicide on his block. Being kind to himself and others was the reason that he was able to move forward, rather than getting stuck in the bitterness of his harrowing experience.

This is the *true* power of our internal conversation.

Imagine this for a moment. How would you feel if you spent a day with someone who kept telling you that you were useless, not good enough, fat, stupid, snapping at you or criticizing you and putting you down? You would surely come back at the end of the day feeling pretty low, fed up, and depleted. Wouldn't you?

What about if you had a friend following you around all day telling you how *great* you were? Who believed in you and was kind to you when things went wrong? Who was reminding you during challenging times that you could do whatever you set your mind to do? That everything would be okay when things didn't go as you expected? After one day with that good friend, how would you feel?

You would surely end the day feeling content. Feeling confident and believing in yourself, even when things went wrong, you would feel empowered to handle them.

Now, think for a moment about the reality that you *could* have either of these people with you all day, every day, simply by choosing *which* conversation *you* engage with in your own mind.

Which one would you rather carry inside your head all day? The critic or the friend?

You choose.

THE CANVAS OF YOUR EMOTIONS

With emotions so fundamental to our stress and behavior, let's spend a bit more time trying to understand what emotions are the most crucial ones to note and observe.

Fear plays a huge part in our emotional stress. We fear what is happening or what might happen. It becomes a driving force in our emotional suffering. Even our decisions. Often being masked by other emotions . . . when the reality is our unaddressed fear is what is creating the action.

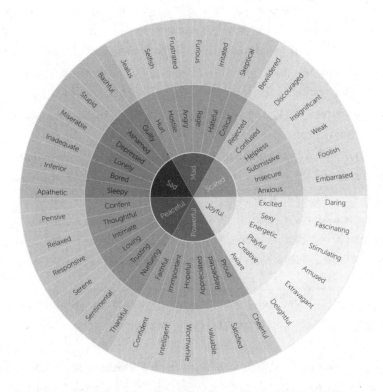

Gordon Corsetti, "Wheel of Emotions," Mentally Agile, March 29, 2020, https://mentallyagile.com/blog/2020/3/24/wheel-of-emotions.

During the 1970s, psychologist Paul Ekman identified six basic emotions that he suggested were universally experienced in all human cultures: happiness, surprise, sadness, disgust, anger, and fear. Later, psychologist Robert Plutchik put forth the "wheel of emotions" similar to the idea of the color wheel. He showed that basic emotions can be combined to form different feelings, much in the way primary colors can be mixed to create other colors.[1]

Between each two spokes, you'll find what he called *mixed emotions*—contempt, for example, rises out of a combination of anger and disgust.

Plutchik's research defined twenty-seven emotions, just as research from the University of California at Berkeley in 2017 later agreed.[2]

If you are intensely aware of all the ups and downs and ins and outs of your emotions, however, you won't be surprised by the findings of Professor Brené Brown's research in 2021.

Brown's team worked with a sample of seven thousand people and asked them to write down as many emotions as they could recognize within themselves. Out of seven thousand people, the average number of emotions able to be named was only *three*: happy, mad, and sad. Just three emotions recognized from the vast array of emotions that a human is capable of feeling. This really puts into perspective how the majority of people today are largely lacking in EQ, lacking the skill of understanding their own emotions, which is our key to feeling good.

Brown's research found that although many people can only identify and understand three emotions, humanity at large can feel eighty-seven.[3]

Is it any wonder that so many of us are lost in the emotional whirlpool of our own feelings? Feeling misunderstood by others; when we argue with our partner, telling them, "You don't understand how I feel"—well, maybe not, but do *you* truly understand how you feel yourself?

Remember! If you don't accurately understand how you feel, how can you expect other people to?

Being able to notice the subtle differences between different emotions is a skill to be learned. With it, emotions can be processed, helping us to truly understand ourselves and our actions.

A great example of this subtlety is the difference between envy and jealousy. Many think of these two emotions as the same: if I am jealous of someone, then I am envious, and vice versa. But what Brené Brown's extensive research showed is that envy is usually an experience between two people, and jealousy is usually an experience between three. Envy is when we want something we don't have. Jealousy is when we are scared of losing something we already have. We feel jealousy when the person we are in a relationship with is flirting with someone else, whereas we feel envy when someone is on the holiday that we would like to be on ourselves.

You can clearly see there are differences here, and even subtler is that within envy there are also two shades. "I want that and I don't want you to have that" or "I'm glad you had that and I want that too."

Understanding the actual intricacies helps us better understand the true source and impact of our feelings.

Envy, in its lighter shade, is directed inwardly. It expands the mind to what is attainable for me, noting that another has it. In its darker shade, it's negative and directed externally. "I don't want another to have what I don't, because I don't feel it's fair," and "I want it for me because I deserve it instead." The darker shade is actually directing me to look at our own self, as it's showing us something internally we need to face and heal that is not allowing us to be happy for someone else who has what we desire.

Remember ! It's not knowing the subtleties of our emotions that make them hard to manage.

Exploring this side of ourselves is what allows us to truly master ourselves. These are the eighty-seven emotions and experiences found to be available to us as humans:

Stress, Overwhelm, Anxiety, Worry, Avoidance, Excitement, Dread, Fear, Vulnerability, Comparison, Admiration, Reverence, Envy, Jealousy, Resentment, Schadenfreude, Freudenfreude, Boredom, Disappointment, Expectations, Regret, Discouragement, Resignation, Frustration, Awe, Wonder, Confusion, Curiosity, Interest, Surprise, Amusement, Bittersweetness, Nostalgia, Cognitive Dissonance, Paradox, Irony, Sarcasm, Anguish, Hopelessness,

Despair, Sadness, Grief, Compassion, Pity, Empathy, Sympathy, Boundaries, Comparative Suffering, Shame, Self-Compassion, Perfectionism, Guilt, Humiliation, Embarrassment, Belonging, Fitting In, Connection, Disconnection, Insecurity, Invisibility, Loneliness, Love, Lovelessness, Heartbreak, Trust, Self-Trust, Betrayal, Defensiveness, Flooding, Hurt, Joy, Happiness, Calm, Contentment, Gratitude, Foreboding Joy, Relief, Tranquility, Anger, Contempt, Disgust, Dehumanization, Hate, Self-Righteousness, Pride, Hubris, and Humility.

Ask yourself how many of yours do you actually notice and understand. Three? Six? Nine?

How many of those do you recognize as an emotion when you read them, even if you don't tend to recognize them when they are happening within you?

There are subsets within all the most obvious emotions that we have. When we can delve into those subsets, like jealousy and envy, then we can ask ourselves better questions, and when we can do this, then we get better answers.

The answers we get when we really understand our emotions and their origins are what we need to live our lives at the highest possible level, to have happiness that is more easily returned to, as we suddenly understand where our stress and anxiety is actually coming from—while also understanding where our calm and happiness originate from too.

Take a moment now to reflect on the intricacies of your own emotions. Find an emotion that's been prominent within you recently and try to analyze it deeply in a long moment of contemplation. What triggers it? Where is it directed? Does it come in different intensities? Different shades?

 Get to know your emotions intimately. Only then will you start to know the real you.

EMOTIONAL BRUSHSTROKES

When I hosted the legendary musician Ludovico Einaudi on *Slo Mo,* I asked him what I thought was a simple question: *Why does your music evoke emotions within me?* His answer was one of a true artist. He said that when he was young, he would listen to his mother play the piano at home. As she played, he would create memories made up of certain events, associated with certain emotions and certain tunes. The association between a feeling and a key or a tune was all mixed up within him, he said, until he was able to home in on what melodies triggered which emotions. As his artistic genius developed, he started to relate to those melodies and the exact emotions they evoked. As he touched the keys on his piano, he used the same vocabulary to make us feel what he felt when he created music. He used his emotions as the brushstrokes that painted the canvas of his music. Brilliant!

We all have similar experiences of associating emotions with memories. We too have those emotions all muddled up inside us. With the right level of emotional maturity, we too should be able to isolate each emotion so it's clear and recognizable as a distinct color with which we can paint the canvases of our own lives. It takes deep awareness, and it all starts with a name.

Using the right language around our different emotions is the starting point. When we are able to notice and name each emotion, we can place them where they belong. So often I, Alice, have conversations with clients who are trying to explain how they feel but they can't name what the feeling is. We learn to move emotions through us by giving them the right attention. The secret is found in untangling the muddled-up mix of emotions into distinctive strands.

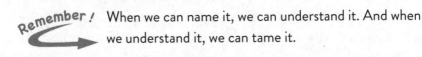 Remember ! When we can name it, we can understand it. And when we understand it, we can tame it.

Using language to describe our feelings effectively is a portal to connection. This identification then enables us to better communicate to others how we *actually* feel. When we do this, those we love become better informed to support us in our toughest moments, just as we support them in theirs. As much as we would love to be telepathic and know what others are thinking, we're not. We can't expect others to understand how we feel if we are not able to effectively communicate the truth of our feelings because we don't understand them ourselves.

Getting intimate within the nuances of our emotions is key to relieving our emotional stress, while also allowing us to not create more, by misunderstanding or feeling "misunderstood."

Understanding the language of emotions isn't just a portal for us to connect to others, it's also a portal to our connection inward. How can we possibly navigate our way through our own highs and lows if we are unable to decipher their details? We need to learn to understand what the trigger is and what the triggered feelings are.

We struggle with other people's emotions as much as we do with our own. Emotions, when unclear, challenge how we see the world, causing us emotional stress. We ferociously try to work out *why* someone else is acting the way they are. Why is our partner reacting to something in a way that we didn't anticipate? Why don't they understand how we feel?

Why is the conversation so heated? Why don't they listen? Why are we tempted to flee?

If you look inwardly, though, you may be surprised by how similar your own reactions are to the situations. When we don't understand our own emotions, we can't explain why we behave the way we do.

While our emotions are the direct derivative of our thoughts, once generated, our repressed emotions are not always recognized by the conscious mind. Those emotions remain hidden inside us while we disconnect from our emotional selves, a disconnect from the truth that lies behind how we are feeling. If we don't connect to the truth of our negative emotions, then we can't possibly connect to the fullness of our positive ones. Often the symptoms of depression are associated with an inability to find joy in the positive sides of life. A person suffering depression may have a loving, caring partner, friend, or parent who wants nothing but their happiness and acts with care and compassion, but often they would ignore that blessing because they avoid addressing the underlying cause for the negativity they feel.

Never, ever blame them for it. In doing so, they are acting in exact accordance with the very design of what it's like to be human.

You see? On top of humanity's highly sophisticated ability to plan and analyze, which made our ancestors store food for a cold winter and helps us save for a rainy day, we are also equipped with the safety mechanisms of less evolved members of the animal kingdom. As mammals, our system is designed for seeking pleasure and avoiding pain, and like reptiles, we are also wired to evade threats and feel fear.

Your monkey brain will do almost anything to seek pleasure and avoid pain. We would even hurt others, in wars of large scale, when that seems more appealing than being subjected to pain ourselves. In reality, your more sophisticated logical brain views things differently.

Remember ! If you do not turn toward your pain and own it, it owns you.

Your lizard brain pushes you even further. It keeps you stuck in negative emotions because of the most primal of all negative emotions—fear. We refrain from facing our negativity because we fear it. We fear that we may not be able to reverse it, which, for those suffering excessive stress or negativity, is a fear that is reinforced with every passing day through which they remain stuck. Your more sophisticated logical brain, however, knows the truth that when we have the courage to turn toward our fear and own it, we can change it.

DIVIDE IT BY TWO

Courage and facing stress come hand in hand, as allowing our stress to live largely stems from our fear of confronting it. So do many of our different negative emotions, which leads to a comforting thought. What if our decisions and actions did not result from as many as eighty-seven emotions? What if they so often stemmed from just two?

In the spiritual text *A Course in Miracles*, Dr. Helen Schucman speaks of how at our basic foundation, human beings are always only ever acting from two basic emotions. We either act from a place of fear or act from a place of love. Every other emotion is a secondary emotion—layered on top.

You may be puzzled by this view. I was too when I first read Dr. Schucman's work. I wondered, *Could this actually be true? How can all my choices and actions be coming from just these two emotions? Am I acting out of fear more than I would like to believe?*

Take a moment to look a little closer now. You will find that quite often this is in fact true.

If you are feeling envious of someone, for example, because they have something that you wish you had, where is that feeling coming from? *Why*, at a fundamental level, are you feeling that way?

Underneath that envy, you are either scared that you will never get that thing you desire or, perhaps, you are scared that you may be perceived as less than that other. So you become envious, then, as a reaction to your hidden, more primitive feeling—fear.

Are you actually angry with your children when you yell at them as they run across the road, or underneath that anger, are you actually just afraid they could get hurt? Yes. It's anger, but deep inside, it's fear.

What about stress, then? Obviously, as we explained earlier in this book, stress is a response to a threat. It is our instinctive biological reaction when something scares us. In that sense, stress has fear written all over it at its origin. More interesting, the reason we remain stressed is because of the lingering of that fear. When we explained the biological machinery that triggers our fear, we explained that after detecting a threat, we keep scanning for its presence. We become hypervigilant, and we find more reasons to be afraid. Then we let the stress linger further when we ignore it. On one side, we allow the reasons for our stress to remain unresolved, and on the other side, we fear that if we address them, by leaving our stressful job or relationship, or by confronting the bully that's making our life difficult, we may face other unfavorable consequences—which, in our minds, translates to more and more fear. Let's face it: Your emotional stress, at its core, all results from fear.

Now, look at the other side—love. If you're really excited about something you've been looking forward to, ask yourself: Where does this excitement come from? What's underneath it, really? Why are you looking forward to this particular thing so much? It is usually because you have a love for the place, people, or experience you're about to enjoy. You feel excited that you are about to experience something you love.

Love is an intricate emotion. It comes in different varieties. It's not exclusive to the Hollywood-type romance we so often are conditioned to dream about. As coined by the ancient Greeks, there are eight different types of love.[4] Philia, deep friendship. Eros, romantic. Ludus, playful. Storge, family. Mania, obsessive love. Philautia, self-love. Agape, selfless and spiritual love. Pragma, enduring love.

These different flavors of love can be combined to paint a variety of different relationships, one deep, fundamental emotion in different combinations yielding endless brushstrokes. This is another example of the subtleties within our emotions.

When we act from a place of love, our other emotions are secondary to that prominent foundation. Could it be, then, that love is the most primal of all our positive emotions? Just as fear is the primal instinctive emotion that keeps us away from all that we need to avoid and evade, love is the emotion that gets us closer to others, to ourselves, to the divine and all other beings.

Remember! You fear to love or you love to fear.

By simplifying the origin of our feelings, to love or fear, we can uncover the more complicated layers that have been built on top. How? Simply ask yourself the question: *Why?*

It's easier than you think if you develop the muscle for it. The next time you find yourself reacting to an emotion or making a decision you are unsure of, just ask yourself honestly:

Remember! → Is this coming from a place of fear or a place of love?

Question your emotions, get curious, and see what you can find. If you find they're coming from fear, ask yourself *what* you might really be afraid of and *why*? Address the source and you will resolve the fear and all the derivative emotions.

It's when we can learn to alchemize our negative emotions that emotions no longer become something to be feared but something to be dealt with, even treasured. Only then do we start to value our emotions and see them for what they truly are—the only reason we feel alive, the road map to our own growth and expansion.

FEELING FEARLESSLY

The first step on the path to let our emotions show is to address the fears that are suppressing them.

Our world values logic over intuition. Thinking over feeling. By pushing people to "toughen up" and just get on with it, we have created a culture that is toxic for ourselves and our emotions, a culture that doesn't teach us to understand and use them effectively, but sadly teaches us to fear what we feel. How were we conditioned for this fear?

In this culture, we normalize brushing off how we feel, rather than deeply exploring it. Hiding our negative emotions, as we are too intertwined in the belief that emotions have no place in success. That they are the traitors that will reveal our vulnerabilities to the world, so they must be kept in line. We want to appear to be who we think we need to be in order to achieve success or have the relationships we yearn for. We get stuck in a cycle of wearing these emotional masks, putting on the various faces we think we need to conform to in that particular place or in front of that particular person. Why? So that we feel *accepted*.

So that we don't have to expose ourselves to being judged by others, conforming to their ideas shaped by society instead of standing true to our own.

We push away this huge part of us as a form of self-protection and self-preservation.

So instead of encouraging us to face the hard emotions and express the great ones, we were encouraged to be seen but not heard, told to stop crying and get on with it.

Instructed to look to the logic of our minds to navigate our lives, when intellect is not the extent of our intelligence, and the guiding compass we desperately need is the emotional intelligence that lies within our hearts.

The courage to show vulnerabilities and to stand in the truth of our feelings is what makes us strong. In Brené Brown's famous TED Talk "A Call to Courage," she summed it up so beautifully when she said, "True belonging doesn't require you to change who you are; it requires you to be who you are."[5]

I love this sentiment; it's the epitome of courage—to find it within ourselves to be who we actually want to be. Despite who we are being *told* to be.

Remember! We will never become who we are meant to be if we're not willing to show who we truly are.

Our feelings are a part of who we are—a part of our truth. When so many of us hide those feelings, they're either too scared to feel or too scared to show how they feel.

I struggled with this myself in my early twenties. I was so scared to tell people how I was actually feeling. I was scared to tell my family, through the tough times we were going through, for fear of upsetting them even more. I was scared to tell the man I was in a new relationship with just how difficult things were for me, for fear that he would think there was something wrong with me.

I feared, like I'm sure you have before, exposing myself through showing my true feelings.

It takes a lot to be brave enough to show our true feelings not just to others but to ourselves.

We get caught up in the idea that emotions are meant to be good, that the happy ones are what we should *always* feel. This is the reason why many influencers on Instagram will only post stories of their happy, confident moments (or fake images of those feelings), making us feel that they are some kind of deity that never suffers hardship and never lives a dull moment.

We are told that negative emotions are not meant to be there for long, or else there *must* be something wrong with us. So we judge ourselves, and we hide them in fear of being judged by others. If we were to learn to live fearlessly, this would be the part we need to change.

Emotions, you see, are neither good nor bad. They are the signaling system that allows us to navigate the subtleties of our lives so we make the right decisions and avoid danger. They help us discern good from bad, help others understand us, and help us understand ourselves. And on top of it all, emotions enable us to experience the true beauty of life as we sense the polarity of our joy and pain.

Those feelings are never random; they are messages that are always true, informed reactions to the moment we are living through. Messages are to be dealt with, not feared. If we want to get anywhere in our lives, we need to let our feelings speak directly to us and tell us what we *really* need and to plot the correct path of action based on how we feel because . . .

Very Important! Our emotions are neither good nor bad. It's what we decide to do with them that is.

Understand that no one ever judges your emotions. They don't even *know* your emotions. Judgment around our emotions, is, in fact, a judgment of emotional reactions. This is the only part others can see. Feel what you feel freely and learn to react to those feelings, positive or negative, in a positive way. This is the key to feeling fearlessly. Once you learn to take charge of your reactions, you will not need to control your emotions anymore.

There are several ingredients needed for you to make this transition: to have courage, observe the signs emotions indicate, and break open.

If you had never seen anyone be judged for showing the truth of their emotions, would you have the courage to stand in the truth of your own?

FEARING COURAGE

Courage is more than fearlessness. It takes courage to feel. To understand and even show our emotions may be the most courageous thing that any of us can do, to have the courage to be truly seen and heard, and to stand in the true essence of who we are without retreating from the truth of what we feel.

I shaped myself well in my midtwenties. Distraction was easier than facing the truth of things. It was when I lost my dad that I couldn't follow that pattern of hiding and distraction anymore. I had become emotionally aware and knew from my past experience that what we push down only reappears in a greater strength or a different capacity, months or sometimes even years later. There was no escape, I realized. Sooner or later, I needed to face the music of what I needed to feel.

Is it easy to show up for our pain? Of course not, but it *is* necessary.

Very Important! Only when accepted does the pain choose to leave.

This acceptance is the most valuable gift you can ever give yourself.

And the opposite is also true. When we fear our pain, or what we might discover about ourselves when we feel it, we create lingering cycles of suffering. The pain holds us back. It blurs our vision of our truth. It then becomes the lens we view our lives through, leading us to make our choices from the fear-based lens of past experiences, either consciously or subconsciously. We erect an emotional wall within us in an aim to never have to feel this again. The pain we ignore is then compounded, adding to its intensity. Our unfaced emotions sit deep within us, like a ticking time bomb just waiting to explode.

Sooner or later, your pain will come to the surface. The longer we leave it, the more unexpectedly it can turn up.

Remember ! In a moment of reflection or an explosion, sooner or later, you will have to face your pain.

If we are to reach the level of happiness and calm we all desire, then we have to find the courage to get intimate with our negative emotions as much as we embrace our positive ones. We have to learn to allow these uncomfortable feelings and sensations to be felt and not just felt but fully accepted and understood. The upside, even to negative emotions, begins when you can face your emotions. You can observe the signs.

Our emotions are an internal compass that is our greatest resource *if* we choose to engage with it.

When something doesn't feel right, it's usually because it's not. If you are feeling anxious, there is a reason underneath it. If you are feeling uncomfortable, there is something that is waiting to be revealed to you, something that you can then act on. When we ignore these little flags that our emotions are desperately waving at us, then we miss the simple clues back to our own happiness and peace.

Fear is a flag that's waving to tell you there is a concern your brain perceives about your state of safety at a moment in the future. Acknowledging and acting upon it makes you safer; ignoring it allows the potential threat to risk what you hold dear. Feel the fear. Don't let it hide. Take action.

A deep disappointment with the behavior of your partner is a flag that's waving to tell you that your current setup is not meeting your expectations and serving your needs. Acknowledging and acting upon it makes you change for the better. Ignoring it allows the behavior to be a habit and your life to slowly morph into the life you don't want to live. Feel the disappointment. Don't let it hide. Take action.

The suspicion you feel when you're watching the news or swiping through the internet is a flag waving to remind you that not all that you are told is true. Acknowledging and acting upon it makes you research further to seek the truth. Ignoring your feelings may lead you to make rash decisions that could harm you when not fully informed. Feel suspicious. It's absolutely okay. Don't let the feeling hide. But don't let it linger.

Take action to make your life and your world a better place. It really is that simple.

Our negative emotions are only ever trying to alert us to one of two things: something with yourself that you need to heal or something outside of yourself that you need to change.

When was the last time that you fully welcomed any uncomfortable feelings that arose within you? Did you sit with them and ask yourself why they were even there? Or did you brush them off with outside distractions, numbing them out and hoping to never have to feel them again?

When we become curious about our emotions, we allow them to be. They no longer get stuck inside the cavities of our bodies and the structure of our energy. They come to tell us what they are there for, and gracefully leave. We see then that we have nothing to fear from our negative emotions when we learn how to deal with them.

Those emotions indicate to us that something is asking for us to pay attention. So it's up to us to ask what that is.

BREAK AND YOU'LL OPEN

The true beauty of what life has to offer is only felt through the polarity of our good and bad experiences. Without the pain, we don't appreciate the joy. I truly believe that until life has cracked you open in some way, you have not started to live. It's the day your heart fully opens up, when broken in two from pain. That's the day you truly learn to enjoy the beauty of life. When you choose to hold your open heart gently, rather than closing it shut even tighter than before. Everything in comparison becomes just a little bit sweeter, and your capacity to love becomes heightened as much as the capacity you have allowed yourself to open your heart and feel your pain. It is like a heart-expansion initiation.

Very Important! To feel pain deeply increases our capacity to love deeply too.

Pain, you see, has a function that goes beyond alerting us to harm. When the pain has passed, the experience increases our capacity to come back to love, to fully feel joy. To fully feel life. To live while alive. To find courage and gratitude from a place of knowing the true meaning of the blessings we are currently experiencing. The true value of the love we are giving and receiving.

Every pain, fully experienced, makes you appreciate life more, and every time you rise from the ashes, you are remade stronger. When we break, we always rise. It's when we resist that keeps us stuck in pain. Breaking down is like letting the pus out of an infected wound—gross, I know, but it's what helps you heal.

Remember! Allow yourself to break.

I used to think that my feelings were my curse, that my ability to feel everything that was going on around me was a torture. I could connect to the pain of my other family members and those closest to me like it was my own. I could be hurt by an unkind comment in a way that stuck with me for a few hours as a stab in my chest.

When I used to go home to visit my dad when he was in the depths of his depression, I used to leave feeling depressed myself. Like a dark cloud of despair and apathy was hovering over me, as it was him. This would stick with me for a few days, confusing me with my own emotions. That was until I finally learned that emotion is just energy. When I stopped resisting it, I learned to move it.

MOVE IT

Psychologist Dan Siegel says, "Emotions are just a form of energy, forever seeking expression."

The Latin derivative for the word *emotion*, *emotere*, literally means "energy in motion."[6]

The emotional energy in itself is neutral. It just charges us with a feeling. That feeling, sensation, and physiological reaction to the energy is what marks a specific emotion positive or negative. The feeling is then what we label as *sadness*, *joy*, or *fear*.

It is then our interpretations or thoughts about emotional energy, the point at which we label the feeling, that gives our emotions meaning. This is critical because it means that if you manage to change the label, you may be able to use the energy very differently and effectively, regardless of if the original label was positive or negative. Keep that thought for a minute. I'll come back to it later. Let's first understand this concept of energy a little more.

Emotion seen as energy is a fluid, moving supply that needs to be directed, expressed, so that it can be released. When suppressed, it is trapped, waiting to, one day, explode.

We've all had those moments when you walk into a room and you just *feel* a negative vibe, or when you've been around someone who's complaining and you leave feeling *drained*. Equally, I'm sure you've experienced spending time with someone who exudes positive or calm energy and they feel wonderful to be around. As you leave them, you feel energetic and *fully charged*.

You see, feeling drained or charged is not a question of how many calories you've consumed that day. It's not just your physical self that's turning food into energy so you can move and think. It's your emotional self too that can make you feel strong, weak, active, or tired. That is why we call it emotional *energy*. It may not be the kind of energy that physics measures. But it's what we carry within ourselves all the time, affecting our ability to perform in life and what we give off to others continually as we affect them too.

So what can you do with this energy? What can you do about it when it makes you feel negative? Well, energy is what we all need to navigate life. Use it! Just learn to make it positively directed or positively charged.

POSITIVELY DIRECTED

Mo here. In a conversation with Arun Gandhi—the grandson of Mahatma Gandhi and the author of *The Gift of Anger*—I asked him, "How can anger be a gift?" He smiled and answered calmly, "Anger is just energy, Mo. You can use it to punch someone in the face, and you can use it to stand up and be heard and even change the world." Profound!

Anger consumes us. It makes our blood boil and then, when it's too much, we explode and harm others around us. This is true of many other negative emotions. They work against us—that is, unless we make them work for us.

Feeling inadequate or disappointed with oneself, for example, is one of the most harmful emotions in the modern world. But that's if we submit to it, sit in a corner, and feel bad about ourselves. This same emotion, when informed by reality—drinking too much has gotten you in trouble repeatedly, for example, and you feel disappointed with yourself—can save us. It's that same disappointment that becomes the energy that helps us quit and be better. Envy or jealousy, when you compare yourself to an influencer on TikTok, for example, could tear you apart or drive you to become as silly as many of them are when directed negatively. That same envy, when directed positively, would become the energy that drives you to reach your potential in life (hopefully by choosing to become something more productive than being an influencer).

Remember ! The power of your emotional energy is always positive in its magnitude and neutral in its direction.

It is you that gets to choose where to direct this energy. Choose wisely. Don't let it destroy you. Let your emotions build you into the best possible version of yourself.

And while at it, please don't let the energy consume you. You see, some of us spend years building a business or seeking a partner in spite—trying to prove that they are better or to get back at someone who hurt them.

They spend a lifetime positively directing their emotional energy externally in order to build something beautiful, while deep inside, it's ugly. The negativity of their energy consumes them into years of suffering that last even beyond their success.

POSITIVELY CHARGED

Emotions originate in your mind where your opinions of a situation are formed. One of the biggest mistakes with the modern world is that for years our parenting and educational systems only knew how to motivate us through the negative.

Getting a B is not good enough; you need to get an A. If you speak in class, you are rude; you need to learn manners. You have too much energy; sit down and be quiet.

Growing up, for most of us, was a series of things going wrong that needed to be fixed. We were most often motivated by the negative. If energy was to be exerted to achieve anything, it was to correct what was wrong. As a result, we grew up doing more of the same. We work hard because we don't believe we have enough, and we riot in the streets only when motivated by hate.

It doesn't have to be this way. We can be equally motivated by the positive. We can work hard because we are excited about the potential of becoming better, not just because we are disappointed that we're not good enough. You are good enough, obviously; you've made it all the way here. But yes, you—all of us—can be better. We can make our voices heard because of compassion for those who suffer injustice, not just because of hate for those inflicting injustice on others. We can take action motivated by the positive impact on our planet if we change, not the negative impact of climate change if we don't.

As a matter of fact, when motivated by the positive, we are much more likely to be able to further advance our agenda and reach our cause. Clearly, positivity energizes us while negativity drains us in cycles of thinking and calculating and plotting. It distracts us as we become hypervigilant and push people away, people that can support our cause.

Remember !   Positively charged energy, positively directed, takes you the furthest.

But how can we turn positive when the fabric of our emotion is negative?

For every negative emotion that could drain you, there is a positive side that could energize you. There are always two sides to every coin. *Always!*

Comparing yourself to another leading you to envy, at its core, is a flag that simply says, "There is something that another has, or has achieved, that you have not yet." At its core, this concept is void of polarity. It is just your perception of reality.

Take that concept and charge it with the thought *I'm not as good as they are*, and it turns negative. Take it and charge it with *There is room for me to develop and grow*, and it becomes a very powerful positive motivator. When you disapprove of acts of injustice, the core of your waving flag is signaling the concept: *As per my moral compass, this is not how things should be.* That in itself is polarity neutral. It can lead you to rage and hate if you direct it at the perpetrator of injustice or can lead you to compassion and heroism if you direct it to the victims.

The energy will lead to action and impact either way. That impact can be very different depending on the polarity you choose. One side may become destructive and revengeful while the other may be constructive and healing. Which should you choose?

When you feel negative, look at the other side of the signal sent to you by that emotion. There is always a positive side to every negative face of your coin.

If you're unsettled in your relationship, the positive side is there could be a better way to be with your partner or a better partner for you. If you're feeling your city is becoming too expensive, maybe your emotions are asking you to consider a different city. If you've scored low on your exam, that means you still have something to learn.

DON'T LINGER

The truth to our emotions is simple: we want to feel good all the time, but that's impossible. Negativity is a survival mechanism. It is there to alert us that something requires our attention and action. It's a bit like physical pain. We don't like it, but without it, you would plug your finger into an electrical socket without noticing that this may end your life. There is a utility to emotional pain too. We experience it to alert us to what we need to act upon beyond the safety of our physical forms. As we move from positivity to negativity, we experience the highs and lows of life, we live life to the fullest, while the twists and turns of our outside experiences affect our inner ones. It's just how life is.

 Our negative emotions need to be felt; they inform us. But beyond becoming aware, there's no need for them to linger.

We have the ability to move them through us far quicker than we tend to. Simply by paying the *right* attention to them.

Neuroanatomist Dr. Jill Bolte Taylor says that at any one point in time there are only ever three things going on inside: you're thinking your thoughts, you're feeling your emotions, and you're having a physiological response to what you are thinking and feeling.

Her famous 90-Second Rule states that it takes no longer than ninety seconds from the instant you think a thought that stimulates a feeling leading your body to produce the physiological response and then go back to normal.

From the second you think about something and feel angry, to the second your body dumps noradrenaline into your bloodstream so you feel the rush of anger and start to act, to the second that hormone is flushed fully out of your bloodstream, it only takes ninety seconds from start to finish.

How, then, can some people remain angry for years? It's because they re-create the anger over and over on a loop by regenerating the thought.

With every repeat of the thought, the ninety-second timer starts again and again and again.[7]

Dr. Taylor said, "There's a ninety-second chemical process that happens in the body; after that, any remaining emotional response is just the person choosing to stay in that emotional loop."[8]

We choose to remain angry. We choose to remain sad. We choose not to take the actions that would make things better, and we choose to regenerate those uncomfortable feelings again and again. How stupid is that?

Every ninety seconds, you are given a second chance to reassess, reevaluate, and choose what you will do for the next ninety seconds. You get a chance to ask yourself if staying angry at the poor customer service agent is going to get you to finish your transaction quicker. Or if being frustrated with the person who cut you off in traffic is going to get you to your destination any faster.

For ninety seconds, you get to watch the process of you getting trapped by an emotion and then being set free; you can feel it happening, and then you can watch it go away. By noticing it happening, pausing, feeling it, breathing through it, and then consciously choosing your thoughts again, you can change the course of your future.

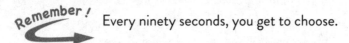 Every ninety seconds, you get to choose.

So how do you break the circuit that keeps you trapped in negativity?

BECOME THE OBSERVER

Before we react, we have to observe. We have to give space for us to become an onlooker to our own emotions, rather than the puppet reacting to them. The next time you notice yourself stuck in a loop of stress, anger, fear, anxiety, or any other negative emotion, pause and take a deep breath.

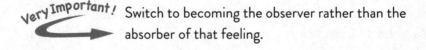 Switch to becoming the observer rather than the absorber of that feeling.

Where is that feeling being held in your body? Breathe into that area. What thoughts are you holding in your mind that create and then re-create that feeling? Ask yourself how you can change those thoughts and choose differently. Just notice your negative emotion, breathe through it, allowing it to pass through, and then consciously choose your thoughts again.

This is the perfect space, once you feel calmer, to disrupt your negative thought cycle. Often all you need to do to disrupt your negative thought spiral is to get in touch with your thoughts and repeat a simple statement in your mind—such as "Cancel, cancel," or "Bring me a better thought" (remember the deal?)—to interrupt the pattern of negative thoughts so you get to choose again.

First, notice yourself when caught up in a negative emotion, and then take a step back, pause, and observe that feeling like we would a friend when they are feeling negative. How would you treat a friend in that state?

 *Very Important!* Pay attention, kindly, with no judgment.

Kind attention without judging yourself for what you're feeling allows your mind to observe the negative without giving it fuel to burn. You become curious rather than critical; kind and supportive, not discouraging and destructive; realistic in acknowledging that negativity comes and, when dealt with, goes.

Please don't berate yourself. Don't let your mind tell you things like, *Ugh. I hate feeling like this. I have no right to be upset about this*, or, *I'm pathetic.* Look at your feelings, instead, as a neutral, objective observer: *Okay, I feel a tightness in my chest. It feels like fear. Why might I be feeling this way?* Let me remind you one last time:

 *Remember!* It's okay to feel.

Create a space between yourself and what you're feeling and then ask yourself the questions you need to ask to get to the bottom of that emotion. Ask four questions every time:

- What emotion am I feeling?
- Where am I holding this feeling in my body?
- Why might I be feeling like this today?
- What can I do about it?

Question your emotions, and your answers become the passage back to your happiness. Those emotions are not there to wear you down. They simply are intended to inform you. Listen and act, and like magic, the feeling starts to dissolve.

Sometimes we need to take space between what we are feeling so that our emotions don't overwhelm us in the moment. This happens when we are flooded.

FLOOD WARNING

Flooding is something that can happen during a conflict with others, when you're having a heated discussion with your partner and suddenly you just lose it. We start screaming irrational profanities that make no sense to the argument or are extremely cutting to the other person and something we wish afterward that we could take back. But the damage is already done.

When our bodies sense a big stressor, which for many of us can be a difficult conversation, an argument, or cutting feedback from someone, we feel attacked and overwhelmed. Flooding, as defined by the Gottman Institute, is "a sensation of feeling psychologically and physically overwhelmed during conflict, making it virtually impossible to have a productive, problem-solving discussion."

Dr. John Gottman, psychologist and founder of the Gottman Institute, explains, "We all have a sort of built-in meter that measures how much negativity accumulates during such interactions. When the level gets too high for you, the needle starts going haywire and flooding begins. Just how readily people are flooded is individual."

When we are flooded, our thinking brains, which allow us to consider other people's sides, shut down, and we lose some of our capacity for rational thought. So we end up saying things that are likely to trigger the other person's flooding and we find ourselves in our own standoff of flooding, hurling unfiltered, unhelpful, and often unkind comments at each other, with neither party backing down nor able to hear rationally what the other side is saying. We end up doing more damage than good.

Like a sealed chamber, the more pressure applied, the more likely it is that the seal will break. And when the chamber finally breaks, the more damaging the flood will be.

Very Important!

The more we let the pressure we suffer mount and grow, the more likely we are to be flooded, and the more damaging the flood will be.

The pressure affecting us before we break, notice, is not all external. The external trigger normally is just the last bit of pressure that breaks the seal. Most of our pressure normally comes from our mounting emotions.

For this reason, taking a step back when we are in a heated conversation with someone we love or beginning to feel ourselves getting irritated, putting it on pause and taking time out is key.

When we are able to go away and self-soothe our emotions, go and ask ourselves why we are feeling this way and why *they* may be feeling the way they are, we shift our perspective, allowing us to not get overwhelmed by our emotional stress and bring others into it with us.

The next time you feel yourself about to be flooded or are in the depths of a flood, pause and take a time-out. Return to the conversation when you are feeling calmer and in a more rational state of mind, better able to see the bigger picture, not just the threatened one your flooded mind would have you believe.

It can save us all a lot of regret for the things we say in this heightened state and save us from creating even more emotional stress for both ourselves and others from what we said when in it.

Better still? Don't let yourself get to the point of flooding in the first place.

Although we don't need to let our emotions out on other people, let-ting our emotions out is essential. Emotions are always welcome. What we need to avoid is an excess of stored, unprocessed emotions.

So, how do we begin to notice what's brewing inside us and free our-selves from the danger of emotional stress and explosive floods? How do we free ourselves from our emotions?

EMOTIONAL FREEDOM

Emotional freedom lies in our willingness to be emotionally curious, so we become more emotionally aware and intelligent. We do this when we observe and acknowledge our emotions in an inquisitive way.

Emotions are just energy in motion. Uncomfortable emotions can be managed by diffusing their energy; we do this by giving them the right at-tention and then moving them through us. We can change our emotional state much quicker than we realize. Here are three techniques to shift your emotional state quickly.

THE THREE EMOTIONAL ALCHEMISTS

Tap It

Tapping—officially known as EFT (emotional freedom technique)—was developed in the 1990s by Gary Craig. It is an expansion of the concepts that make acupuncture and acupressure so successful.

Chinese medicine works on energy meridians throughout the body. These are the channels that connect acupressure points through which a person's life energy force—which the Chinese call *qi* (also spelled *chi* and pronounced as "chee")—flows.

When qi is in flow we feel emotionally and physically healthy, but when it gets blocked or stuck, we suffer imbalance. The energy of our uncomfortable emotions becomes stuck in certain parts of the body. We hold these emotions in our bodies as a sensation—tightness in our chests, aches in our shoulders, or knots in our stomachs. Sound familiar?

EFT works by tapping on certain acupressure points in the face and upper body, while acknowledging the emotions you are feeling. It is the *acknowledgment* of the emotion, while tapping on the energy meridians, that allows the stuck energy to be passed through the body, returning us, once again, to our state of balance.

Throughout this book, we will remind you that if your stress is extreme, such as in the case of trauma, you should seek the support of a professional practitioner of the technique we discuss. There are, however, effective uses of tapping that you can practice on your own.

Step 1: Identify the issue

Acknowledge how you are feeling, about what and where. For example: *I feel anxious about starting my new job, because I am worried about what the people I work with will be like. I feel a tightness in my chest.*

Step 2: Rate the initial intensity of your emotion

Rate the intensity of how you are feeling on a scale of 0–10, where 10 is the highest and worst you could possibly feel, and 0 is totally calm and at ease. Keep that rating in mind.

Step 3: Create your statement

Create a statement with two parts: a statement of acknowledgment of the specific problem, followed by a statement of acceptance of yourself despite the problem.

For example: *Even though I feel anxious to start my new job, I deeply and completely love and accept myself, and I'm willing to let my fear go.*

Step 4: Begin the tapping sequence

  1. Sit comfortably with your back supported, take a deep breath, and gently close your eyes.

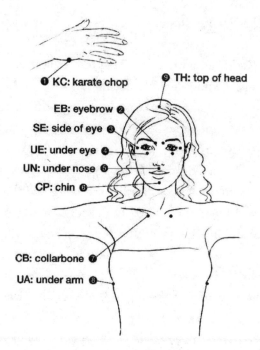

2. Bring the issue and the feeling you have around it—your statement—to the forefront of your mind.

3. Bring the outer sides of your hands, the parts you would use to karate chop, together for a couple of minutes while repeating your setup statement: *Even though I feel anxious about starting my new job, I deeply and completely love and accept myself.*

4. Now begin tapping each point, as shown in the figure, in order, starting from the top of the head and ending at the points under your arms. Tap on each point rhythmically, for around twenty to thirty seconds, using both hands with your index and middle fingers.

5. Breathe deeply as you move through each point, keeping your awareness of your issue and statement. When finished, repeat this whole sequence for another round.

6. Drop your hands down with your eyes still closed, take a deep breath, and rate how you feel again. Notice if it has gotten quieter or louder, without judgment—take note of the rating.

You can repeat this process till you get it down to a manageable rating (1–3) or till it is gone completely (0).

Because tapping is such an easy process and because it works like magic, I urge you to not let issues linger. Whenever you feel emotional distress, tap it away. Don't wait. Even better, make it your habit to tap your negative emotions away as part of your evening routine, once or twice a week.

You can even use EFT to move through a negative emotion that you don't understand the reason behind. Use a statement like, "Even though I feel this anxiety in my chest, I deeply and completely love and accept myself."

Shape It

Being curious about our emotions is the key to befriending them, rather than making them our enemies. When dealing with intense emotions, our pain will naturally keep returning as we move through the process. Once we become inquisitive with our emotions, there becomes no need for them to persist to get our attention.

It's wise to take time every day to check in with yourself and ask how you are feeling and why you may be feeling that way. To make this an easier process, we can turn the emotional into the physical so that it is more recognizable to the mind. For this, I use a process I call *shape-shifting*. It allows attention to be paid to the physicality, beyond just the physical signatures of our feelings so we can give the emotion life and describe it like any "shape" we can see.

When we do this, we learn to locate it within the body and pay attention to it in detail. It's a great way to become the outside observer of your emotions. Reiki masters learn the first part of this technique for healing, but I have further developed it to add a way to release the emotional energy at the end once it's been located.

Through thorough observation, we can ask each emotion what it's trying to tell us and then move forward, releasing it through our breath now that it has been fully given the correct attention.

Step 1: Find somewhere quiet

Sit down comfortably, take a deep breath, and close your eyes.

Step 2: Scan

Breathe deeply as you scan your body from head to toe. Notice where in your body any negative feeling is being held.

Step 3: Observe and describe

Place your awareness on this area of your body and continue to breathe deeply. Start to describe the feeling as a set of physical attributes: What shape is it? What size? What color? What texture? And what temperature?

Step 4: Identify the feeling

Once you have identified it as a physical form, ask yourself what *feeling* this shape represents and what this shape and feeling may be trying to tell you.

Step 5: Acknowledge it

Now, breathing deeply, start to release the emotion as follows: *Thank you, (emotion), for showing yourself to me as (shape, size, color, texture). I know the reason that you are here is because (your realization for why you are feeling that way), and I am now ready to release you.*

Step 6: Release it

Finally, place your awareness on this area of your body (even place your hand gently over that area if you can). Inhale deeply through your nose and exhale through your mouth. On every inhale, imagine breathing in calm, and on every exhale, imagine that the emotion is being released by visualizing the shape shrinking.
Repeat in your mind continually, *I release you.*

Repeat this process over the day or over a few days until you feel the feeling has shifted.

Okay, it's me again, the annoying masculine engineer who reads this and does not see how the human machine would benefit from this. But this whole process is truly beautiful, and it does work. It's a tender, kind way to acknowledge and accept what you feel. It is attentive in a way that appeals to your inner child and it's nourishing, life-giving as the motherly feminine that we all so crave. Shut your engineering mind up, Mo. We're dealing with emotions here.

Getting tangible with our emotions and turning them into something physical that we can visualize is a powerful way to shift them. Here's a final, more practical way to do that.

Write It

Sometimes what we can't say, we *can* write. You may notice this when you are texting a friend. It's easier to write down what you feel and reflect on it deeply than it is to say in a conversation. I, Alice, know that writing my emotions concisely to someone else has always been helpful when broaching a more difficult conversation. Our feelings surface more effortlessly when we allow them the right non-judgmental space.

Very Important!   When you want to deeply connect to your emotions, write them down.

Writing has been used as a way to prompt us to delve into our emotions by asking ourselves better questions for millennia. The concept was formalized into journaling, however, only in the 1960s in the work of psychologist Dr. Ira Progoff's intensive journal method.

By answering journal prompts, we get to the reality of what's inside, provided that we write down whatever comes up within us—uncensored. Because no one ever needs to read what we write down, we can be true to our emotions without the fear of being judged. This uncensored free flow is key for us to process our emotions and increase our self-awareness.

I so strongly believe in the power of journaling that I encourage every client I work with to use a journal so they can better understand their own stress and anxiety. This very often works as research from the University of Rochester Medical Center has shown. Journaling on how we feel is proven to reduce our anxiety and stress and even help with depression.

What starts from this evolves into a much deeper practice of exploring their own sense of self and really getting to know themselves on a deeper level.

Putting a pen to paper is a magical path from being lost to feeling found, from confusion to clarity, and from a chaotic mind to a calm one. When we later take the time to read what we wrote, we make ourselves an implicit promise to fix what's broken, recognize what's hidden, and act when what needs to be done becomes clear.

With consistency and discipline, the habit of journaling, knowing ourselves and what causes our stress, is the key to being able to better manage it. As the Chinese philosopher Lao Tzu wrote:

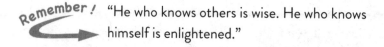

Remember!   "He who knows others is wise. He who knows himself is enlightened."

Another significant benefit to writing your emotions down is that the moments you spend journaling are moments spent in a state of reflection, focus, and deliberate attention. Those moments bring you to a state similar to what you experience during meditation, only instead of focusing on your breath, you focus on your emotions. Do this regularly and you will bring a state of calm to your life even if the emotions you experience are stormy.

Earlier in the chapter, we agreed that the biggest reason for emotional stress is that we don't know the language of our emotions well enough. Turn those emotions into words you can read and you've gone a long way toward translating them.

Journal and ask yourself:

- How am I feeling today?
- Why might I be feeling this way?

If what you feel is negative, ask yourself:

- How would I like to feel instead?
- What is one thing I can do that can help shift me toward this feeling I want to create?

And if it is positive, ask:

- How can I cultivate this feeling and bring more of it into my life?

While at it, ask yourself one last question that will help you end on a high, as we mentioned around mental stress in chapter 4: *What do I feel grateful for today?*

Don't take life for granted.

 Be grateful for every little blessing that you have today.

KILL IT WITH KINDNESS

If gratitude can help alchemize our negative emotions, kindness can help us alchemize our stress into calm.

When we are feeling stressed, anxious, or just plain old down in the dumps, we go through cycles of analyzing life and all its tricks, believing that its mighty wheels and everyone in it revolves around the center of the universe—"I, me, and my." When so absorbed, the last thing we feel like doing is to get out of our own way to look outside of ourselves and do something for someone else. We get so absorbed in the stories playing inside our minds that we even ignore the need to be kind to our own selves.

Very few things we can do at those times would help more than to practice self-kindness toward ourselves in times of struggle or to practice kindness to others.

The Random Acts of Kindness Foundation, established in 1995 to inspire people to practice kindness and to pass it on to others, put together research from studies done by various universities to show the overwhelming benefits of kindness. They found that giving random acts of kindness to others decreases stress, with perpetually kind people being found to have 23 percent less cortisol in their bodies and to be aging slower than the general population. Shocking, isn't it? In a way, they found the fountain of youth, when you think about it.

A study published in the journal *Motivation and Emotion* by University of British Columbia clinical psychology professor Dr. Lynn Alden showed a group of 115 highly anxious undergraduates who were asked to do at least six random acts of kindness a week for one month. Simple as those acts might have been, the participants, across the board, experienced a significant increase in positive moods and relationship satisfaction, and a decrease in their social anxiety and avoidance of social gatherings due to anxiety.

Studies also found that kindness increases our energy, happiness, serotonin levels, life span, sense of pleasure, self-esteem, and optimism.

Research from Emory University showed when you are kind to another person, your brain's pleasure and reward centers light up as if you were the recipient of the good deed—not the giver. This incredible phenomenon is called the *helper's high*.

Very Important! Being kind is both the most selfless and most selfish thing you can ever do.

Next time you are feeling particularly stressed or deflated because of something you can't change, ask yourself:

Remember! What can I do as a random act of kindness for someone else instead?

Buy a coffee for a stranger, let someone go in front of you in the line, send a loved one a kind and loving message. See how your mood shifts afterward, and yes, please be kind enough to reach out to us both on social media, to make us happy and tell us that this worked for you too. It would be most kind of you.

BOUNDARIES CREATE CALM

Being kind to others decreases our stress and increases our happiness, but we mustn't then forget to be kind to ourselves too.

One of the kindest things you can do for yourself is to prevent the madness of our modern world from negatively affecting you. This only results from being able to set boundaries, something that so many of us often struggle with.

Most people are not evil, though sometimes they are self-centered. They do, however, act with no understanding of what our needs truly are. Our needs, then, don't get met, and we find we become frustrated, even depleted—becoming emotionally stressed with ourselves and others. You can't blame anyone else for this.

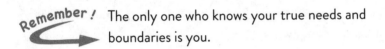 The only one who knows your true needs and boundaries is you.

Setting those boundaries is key to our emotional health and a sure way to help ease our emotional stress.

When we know what our own boundaries are and we have the conviction and courage to act on them, we create a better sense of self, as well as an ease in our relationships with others, as we have shown what we will and won't allow.

The next time you are in a situation where someone is demanding a lot from you, notice how you start to feel depleted as you allow this person to overstep into your energy reserves and spread your attention resources too thin.

Often you will find yourself saying *yes* just to please other people. Alice here. I know that I have been guilty in the past of not telling my own family, friends, or past boyfriends what my needs are. As someone who likes a peaceful environment, I find that sometimes my own needs get pushed to the side for the sake of others' peace and happiness. But I have come to learn that in doing this, I only end up feeling exhausted or frustrated later down the line and not as happy as I would be had I just been honest about what my own needs were in the first place.

When we don't communicate our needs, we end up drowning in stress and frustration, and we end up letting down those we care about as a result. Boundaries are not only needed to protect you, they are also needed to protect your loved ones by keeping your limited energy and attention reserves dedicated to them.

As Gandhi once said:

Very Important! "A 'no' uttered from the deepest conviction is better than a 'yes' merely uttered to please."

The irony is that without boundaries, the very objective of giving is eventually missed. When we stand in the truth of what we want and most important what we need, we allow ourselves to help those that matter most to us because our own resources are not depleted. The result is someone who has enough to give because we become someone who is able, and committed, to give to ourselves.

Remember the stress equation. Stress is not just the result of the load applied to us but also the result of our ability to handle it. When we set healthy boundaries, be that in our relationships, our time, or our work, we address both sides of the equation. From one side, we reduce the load affecting us and from the other side, we build our skills to eliminate future loads, simply by saying no to them before they are even applied to us, and we leave some of our time and energy to deal with other unavoidable stressors.

Boundaries reduce our emotional stress because they help us avoid resentments toward others from having said yes to something we didn't actually want to do.

Ask yourself where you might be in need of setting better boundaries in your life. Are you currently saying yes to things just to avoid disappointing others, at the expense of your own happiness? Are you able to set boundaries between your work and your homelife so that you can switch off and properly relax in the evening? Or do you know deep down that you need to work on your boundaries because your own needs are often not met?

How do you know that you need to set more boundaries? Well, that's easy. When boundaries are crossed, they deplete your time, energy, and emotions.

Observe how much time and energy you are giving to people, activities, and work, then look at how much time and energy you are giving to *yourself*, your own wellness, connections to loved ones, and your physical and emotional needs. List what you feel is missing. How do you know what that is? By thinking what you would want to see more of in the life of someone you love dearly. If you would give something to a loved one, you should give it to yourself too.

Carve out the things you want to do for yourself.

 Plug the things you want to do for yourself into your schedule first!

Mo here. During my extremely busy executive life, this one tip was the biggest game changer for me. Time to meditate, to go to the gym, or with my daughter always went into my calendar first. No other commitment was allowed a higher priority than those. If the CEO of Google wanted time with me to discuss an important project and that time overlapped with an appointment that I had with my daughter, I would answer that I had a conflict in my agenda and would call Aya first to make sure that her time would allow another possible slot for us to meet. If it wouldn't, I would, believe it or not, ask our CEO to suggest another time. That's how important your personal care and boundaries should be for you too.

Block your me time in your schedule just as you would any other meeting.

Then look at the bigger picture and ask yourself how much of your work is creeping into your social and personal time—and how much of your awake time is going to work and others rather than to you. A good rule of thumb is fifty to sixty hours a week. This should include your work and chores and positions your life, approximately around a third being for work, a third for sleep, and a third for living and self-care.

Finally, look at your me time and check how much of it is going to social media, negative news, and technology. Ask me what a good rule of thumb is around that, and I will always say, controversial as it may sound . . . always strive for zero. If you are spending a minute of your quality care time on those, it is a minute too much.

Now that you have clarity around the actual allocation of your time and energy, start to look at how much emotional energy you tend to give to certain people and situations. Identify where you may need to take a step back and reserve those emotional resources for yourself. If you find that you often get caught up in emotional situations and make them your own problem, with family members or friends, perhaps cut back on the emotional investment you dedicate, especially when those issues can only be resolved by those experiencing them. Continue to support your loved ones, but don't let it compromise your own emotional reserves.

Very Important! Get really honest with yourself about where you need to set some better boundaries.

Boundaries, whether physical, emotional, or time-based, are key components to our emotional well-being, but I also believe, Alice here, another important but often forgotten aspect is our energetic boundaries. We can create boundaries and look after our own energy body through energetic intelligence.

ENERGETIC INTELLIGENCE

Our energy body is a complex mix. According to ancient Eastern wisdom, there are several layers of our being, sometimes known as *koshas*. Within these several different layers, which include our mental, emotional, physical, and spiritual bodies, also lies the energy body.

Our energy body holds within it multiple channels and pathways (meridians) and centers (chakras). Within this energy system is where our life force energy, qi or prana, moves.

Energy, like water, should be moving to keep it fresh; otherwise, we create a stagnation. This stagnation is caused by disruptions from, of course, our *unprocessed* emotions.

Energy therapies like acupuncture and EFT, as shown earlier, help keep our energy flowing and healthy. But a simple way to easily enhance your own energetic health, here with your emotions, as emotion is just energy in motion, is through creating energetic boundaries and practices.

Something to take into account about your energetic health is it's not just what you are doing but what other people are. Just as an unkind comment can have an effect on our mental and emotional well-being, intense energies given off from other people have an effect on our own energy and how we feel.

Denser emotional energies, such as fear, anxiety, stress, depression, anger, and envy can attach onto our energy body from others and deplete our own energy.

This is why certain cultures believe in energetic protection—the Greeks, for example, use the evil eye, *mati* (μάτι), which is a symbol to be worn for protection against the envy and jealousy of others.

When you are "evil eyed" by someone, it is believed to be an energetic curse (powerful intention) given by an envious and malicious glare to make the person experience bad fortune or loss. When unprotected by the evil eye symbol, this can even cause the recipient to feel unwell, which I have even experienced myself. Still to this day, the evil eye is a prominent part of Greek culture and worn by millions of people worldwide for protection and something I wear every day.

The effect of other people's energy on our own is something to be aware of when you are feeling particularly drained, stressed, or anxious, as so often we pick up these energies and confuse them with our own feelings.

Becoming aware of when you are feeling something that is actually someone else's emotional energy is a skill that takes practice as you build up your own emotional and energetic awareness—how your own emotional energy feels versus how the foreign energy of others feels instead.

Understanding some simple energetic intelligence to be able to look after your own energetic health is vital toward feeling good and helping you become unstressable.

You can start by cultivating a simple practice to look after and protect your own energy with what I call your energetic **CPR**.

CLEANSE, PROTECT, RE-GROUND

Cleanse

Cleansing our energy of the energetic rubbish that we pick up throughout our days from people we know and the collective is a great way to help us to feel lighter again.

The stress, fear, anxieties, anger, and jealousy of others are all very dense energies that bring our own energy down, causing us to feel energetically drained and emotionally imbalanced.

If you're feeling drained and tired, try the following. I recommend doing this at least once a week to keep your energy body clear.

Salt is a natural energy cleanser. When combined with water, it has the ability to cleanse our aura (the energy body that surrounds our physical one) from any negative energies it may have picked up. Do you tend to feel lighter after you've swum in the sea? The natural salt water cleanses your energy body while you are immersed in it, making it an energetic practice as much as a physical one. But if you're reading this from somewhere that doesn't resemble a paradise island, don't worry; you can do it quickly at home too:

- While in the shower, get a salt scrub and scrub down your whole body.
- When you go to rinse it off, close your eyes for a minute and

visualize the water from the showerhead washing away any negative energy and swirling it down the drain.

You can also do this by having a bath with Epsom salts and setting the intention in your mind, as you get in to soak, for any heavy energy to be cleansed away. Allow the salts to work their magic. This may sound strange, but just notice how you feel after you have done it, compared to before.

Protect

Once we have cleansed any unwanted outside energy, it's important to protect ourselves from it so that our energy body is not as open for outside energy to easily attach to it again.

Energetic protection is done through intention or visualization.

Visualization can be done by closing your eyes and visualizing a protective translucent bubble coming down and around you, from the top of your head all the way down over your feet. Finish by setting the intention in your mind for this to protect your energy.

Or we can simply do it as and when we need, through verbal intention.

I was given this really simple and effective energetic prayer by a teacher of mine, Tori Jenae, and it is my go-to; it's quick, easy, and you can do it anywhere.

Repeat this intention in your mind, either before you go out to somewhere you know may be a little intense or during a conversation where someone is getting angry, stressed, or making you feel uncomfortable by doing something that drains your energy, like complaining or gossiping.

Simply repeat three times in your mind:

What's mine is mine, what's yours is yours.

You'll notice this is particularly effective when you are cornered in an uncomfortable situation with someone. Even if you are speaking to them on the phone, do it. It will help you to not come off the call feeling so emotionally drained and exhausted.

Re-ground

To feel steadfast, calm, and grounded in ourselves, we need to re-ground our energy.

Grounding our energy is an amazing antidote to our anxiety. When we are anxious, our energy is erratic and all over the place. When we are calm, we feel grounded and stable in our energy and ourselves.

If you are feeling anxious, one of the first things to do is to make sure you ground your energy, to make sure that this part of your being is stabler.

We can do grounding in two ways. One is by simply walking in nature barefoot, which is often referred to as *earthing*. This also helps calm our nervous system, while it grounds our energy to the earth.

Here is the second way:

- Sit with your feet firmly on the ground or stand with your legs shoulder width apart.
- Close your eyes and take a couple of deep breaths.
- Feel the weight of your body into your seat and the weight of your feet into the floor.
- Then visualize energetic roots coming out of your feet like the roots of a tree and going all the way through the floor, through the ground below you, and down into the center of the earth.
- Imagine them wrapping around the core of the earth and coming all the way back up and into you, up through your feet, up into your heart space and wrapping around your heart.
- Repeat this visualization one or two more times.

When you are finished, take a deep breath and repeat in your mind, *I am grounded.*

 When our energy is balanced, it allows us to cope with stress more easily and to feel less anxious.

We feel clearer and more balanced within ourselves, so we become better able to manage the challenges we are faced with throughout the day.

The power and importance of our energetic health has been recognized within many cultures and countries such as India, Turkey, Japan, and China for centuries. They recognize the effect that our own energy and the energy of others has on both our emotional *and* physical health, practicing alternative energy therapies, such as acupuncture and, one of my favorites, Reiki.

REIKI

Reiki was founded in Japan by a man called Mikao Usui in 1922. Usui went to meditate atop Mount Kurama in Kyoto, Japan. He went to try to experience a type of enlightenment called *anshin-ritsumei*, where one is continually in a state of supernatural peace, and when in this state, one is guided to fulfill one's life purpose.

After succeeding through meditation to enter this state, he ran down the mountain to tell others what had happened, when he tripped and injured his toe. He placed his hands on his toe to try to soothe it, to find he felt a wonderful warm feeling, and the pain in his toe disappeared. It was then that he discovered he had received an ability to heal—Reiki.

From this, he went on to teach Reiki, opening a Reiki clinic. Reiki has since spread to the West and become a recognized alternative therapy, even recognized by the National Health Service in the UK.

Its ability to help both our physical and emotional health, due to the link between the two, is something quite extraordinary. It is performed with a hands-off technique, which allows the practitioner to channel healing energy into the client and to be able to notice where any energetic blocks are within their energy system and move the energy back to balance again.

The idea of Reiki may sound strange to you at first, but let me tell you about the experience I had with it, which got rid of the doubts of my own.

In the time after Suzanne passed away and our dad was taken over with depression, I was struggling hugely myself to come to terms with the new reality of what the dad in front of me was like now, my own grief, the reality of what my family life now looked like with no financial security, and moving from our home, with no end to the stress in sight.

I had this feeling of an elephant sitting on my chest every day. This feeling had been building up and up over the months before my sister died and then continued to just grow and grow.

I had become so familiar with it that I had forgotten what it was like to not feel that heaviness in my chest—that is, until it was gone.

I had sought the help of a therapist to try to come to terms with my new reality, but she and I were just not the right fit. As with any good relationship, there has to be the right chemistry.

This particular therapist didn't get that my twenty-five-year-old self struggled to talk about what I was dealing with unless I was asked questions to coax it out of me. She would sit in silence staring at me and waiting for something that would never come.

Eventually, after ten weeks of frustration and seemingly getting nowhere, she told me there was a Reiki practitioner in the building and that she thought I should try a few sessions alongside ours.

I had no idea what Reiki was, no understanding of energy healing, no belief in it even. But at that point, I was feeling so deflated by life that I was willing to try anything.

I went to the first session and felt more at ease than I had in a long time, being able to feel the sensations of energy around my head and chest as I lay there with my eyes closed, relaxing while she worked on me. I was intrigued, so I returned once more and again felt the sensations and was deeply relaxed. But it wasn't until I was walking home after the third session that I suddenly stopped in my tracks, holding my hands up to my chest. It was then I realized that the familiar elephantine pressure was finally . . . gone.

That physical feeling had been with me for nearly nine months. Ten weeks of talk therapy had done nothing to ease it, but it had been shifted with just three sessions of Reiki in a way that could actually be felt *physically*. I was amazed, relieved, and, of course, curious.

From this, I tried out as many different energy practitioners and healers as I could over the next few years before studying energy modalities like Reiki, EFT, and clearing myself. I began understanding more about the power of energy therapies firsthand and later became a Reiki master.

Reiki and other energy therapies, like EFT, are one of the most overlooked aspects to stress management and to preventing our physical health declining. There is a link between our emotions and our physical health. This link is connected by the energy that our emotions store. When we are emotionally healthy, then we can have the free flow of energy within us, our qi. We need this free flow of energy in our systems in order to be well and feel good. When it becomes stagnant and blocked by emotional experiences we have not dealt with, emotional and even physical problems can occur.

I have often seen clients who are having stomach troubles because they are holding on to a negative emotion in their stomach and unknowingly storing their emotional stress there.

A good friend told me once of his digestive troubles, which were causing him a lot of discomfort. He had been to the doctor and had every test he could. But nothing could be found, and he was still experiencing the same symptoms. When he told me about a recent stressful event he had been through, I knew intuitively that it was an emotional issue that had caused an energetic block, which had now turned physical. I told him to come for some Reiki, as at that point he might as well just try, having exhausted everything else. An hour after the session, he messaged me to say he couldn't believe it, but all of his symptoms were gone.

We so often need to experience something ourselves, if it challenges our own beliefs, to be able to see the power of it. Reiki can be this way for many people, as it was for me. Knowing the true benefits of Reiki, I would urge you to explore it for yourself and try it out if you are feeling particularly drained or stressed, as well as just to relax.

In our monthly membership, there is a chance to explore this, as we give members Reiki-infused meditations I've created that work to keep your mind, emotions, and body balanced, giving people the benefits of Reiki and meditation in one.

We've been talking about emotions for quite a few pages now. Though those tricky sensations occur trillions of times across humanity every day, and though they completely drive many of our actions and moods, few of us truly acknowledge them, let alone speak their language and understand them.

In a nutshell, emotions are not hard to deal with *once* you pay them attention and you know how. They are the signaling flags that are there to alert us about the subtleties of life, the stuff that demands our attention. Though they are triggered by a thought, it's hard to trace them with logic because that thought often originates subconsciously and very frequently gets buried deep so we are left with the raging emotion but sometimes with no clear logic that explains why we feel the way we feel.

To get intimate with your emotions is to observe them in a neutral fashion with no judgment, accept them, even celebrate them and view them as a form of energy that can be moved, positively charged, and positively redirected. Ask where, why, and what so that things become clear. Whether you tap yourself through your emotional tides or set clear boundaries so they don't arise in the first place; whatever you do, don't let your negative emotions linger.

Emotions are the fuel of life, but when they are uncomfortable and we allow them to loiter, they lead us into chronic stress and eventually bring us down. Understand the flag as soon as it's waved and address what it's telling you and act upon it. It can actually be that simple.

The next layer of what makes us human, your physique, is theoretically easier to understand. It screams and causes you discomfort and even pain when it wants to be heard, and yet we still ignore it. In honor of your body, please put this book down. Get up and stretch. Take a break, feed your body, or let it enjoy a nourishing drink.

Connect to you and you may not even need to spend the time reading the next chapter.

But we recommend that you do.

6

Your Hips Don't Lie

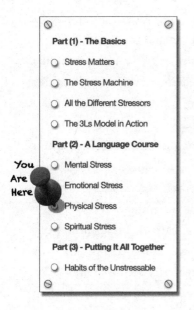

You
Are
Here

Butterflies in your stomach. A pain in the neck. Those are not just expressions that we use as metaphors. Those physical sensations truly are felt when we feel certain emotions. Shakira sang it. It's the truth. Hips don't lie. Neither does any other part of your body. The link between our bodies and our emotions is as real as the link between our thoughts and what we feel.

But while our minds can play tricks on us, and while our emotions may hide and morph, our bodies say it as it is. The signs our bodies give us are unmistakable, for those who pay attention. Those signs can only be pushed away for so long before something starts to give. When our bodies speak, we should listen.

You may be missing some of those signs and choosing to ignore some. Those signals, when ignored, can put you into a deeper state of stress—a spiral that is bottomless and surely one that deserves your attention. Bessel van der Kolk, author of *The Body Keeps the Score*, stated, "We have learned that trauma is not just an event that took place sometime in the past; it is also the imprint left by that experience on mind, brain, and body. This imprint has ongoing consequences for how the human organism manages to survive in the present."[1]

Your hips truly don't lie about the experiences they have been through, physical, mental, and emotional. Neither does any other part of your body. It all keeps the score. You just need to learn to listen to it.

THE PHYSICAL SIGNATURES OF OUR EMOTIONS

Ancient Eastern medicine and healing philosophies have known for centuries what the West is only just starting to catch onto in the last decade. They teach us that when we look closer, we see that the emotions we experience but don't fully process manifest in our bodies, causing physical aches, pains, sensations, and all sorts of illnesses and troubles.

Those relationships between our physical conditions and our emotions can be found in traditional Chinese medicine in which it is believed that seven emotions—joy, anger, worry, longing, sadness, fear, and shock—affect the health of five internal organ groups.

When the emotional stimulation is strong, negative, and long-lasting, it surpasses the body's capacity and capability to handle it, which results in damages to the body's internal organs and obstructions in the flow of our vital energy, which the Chinese call *qi*.

Your heart reacts to negative emotions of hate or impatience. Worry, anxiety, and mistrust are controlled by the spleen, leading to physical symptoms such as fatigue, memory loss, poor appetite, bloating, and weight loss. Is it any wonder we get tired when we are stressed and worrying?

Sadness, grief, and depression are closely associated with the lungs. Tightness in the chest, shortness of breath, asthma, and frequent colds can be part of your life when you're sad.

Fear is associated with the activity of the adrenal glands—the glands that secrete adrenaline when stimulated by the body's flight-or-fight response.

Anger, frustration, jealousy, and envy affect the liver, which is easily understandable because it is responsible for storing and rapidly releasing glucose into the blood when the energy of anger takes us over.

From seeing what organ is in distress, a practitioner of Chinese medicine can look to heal the emotional issue in order to cure the physical symptom. The belief is that if we only cure the physical and leave the emotional unresolved, the illness may disappear for a while, but it will return again so long as the emotional issue is not healed.[2]

It is fascinating when you think about it: an emotion directly controlling your physical form leading to sensations and even illnesses. The good news is this works both ways.

Positive emotions keep us healthy, and being healthy—when our bodies are well taken care of—contributes to our positive emotions, such as love, trust, courage, and gentleness.

Positive emotions, such as love, joy, and happiness, in traditional Chinese medicine, are considered elements of fire. Feelings of love and appreciation, accordingly, are believed to influence the heart's health and rhythm. You can love your way to a healthy heart. How beautiful is that?

Emotions like fairness, openness, and trust are seen as elements of the earth. They ground us and in the process keep the spleen, stomach, and pancreas healthy.

Courage and righteousness, considered elements of metal, affect the lungs and skin. Gentleness, calmness, and stillness, considered elements of water, are felt in the kidneys and bladder. And generosity is healthy for the liver.

Traditional Chinese medicine has worked for millennia to keep the largest population on earth healthy. But even if you choose not to believe in any of it, try to enjoy the beautiful metaphor.

Remember! Emotions manifest in our physical form. We can physically sense them in our bodies.

Louise Hay, author and founder of the publisher Hay House, looked at this link extensively. She studied how to identify what emotional issues are in need of healing based on what physical symptoms we feel. In her book

Heal Your Body, she shares a comprehensive list of physical illnesses and the believed emotional cause. She said, "I believe that we create every so-called illness in our body. The body, like everything else in life, is a mirror of our inner thoughts and beliefs. Our body is always talking to us; we just need to take the time to listen. Every cell within our body responds to every single thought we think and every word we speak. Continuous modes of thinking and speaking produce body behaviors and postures and 'eases,' or dis-eases."[3]

She believed that our emotions are also what can manifest our physical imbalances, just as much as an outside virus can—they can be our own internal virus that we create.

EMOTIONS MANIFESTED

I experienced this link with my own body, when I was a fit, healthy thirty-year-old and I caught pneumonia.

I had never had pneumonia before in my life. I was healthy, I ate well, I had no underlying conditions that could have caused that reaction—nothing obvious, except the fact that at the time I was dealing with one of the toughest emotional experiences we as humans can go through: grief.

I had lost my wonderful dad just eight months prior and was still going in and out of the depths of my grief. My immune system was affected by the stress. That would probably be a reasonable Western medicine explanation—a lowered immunity allows a disease. What was fascinating to me, however, was that in traditional Chinese medicine, the organs that they associate with sadness and grief are, of course, the lungs.[4]

When I got pneumonia, I had every antibiotic and steroid imaginable thrown at me to try to attack what the Western doctors believed was causing the disease. By the fourth round of antibiotics, I was either suffering from an allergic reaction to the antibiotic itself, or I was now in a stage of pneumonia that would mean I needed to be admitted into the hospital immediately. I was in very bad shape. I was told to stop the antibiotics and wait till the morning. This was not the most restful night's sleep, as I am sure you can imagine.

When I woke up and felt a bit better, the doctor explained that it was the antibiotic that had been making me sicker. So when the doctors offered to give me a fifth round, I declined. Instead, I decided to look to my own body to heal but also to my emotional health.

I gave my body strength through rest, fluids, steam and tea tree oil inhalations, and as many vitamins as possible. What mattered more, I believe, is that I also allowed myself to process a lot of the pain resulting from my grief.

I was totally alone for six whole weeks, unable to leave my home. When you are given that much time alone, with no choice but to stay inside, no choice but to be with yourself; if you're open to it, you'll get to meet your emotions on a very intimate level. I did.

I journaled every day on how I was feeling. I meditated. I cried whenever I needed to. I practiced breathing techniques to get the emotion to move through me and my lungs. I wrote letters to my dad as if he were still here and told him all I needed to say. I did Reiki on my chest every day, and I listened. I listened to the emotional signatures in my body. Lungs are for grief. I worked through more of the grief, and I got better with no more medication, all on my own.

Now, it's obvious we should seek medical assistance. I'm not saying that anyone should slack about that. All I am pointing out here is that the issue for me in this instance wasn't solely the virus but the environment my unprocessed emotions had created to house the virus in my body and that, to heal, I needed to start to heal my emotions first.

Remember ! To heal your body, you often need to heal your heart first.

Just as the Chinese associate different parts of the body with various emotional signatures, they do the same for stress too.

THE THINGS WE ALL IGNORE

Just like the modern world teaches us to ignore our emotions, we also learn to ignore the physical signatures of stress just to keep up with the relentless pace of our modern lives. We ignore the clear entanglement of our physical pain and the stress we suffer. We delay interventions and tell our loved ones that we will sort our aches and pains out "soon." We convince ourselves that things will slow down sooner or later and that when they do, we will have the time to attend to those inconveniences, but the pace keeps going and we stay in pain.

We brush off the continually aching back as having pulled it lifting something weeks before. We ignore the returning migraines as too infrequent to remember or do something about, until the next one comes crashing back around to remind us. We try to fumble through the digestive issues, blaming purely our overindulgence of one meal, and we simply dismiss the tightness in our chest that has been growing in the background until the cost of it is too high to bear.

BACK AND FORTH

The thoughts we create and the emotional reactions we don't process keep our system in a state of stress. This leads to the majority of our physical stress. This cycle, however, works equally in the opposite direction too. The constant aches and pains in our bodies, the headaches, the back pains, and the bloating act as stressors that affect us profoundly. I mean, think about it: Have you ever snapped at someone not because of what they said but because you were exhausted or in pain and they kept talking? Have you ever felt irritated because you were not sleeping well or because you had not had sex for a while? Have you ever skipped a friend's invitation and stayed home thinking lots of dark thoughts because of a sports injury or a need for rest? You apologize afterward and say you don't know what came over you, but we all know that it was your body causing you stress. Just as much as our thoughts trigger our emotions and our emotions trigger our physical pain, your pain triggers your emotions, which trigger your thoughts. Stress happens in a closed loop, and one thing leads to another.

Remember! Your pains and aches stress you as much as your thoughts and emotions.

Our brains constantly monitor the information from our environment for threats, but they are also constantly monitoring the information from our bodies. If signals sent by our bodies indicate something is wrong, then our stress response goes on.

Simple things like how we eat, move, sleep, and even breathe all have a direct impact on the effect of our physical stress. Each of those impacts the information that our brains are being given by our bodies, telling them whether we should be stressed or not. If, for example, you are unable to sleep and rest, this may translate to your primitive survival system into a sign of a present danger. If you're not eating food that nourishes you, this could be interpreted as famine. And while our logical brains can assert that neither is true, our more primitive survival instincts truly don't care to distinguish the differences. They just want you safe, and for that, they take those signals as reasons to stress you more.

This downward spiral is vicious. No matter where the stress originates, it will eventually show up in the body, either as the cause of our stress or as the product of it. And then the stress in our bodies will feed back into the other systems, causing more stress that causes more physical stress, and the cycle continues.

THE VICIOUS CYCLE OF PHYSICAL STRESS

The work of developmental biologist Dr. Bruce Lipton indicates that the body is always listening to every single thought we have—every cell is constantly receiving information from our minds. As a result, what we think and speak has a profound effect on our physical selves and the environments we create inside of them, which in turn affects our health.

Dr. Lipton coined the term *nocebo effect*. This, essentially, is the opposite of the placebo effect, which is the belief that we can change our health only through our positive beliefs. The nocebo effect, conversely, is the effect of our negative thoughts and emotions on our health and how *these* have the ability to create a negative health effect in our bodies just from our beliefs.

Stress takes over when your body is knocked out of homeostasis—the state of steady internal, physical, and chemical conditions maintained by living systems. This state is the condition of optimal functioning for any organism. Stress knocks the body out of balance while it concentrates on survival.

If our thoughts are constantly telling our bodies to stay in stress or even to be ill, through worrying about health outcomes, what we tell our bodies will become our reality.

Countless medical reports refer to the impact of our thoughts on our bodies. In 1992, the *Southern Medical Journal* reported a case of a man back in 1973 who had been diagnosed with cancer and given just months to live. After his death, around that time, his autopsy showed that the tumor on his liver had not even grown. The conclusion in his death report read: "I do not know the pathologic cause of his death." Instead of the cancer, it may have been his expectation of death that killed him.[5]

The physiology in our bodies that our thoughts can create is very real.

Remember ! The body turns what you think into your physical reality.

This is true for your unconscious thoughts too. Just recalling a previously stressful event can cause you stress.

If you had a bad experience with your mother-in-law, for example, one that caused you angst before, your stress response can turn on again on your way to see her with your partner, just by remembering how she made you feel.

You sit in the car remembering the last time you saw your mother-in-law, and your body produces the same stress response by thought alone.

In that moment, you produce the same chemistry in your brain and body and feel exactly as you felt when that moment actually happened.

No organism in nature can tolerate living in emergency mode the majority of the time, yet we as humans manage to simulate emergencies even when everything is okay.

We have an ability to imagine the worst-case scenario and allow our behaviors and emotions to mirror the fears in our mind.

THE STRESS OF OUR LIVES

Stress can be debilitating, even life-threatening, when it turns up in our physical forms. This is something I know firsthand from both myself and my wonderful dad.

During the time when my dad was refusing to deal with his own cancer and health troubles, I suffered from stomach troubles myself. I was grieving for the way my dad was before, and was so worried for his health, mental and physical, that I was, obviously, causing myself a lot of stress and holding on to all of it in my stomach.

My digestive issues only got worse and worse as the months went by. Eventually, they got so severe that when I went to see the doctor, because of my family history, he was worried that I might now have colon cancer and prescribed further tests.

That time when I waited after the procedure to see if they had found anything was one of the most nerve-racking thirty minutes of my life. I had just seen my sister go through the horrors of cancer, I had just found out my dad had cancer again, and I lay there wondering if I now shared this horrific family fate at just twenty-six.

The tests came back clear, and the doctor diagnosed me with severe IBS from stress. That was a wake-up call to me that I needed to do something about how I was dealing with my dad's health decision. A wake-up call that stopped me from making myself truly ill. I needed to start changing there and then, and I did. My stress got to me, but I chose to do something about it. My dad, however, very sadly chose not to.

My dad chose to ignore his early physical wake-up calls, partly on purpose out of depression and apathy for life, and partly because he was so adamant in his mind that the physical issues he felt in his stomach were a result of the cancer he didn't want to treat. They were actually the reality of a stomach ulcer that was silently growing, because of his state of stress, in the background.

It was that ulcer, not the cancer, that took him. Had he gone to get it attended to, we would have had him with us longer. He may even still have been here today. But I don't think like that. I know that every soul has its path, and he took his, which is what has led me to write this book for you.

As my dad lay in intensive care after a cardiac arrest caused by the internal bleeding in his stomach, the ICU doctor questioned if he had been under any stress. Well, you already know the answer.

When I remember my dad, I remember the earlier version of him. He was happy within himself, healthy, very sharp for his age, he laughed a lot, and he had an incredible charm and mischief about him. He had always looked and acted ten years younger than he was. Always, that is, until stress took charge of his every day. Seven years of that, and there he was, battling miserably in a hospital because of an illness brought on by stress.

The vibrant person I was raised by is not the one that I got to spend time with in the years before he left. It is not the dad that lay in the ICU after the doctors had brought him back to life, the dad who turned to me, holding my hand with wires coming out of every part of his body, as I looked him in the eye and asked him if he wanted to die, and he replied by nodding gently—yes.

This devastating image of him acts as a reminder for me, as it should for you, that we should never allow our physical stress to linger until it's too late.

Your emotions, illness, fatigue, pain, and other physical issues are not just a symptom; they are a flag that your body waves vigorously to tell you that something is not going right, that you need to slow down and change course.

Learn the language your body speaks. Observe the flags.

GIVE ME A SIGN

Studies show that in the US alone, between 70–90 percent of *all* doctors' visits are somehow related to stress. This means that two out three times you suffer physically, you can safely assume it's because of stress.

When we get a minor physical problem, then the first questions we should ask, before reaching out for the painkillers, are: Am I currently stressed? What could my body actually be trying to tell me? How long has this been going on?

Remember ! Every minute when your stress response has been ignored beyond its purpose wears your body down.

Why? Because the infamous stress hormone cortisol affects your body differently, depending on how long it remains elevated in your system. Under normal conditions, it is anti-inflammatory. It binds to the glucocorticoid receptor (GR) and in doing so helps your body be healthier. Prolonged or excessive secretion of cortisol, which is what happens when we are under cumulative, ongoing stress, however, results in a resistance of the GR that blocks cortisol binding. Similar to the mechanism underlying insulin-resistant diabetes, when this happens, it increases inflammation in the body instead.[6] What was once a healthy physical stress response turns dangerous long term.

Short-term inflammation from our stress response is good because it's the result of your immune system kicking into gear to help you deal with a threat, and it allows your body to prepare for you to heal quickly, in case you should get a wound from an injury that becomes infected. It prepares you for battle.

But once again, what works for you in the short term turns against you after a while. Long-term inflammation, which becomes chronic and unresolved, increases our risk of diseases like heart disease, type 2 diabetes, obesity, depression, and even cancer.[7]

When we are constantly being pumped full of cortisol, inflammation becomes chronic and acts as an immunosuppressant, making us more vulnerable to the attacks of germs and accordingly more susceptible to more disease.

So as we become more inflamed, physical issues in the body naturally start to arise. Our bodies focus on the things they think we need to survive, rather than the things we need to thrive.

A common example of this is digestion. When the stress response is on, our bodies' resources are directed away from digestion. Our wise bodies know chomping away on our steak and french fries is nonessential to our immediate survival when we are under a real threat. The stress response sends resources away from the digestive system. We can do fine without focusing on digestion for a few hours or days, but when the attention is diverted away for too long, we start to develop digestive issues like bloating, constipation, and irritable bowel syndrome. With less blood and oxygen in the stomach, stomach acid increases, leading to complications like stomach ulcers.

Digestive issues are just one of many physical signatures of stress— perhaps one of the common, obvious ones. Other physical signatures are often ones that we all have. Surprise, surprise.

Many of the less severe ones, though, are just deemed so "normal" that we don't think of them as a problem worth taking the time to work on.

And while those stress signatures may be less problematic when they first appear—no one has ever thought they might die of a mild stomachache— over time, they may be life-threatening. Remember my and Mo's dads.

Do any of these signatures of stress apply to you?

- Headaches
- Fatigue
- Tightness in your chest / chest pains
- Aches and pains—particularly back, neck, and shoulders
- Muscle tension
- Tension in your jaw / grinding your teeth
- Trouble sleeping
- Digestive issues—constipation, indigestion, bloating, stomach ulcers, etc.

- Racing heart
- Lowered immunity (more easily picking up common colds, etc.)
- Lowered sex drive
- Higher blood pressure
- Higher cholesterol
- Weight gain
- Acne and other skin breakouts
- Reproductive issues

If you're experiencing any of the above, then you can assume that they could be the result of stress. Now look for a few more.

- A churning feeling in your stomach
- Nausea
- Restless motion in your legs and being unable to sit still
- A thumping and irregular heartbeat
- Sweating or hot flashes
- Faster breathing
- Dry mouth
- Pins and Needles

Those are specifically the result of anxiety, which, as we discussed when we spoke about the equations of emotions, is not just the result of a concern about a future threat but also a concern about your ability to handle it—a double whammy of stress.

These signs tell us that stress hormones have been pumping around our bodies so much that we are now under strain from having to deal with them for so long. But things don't have to be this way.

You could, obviously, prevent further physical stress when you remove the reasons for your stress by looking after yourself mentally and emotionally. They can also be prevented by attending to the physical issues themselves with love and care. Either way, it all starts with one simple decision. Do you want to do it? Do you want to feel physically better?

Ask anyone who's been admitted to a hospital for a serious medical condition or is sitting on the dentist chair with drills pointed at his teeth and what do they all say? *I wish I were more careful. I wish I had taken better care of my body.* Sadly, we tend to think everything else is soooo important—that is, until we are actually sick. We borrow from the bank of our health; we take loans on stress to pay for getting things done.

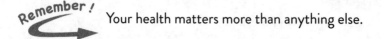 Your health matters more than anything else.

We often only remember this when our ill health suddenly becomes the unavoidable focal point of our days. We so often only value what we have when it's gone.

WISDOM IN THE CELL

Away from the tricks our negative thoughts in our minds can play, our physical bodies are wise; they don't play up on us for "fun." They try to guide us when something is off. They alert us when something needs our attention. And they increase the intensity of the alarm when we ignore the guidance.

Those bodies of ours are a bit like German cars. They perform so well and rarely ever fail, so we take them for granted. We think running this extremely complex biological machine is simple, but think about this. Eight pints of blood are pumped around your body every day.[8] This red liquid carries nutrition to 37 trillion[9] cells so they live and help you carry things and run and think all on just 2,000 calories a day. With each food calorie generating approximately 4.2 kilojoules of energy, your entire, highly tuned machine as a body runs on the equivalent of a 100-watt light bulb. That's how efficient that machine is. Oh, and as some of those trillions of cells die, even better than German machines, your body rebuilds itself and replaces 330 billion cells every day.[10] When something attacks this body, it dispatches enough of its white blood cells to defend itself. Of those, there are between 4,500 and 11,000 white blood cells per cubic millimeter of blood.[11] Your body warms you when it's cold and cools you when it's hot. It's a power plant, a repair workshop, a mobile vehicle, a committed army, and a supercomputer all in one, and it does it all, automatically, without being told to do any of it, while keeping you moving, breathing, digesting, thinking, complaining, mistreating it, and overthinking to make yourself stressed.

Respect your body. Don't take it for granted.

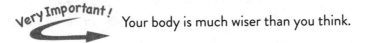 Your body is much wiser than you think.

BODY LANGUAGE

Annoying as it may be, the only language your body speaks when something goes wrong is pain and its derivatives—discomfort, agony, injury, and fatigue. If you plug your fingers in the power socket, you feel that buzzing sensation that is so uncomfortable that it swiftly engages your immediate reflex to pull your hand away and also teaches you to not do that again. As much as you dislike pain, you wouldn't want to live without it, because without it, you wouldn't live for long.

Pain is not there to annoy you. It is there to save you. It works for you when you listen to what it's telling you and react. The exhaustion you feel as a result of your lack of sleep is a clear sign that your body disapproves of your hypervigilance and constant incessant thinking. It is telling you to turn them off so you can rest. The depleted energy you feel when you are stuck in a job or a relationship that's not benefiting you is a sign that you are not where you should be and you should make a plan to change this. The burning sensation you feel when you're irritable and about to explode is a warning signal to calm down and avoid the situations that are stressing you, and the burnout you feel when you are overworking is just telling you that it's time to really take a break.

What's the right thing to do when someone is talking to you? Listen!

What's the right thing to do when your body is talking? Listen!

It's easy to get on a downward spiral of unhealthy habits and keep on going. We drink too much, and when we feel hungover, we swear to ourselves that we will never drink that much again, but then we do. We eat junk, and when we feel like junk the next day, we promise that we will keep a healthier diet, only to reach out for the next burger and fizzy drink in a matter of days. We stay up at night as our restless bodies struggle to deal with what we do to them. Then when they feel exhausted from all the abuse, instead of looking after ourselves, we think, *You know what? I'll just eat a bit more comfort food with a glass or two just for the day. It's been a tough day, and the sugar will make me feel better for now.* But does it?

LOST IN TRANSLATION

At first glance, it may seem that comfort food is the message your body is sending through its cravings. After all, we crave a sugar or carb hit when sleep deprivation causes our hunger-stimulating hormone ghrelin to increase, while also decreasing levels of the appetite-suppressing hormone leptin. In that state, our bodies look for a quick bit of energy to help us feel more awake, and this is most easily accessed via carbohydrates, which break down quickly into glucose before entering the bloodstream. But these temporary hits are not the answer. As with little kids when they eat too much candy, our quick sugar high is followed by a sugar crash. This leads us adults to consume more carbs, supplemented with too much caffeine.

What the body really needs is rest, not a temporary fix. It's trying to keep up like a trooper, but sooner or later, it breaks. Our reliance on the wrong habits is simply the result of allowing our minds to drive us into stress. When we do, our bodies speak. Not the healthiest of habits.

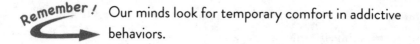 *Remember!* Our minds look for temporary comfort in addictive behaviors.

We numb out on junk food, Netflix, work, alcohol, or meaningless sex and even drugs, just to feel a temporary slither of comfort from our stressed bodies and anxious minds.

That is, until our bodies decide they've had enough. They scream to ask us to pay attention.

I was asked to pay attention when I started getting chronic fatigue in the winter. I finally got diagnosed with recurring Epstein-Barr virus, which doctors believe to be triggered by stress, as a large majority of the population have this virus lying dormant in their bodies, only becoming active when under severe stress. Unsurprisingly, mine only became active when I lost my dad.

Dealing with migraines and severe fatigue resulting from the EBV, I needed to become conscious of what I was putting into my body and how I was treating it.

I changed my skin-care products to natural ones, and I started to eat a strict anti-inflammatory diet. I took the recommended supplements, got into the habit of walking, and found a low-impact strength training regimen that suited me. Via fatigue and my migraines, my body was asking me to pay attention. So I did.

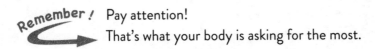

Remember ! Pay attention!
That's what your body is asking for the most.

You can pay attention by observing what affects your body and how it feels as a result.

Ask yourself how your body is actually feeling. What tension are you holding and where? Also ask yourself how you're treating it. What foods are you eating? What exercise are you doing (or not doing)? How much sleep are you actually getting?

What is really going on within and around your body?

TAKEN FOR GRANTED

Nobody is invincible. As impressive as our bodies are at performing the tasks we need to navigate the physical world, they are not just machines. Or at the very least, they are machines that demand frequent maintenance and preventive care.

A better view of the body, however, is to regard it as the temporary home the soul has anchored itself in while we are here. This home deserves respect and care. Like anything, the more we nurture it, the better it becomes, and the more enjoyable our time spent living in it will be.

The truth is so many of us take our health for granted until it's too late. We take it for granted because we haven't yet had an experience in our lives that makes us understand the true value of it.

Remember ! We don't appreciate the value of our health until we lose it.

One day, we finally get the wake-up call, whether that's from our own health declining or seeing someone we treasure suffer and leave. Only then do we wish we had taken better care.

Very Important ! Don't wait. Take care of your body's needs as of today.

How? It all starts with awareness.

The first whispers are key to early intervention.

SCAN IT

The physical sensations of the body are the language it uses to speak to us, its words. How do you start having a conversation? Start by asking every part of your body how it feels, then pay attention to the response.

Notice even the smallest of changes, the little nuances of tension long before you notice the extreme aches, pains, and chronic symptoms. Pay attention to it in an *active* way.

This technique is often called a *body scan*, a mindfulness practice to help you tune in to your body, actively, and as you become aware, it helps to release the discomfort.

Mindfulness demands kind attention. So when you notice something in your body that is uneasy, don't berate or blame yourself. Don't panic and tell yourself that you're falling apart. Notice it neutrally like an outside observer and then relax it in that moment and get support from a bodyworker or clinical physician when you know you can't ease it alone.

Stress Hack

Let's walk together through the process:

- Find a comfortable position, either sitting or lying down, in a quiet place.
- Place your feet firmly on the ground and lay your hands in your lap with your palms facing upward.
- Take a deep breath in through your nose for five seconds and exhale deeply out of your mouth.
- When you're ready, gently close your eyes.
- Continue to breathe deeply as you relax into your breath.
- Begin to slowly scan your body, starting at the top of your head, moving from the crown of your head, just noticing any tension you may be holding as you go.
- Move gradually all the way down . . .
    * Into your eyes, face, and jaw,
    * Down into your neck and shoulders,
    * Moving down into your chest and upper back,
    * Your upper abdomen, your lower abdomen,
    * Moving down into your lower back and hips,
    * Your thighs and all the way down your legs to your ankles,
    * And finally into your feet.
- If you become aware of any part of you that feels any tension or discomfort, with your eyes still closed, consciously breathe deeply into that area of the body.
- Direct your awareness on that area, directing your breath to it.
- Actively visualize a white light expanding in that area when you breathe in, then let go of any tension there when you breathe

out. In your mind, picture how it feels to have no tension or
pain in that part of you.
- As you breathe deeply into this space that needs your attention,
repeat affirmatively, within your own mind or out loud, *Body,
why is there tension in my X?*
- Breathe deeply and wait for the first answer to come to you; this
isn't about receiving a medical diagnosis but an emotional clue.
- Then ask, *Body, what do you need?*
- Breathe deeply and wait for the first answer to come to you.

It may be something simple like more rest, or to stretch, all the way to
a lifestyle change or an emotional need. Just wait to see what your body
and emotions reveal to you in stillness.

Do what your body asks you to do. It's that simple.

SHAKE IT

In his book *Why Zebras Don't Get Ulcers*, Robert Sapolsky jokingly alludes
that the reason zebras don't get stomach ulcers is because when their stress
response goes on, they use up their stress hormones as they are meant to.
They run from the lion, and if they manage to get away, they do a massive
shake of their whole bodies afterward to tell their systems that they are
now safe. They then go back to relaxing and munching blissfully on the
grass around them.

Wouldn't it be awesome to agree to a signal that lets your body become
aware that it needs a release, that all is okay because the "threat" that
stressed it is finally over?

A great way of doing this quickly is by following the lead of
nature and shaking your stress out, just like a zebra. By taking
a couple of minutes to shake our bodies properly, we can release the stress in our systems, massively decreasing any anxiety
we may be feeling and helping to put our systems back into a
relaxed parasympathetic state.

Stress Hack

- Standing with your legs shoulder width apart, raise your arms above your head (also shoulder width apart) and start to work your way from your hands all the way down through your body.
- Shake your hands and wrists.
- Shake your arms and shoulders.
- Shake your head and chest.
- Bounce up and down at your knees, and shake your whole upper body together with your hips.
- Then continue as you individually shake each leg and foot.
- Then make your way back up again.
- Shake your body out for a couple of minutes.

Shake it out vigorously, don't be shy. Really let loose for a couple of minutes.

 Act like a zebra. Shake it out.

LET IT OUT

Remember Taylor Swift's hit song "Shake It Off"? She was spot-on. You should let out and shake off the things you can do without. This can release stored stress actively from our bodies in the form of a strong emotional release.

Take crying, for example. Professor Stephen Sideroff, a clinical psychologist at UCLA, explains that stress "tightens muscles and heightens tension, so when you cry you release some of that tension. [Crying] activates the parasympathetic nervous system and restores the body to a state of balance."[12]

Studies of the various kinds of tears have found that emotional tears contain higher levels of stress hormones than basal (a.k.a. lubricating) tears or reflex tears (when you get something in your eye). The hormones are flushed out from the body and into the tears, leaving you feeling less stressed.

Crying, therefore, is now known to be a great way to release stress, especially in Japan. The Japanese are such great believers in the health benefits of crying that some cities in Japan now have crying clubs called *rui-katsu* (meaning "tear-seeking"), where people come together to cry.

Crying, laughing, or screaming are some of our natural human responses when exposed to threats of stress. By simulating those responses, our bodies regulate to the state they normally induce. Yes! Just let it all out.

Forget the social conditioning that convinced you that those are emotions of vulnerability that should be kept to yourself. Those release valves are there for a reason; they were a planned part of your design. There to regulate your state of stress. Use them as intended.

Warning: To ensure you don't cause even more stress, make sure your screams are consciously directed at a pillow or in a secluded garden, not at your poor, unsuspecting partner.

Oh, and one more thing. Turn that frown upside down. Don't forget to smile.

TRICK IT

Close your eyes and force a smile on your face for two whole minutes.

Stress Hack

The physiology of a smile tricks your brain into releasing the same feel-good hormones it would if you were actually smiling. Don't believe me? Stop now. Close your eyes and smile.

Then see how long it takes for you to feel instantly happier or, if you're like me, to end up laughing from your dopamine hit.

Another quick trick to get yourself to calm down when you are feeling really anxious is to bring yourself quickly back into the presence of your own body.

When we feel extremely anxious, our energy is all over the place, and we don't feel grounded and steady in our bodies, or even like being in our bodies, as our anxiety makes our hearts pound and breaths shallow.

But bringing yourself back to your body is one of the best things you can do in that heightened state. So just like shaking it out, you can bring your anxious mind back into your body by freezing it out too.

 Stress Hack The next time you feel overwhelmed physically by your anxiety, get a bowl of water and ice and plunge your hands or face into it, keeping there for a few moments before it becomes too uncomfortable.

This shock of cold immediately stimulates your senses and brings your awareness back into your physical self, away from the difficult sensations of anxiety. You trick your mind to come quickly back to your body by giving it an overriding sensation.

 Remember! When you are anxious, you feel uncomfortable in your body, but you need to do what's counterintuitive and ground back into your body.

Full cold-water therapy (full-body cold plunges, cold showers, or cold swims) is known to help boost immunity, decrease pain, and increase focus. It stimulates the body's adaptive stress response, which can improve its ability to handle stress in the long run.

Research also shows that cold water therapy can not only make you extra awake, it can also help boost your mood as the cold receptors in the skin send electrical impulses to the brain, which increases norepinephrine, which thus increases brain focus and the release of endorphins, which makes you happy.[13]

DON'T WAIT TO BREAK

Even better than saving your body when it is stressed are the habits that ensure things don't get out of control in the first place.

We've all heard the age-old expression "Your body is a temple." It's nice to think of your body as sacred, but I prefer to change the narrative from a temple where we worship, to a home where we get one chance to live. When we don't clean our home, over time, it gets dirty. When we don't maintain it and look after it, the paint cracks, the roof leaks, and the plumbing backs up.

Don't let your body suffer the same. Listen to it, don't neglect it, don't wear it down. Unlike brick and mortar, you will never be given another home if the body you are in breaks down. So don't wait till your body breaks.

EIGHT BODILY PLEAS

Move, restore, stretch, relax, breathe, fuel, digest, and snooze. Those are the things your body needs to stay healthy and unstressed. It's not that complicated, it's nothing new, but we seem to go about our days like we have never heard of these requests before. So let's dig into why they even truly matter to ease your stress.

Move

Exercise has a profound and positive effect on our stress levels and in turn our mental and physical states. Stress hormones, primarily, are signals that trigger our bodies' fight-or-flight response. In their very design, they are there to trigger our bodies to move. As we move, the hormones are consumed, leaving us ready to get into our relaxed state once again. But stress in the modern world does not always lead to movement, because the stresses we deal with, most of the time, are not even physical in nature. Movement, therefore, is something we need to introduce into our lives, not to run away from threats but to restore our state of balance.

Leading functional medicine doctor and author Dr. Mark Hyman advises thirty minutes of exercise a day as a powerful and well-studied way to burn off stress chemicals and heal the mind. He states that exercise is more effective than the drug Prozac for treating depression.

The next time you feel particularly anxious or overwhelmed, do a quick hit of exercise like a power walk up and down the street or two minutes of jumping jacks. You'll be amazed how you will feel afterward.

A good exercise also instructs our bodies to release endorphins, which give us that natural feeling of being high. Add to that a tiny jolt of dopamine, the reward hormone, when we notice our physical image improve and get that magical comment when someone asks, "Have you been exercising?" "Oooooh, yes, I have. Why, thank you, you observant, wonderful friend."

As we get in better shape, our self-image improves, and we increase our self-esteem and confidence.[14] This encourages us to improve other areas of our lives, as people with more self-confidence are shown to perform better at work and more easily achieve their lifestyle goals.[15]

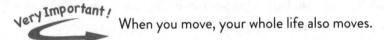 *Very Important!* When you move, your whole life also moves.

Then there is the impact exercise has on physical health and how it helps support our bodies in preventing illness.

A study published by the Harvard Medical School, among various others, showed that regular physical activity helps lower blood pressure (which is known to increase from ongoing stress), improve cholesterol levels, and reduce blood sugar levels. Exercise also cuts down the risk of heart attack, diabetes, colon and breast cancers, obesity, osteoporosis and fractures, depression, and even dementia. Joyfully, it also helps in slowing the aging process, which the majority of us in the Western world are hell-bent on defying.[16] But I guess you didn't really need research to prove any of that. That active friend of yours seems to be all the proof that you need.

What are you doing still holding this book?

 *Remember!* Get up and move.

Restore

Exercise, generally, is a great way to release our stress by burning the excess hormones. When your body is in extreme states of stress and fatigue, however, high-intensity exercise becomes the opposite of what it needs.

When the body is in a state of extreme stress, one of the worst things we can do is to pump it with more adrenaline and cortisol from cardio exercise, as it is already brimming with it as our adrenals are in overdrive. When we are in this state, what you need is to allow your body to replenish itself through low-impact, anti-inflammatory exercise. The best way to do that? A leisurely walk.

Walking is proven to reduce inflammation, reduce stress and anxiety, and help clear your mind, while also promoting weight loss. It is gentle enough for your body not to tip it over the edge with more hormones.

Better still, the long-term benefits of walking include improving cardiovascular fitness, strengthening your immune system, improving your balance and coordination, improving muscle endurance, strengthening your bones, increasing your energy levels, and reducing your risk of stroke, diabetes, heart disease, high blood pressure, and even cancer.[17]

And it's free. Sounds pretty good to me!

Another form of gentle exercise that I would urge you to practice in a state of extreme or hypervigilant stress is restorative yoga. A few poses to hold before bedtime will really help you relax and wind down with minimal effort.

Restorative yoga is generally made up of five to six relaxing poses that you can choose a couple from to try and then hold each for six to ten minutes while you breathe deeply and relax. One quick search online will show you how each of the poses looks. My personal favorites are balasana and legs up the wall. Try them out and see which relaxes you the most.

 Remember ! Allow your body to unwind.

Add some relaxing music for your mind to unwind to. Then just . . . let go.

Stretch

Stretching is a powerful and often underrated way for relieving tension within our bodies and our minds. Stretching reduces our stress levels by stimulating receptors in our nervous system that help slow the production of stress hormones, while also increasing our blood flow and circulation, which in turn helps create a clearer state of mind and a better mood.

You can stretch anywhere, anytime, and for free. It's quick and easy. All it takes is for you to decide to do it.

Explore some different types of stretches and see what you enjoy most. Hip stretches, for example, are a great way to release anger. This is why occasionally, in a yoga class when doing some deep hip stretches, participants can find themselves having an emotional release of either laughter or tears. Your neck and shoulders hold tension. Some believe that your pain in your left shoulder indicates low self-esteem or lack of self-love while pain in the right indicates that you are carrying too much workload and need assertiveness and to learn to say no. Stretch each of those and release those negative feelings. Stretch your lower back and open your chest to release anxiety.[18]

Whichever it is, if there is a pain or a tension in your muscles and bones, there is a negative emotion to release. It takes just a few minutes to find comfort.

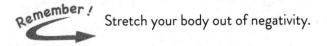 Stretch your body out of negativity.

Relax

Finding two minutes to relax sometimes seems like a task itself when we are swirling around in our stressed minds, just trying to get more done. But, get real, you're not really that busy. We all have a few minutes to relax.

Remember the parasympathetic nervous system? Yes. You need to relax to stay alive. It is as important for your survival in the long term as running away from the tiger is in the short term. When we make it a priority, our relaxation, when we truly relax, is paramount to relieving stress from our bodies.

How do you truly relax? Let me give you a hint.

Lying on the sofa to watch your favorite TV series with a glass of wine in your hand may be enjoyable, but it doesn't count as truly relaxing. It plugs your stream of thought into the emotional drama of what you're watching and keeps you on alert. What you need is active relaxation.

This involves doing an activity that instills relaxation. Walking, gardening, yoga, journaling, meditating, and coloring are but a few examples. I, Mo here, unhealthy as it is, sometimes light a cigar. I'm not really a smoker, but a cigar will force you to spend an hour of your time outdoors as you puff it, slowly, so you don't choke yourself. That hour is an hour that you spend relaxing if you manage to slow down the rush of your inner thoughts. For you, let me suggest a cup of herbal tea instead. It's healthier for you. Put your phone down and remove all distractions. Or if you have access to the ultimate relaxation tool known to humanity, immerse yourself in it. It is known as the . . . hug.

One hug of about twenty seconds signals to your system that everything is okay and tells your system to release the hormone oxytocin (aka the cuddle hormone). Which research shows can induce anti-stress like effects such as reducing cortisol and blood pressure levels.[19]

Think of stress as contraction and relaxation as expansion, Alice again: it gives you the space you need to be in peace. When stressed, we go on high alert and feel ourselves contract, tensing our muscles to protect ourselves and preempt the threats. When we engage in methods of active relaxation, we allow our bodies and minds to go into a much deeper state of relaxation.

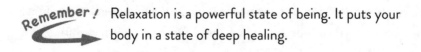 Remember ! Relaxation is a powerful state of being. It puts your body in a state of deep healing.

No hugs around? Here's the simplest thing we can all do to relax even when alone.

Breathe

We have the power to shift into a relaxed state just by using our own breath. This resource is always there and ready for us to direct it, but so often we ignore the impact of it.

When we breathe in, our heart rates speed up a little, but the opposite is also true. When we breathe out, our heart rates slow.

This is why if there is one thing to remember about how to use your breath to calm yourself down, it's to *lengthen your breath on the exhale.*

A fast heart rate is a signal for your body that something needs its effort, perhaps a possible threat, and a slow heart rate is a signal that all is okay and you can chill and put your body back into a parasympathetic state.

Stress Hack

My favorite breathing technique is the **four-four-eight** breath, as it's quick and easy to remember.

- Breathe in through your nose for a count of **four**.
- Hold your breath for a count of **four**.
- Breathe out of your mouth for a count of **eight**.

Repeat this sequence for two to five minutes or until you feel totally calm again.

Our breathing tricks our bodies out of fight or flight. When we slow our breathing and consciously choose to breathe deeply into our diaphragms, instead of shallowly from our chests, we switch our nervous systems into rest and digest while calming our minds, concentrating on the rhythm of our breath rather than the worries in our heads.

Sadly, though, the way that we breathe today has become very different from the way that we were born to breathe naturally. When you watch a baby sleep, you will notice that they are breathing from their diaphragm, not their chest. You watch them effortlessly raise their stomach up with air and drop it back down uncontrolled.

In today's world, however, the majority of us breathe very shallowly from our chests, rarely taking a full deep breath in. This shallow breathing signals to our bodies that we are under stress. This is natural because when we are stressed, our breathing quickens and becomes shallower.

Your body knows that shallow, upper-chest breathing is part of the typical stress response.[20]

There has even been a concept coined called *email apnea*, which is what James Nestor describes in his book *Breath: The New Science of a Lost Art*, as when office workers who are trying to get as much done as possible breathe irregularly and very shallowly from their chests, often holding their breaths as they are typing, for thirty seconds or more.[21]

Try to notice yourself unconsciously holding your breath when you answer the next email. I bet (like me, while writing this last paragraph), you do too.

I ask all my clients to put labeled alarms into their phones to go off silently every few hours to remind them to pause and consciously take a few deep breaths so they release some of the micro stress from their system. I encourage you to do that too. A reminder to just breathe deeply.

Stress Hack

Let's do it now. It is more important than reading further.

- Lie down somewhere comfortable with your knees bent and your head supported. If you are not in a place where you can lie down, sit comfortably.
- Place one hand on your upper chest and one hand on your diaphragm (just below your rib cage).
- Close your eyes.
- Bring your awareness to your breath.
- Take a deep breath in through your nose and concentrate on breathing into your diaphragm, so your lower hand that is on this area rises and the hand on your chest stays as still as possible.
- Breathe out through your mouth. Your hand on your diaphragm should then lower and your hand on your chest will then rise a little.
- Repeat this breath cycle till you feel deeply relaxed, or for three to five minutes.

How do you feel now? Isn't it amazing just how different a few deep breaths can make you feel?

Those few breaths come with a bonus. They oxygenate your blood and give you energy, so you feel more alert if you do this during the day. And if you do it in bed before you sleep, the engagement of your parasympathetic system will help you get a better night's sleep. This whole breathing thing, honestly, feels like a cheat. It's so good that you sometimes feel there must be a catch, but there's not.

 *Very Important!*   Just breathe.

Breathe it out and release some of that tension you're holding on to when you need to. We're all guilty of getting a little bit tense.

Fuel

We all know we need to eat food and drink water to simply survive, but when it comes to preventing excess stress in the body, we need to become choosy and stop putting the wrong fuel in the tank for our bodies to run on.

It is no longer a secret, despite the industry lobbies attempting to show otherwise, that refined sugar and excess alcohol, for example, are considered poisons that cause stress to an already strained system. Food that is not a good balanced, healthy diet just gives you calories to burn or store as fats. It doesn't energize you. Instead, it drains you and stresses your body.

 *Remember!*   Not all food is equal.

If we eat a doughnut with coffee for breakfast, the refined sugar is absorbed quickly into the bloodstream. This spikes our blood sugar rapidly, signaling the body to produce an influx of insulin to help lower the blood sugar level so we don't become diabetic.

Blood sugar dropping quickly tells the body to go into survival mode, as it signals famine. Do this frequently, and the ups and downs of blood sugar triggered by processed and sugary foods are very stressful for the body. Every time you consume foods like sugary drinks, refined white carbs, fast food, or even starchy vegetables, you are injecting an additional dose of stress into your body.

Another side effect of those foods is that the cortisol, associated with our bodies' stress response, is in itself very inflammatory when continually pumped around our system. Inflammation is a breeding ground for illness and disease, making our bodies vulnerable for illness-led stress.

I experienced inflammation from the stress of my grief, and it caused me to put on weight for the first time in my life. I felt tired all the time. I gained an extra twenty-five pounds, which, for someone who has always been naturally small, was excessive, and it put me in an even lower mood.

I tried lots of different diets, but my body was holding on to the weight because it was inflamed and stressed.

Then, when I hosted Yalda Alaoui on my podcast *Unstressable*, she spoke about her anti-inflammatory lifestyle, Eat Burn Sleep, and so I tried it. The weight just fell off me and reset my metabolism back to what it had always been. Alaoui's research confirms what I just shared: refined carbohydrates and grains are working against you, and working on a six-week reset for the gut can decrease inflammation and bring your body back to balance.

MD and nutritionist Elizabeth Boham recommends that our diet include a good source of protein, healthy fat, and fiber at every meal to limit the carbs percentage of our food to a reasonable level and to help us to both nourish the body and keep the blood sugar balanced.

She also talks about limiting caffeine when we are anxious and eliminating it when we are burned out. We think we need the caffeine to function, but we are actually just putting even more excess stress on our adrenal glands as a result while the caffeine fights the body's plea for rest and gives us additional, though unnatural, alertness to keep doing things that stress us.

We've all had those moments of anxiety where our coffee on top has sent our already pounding chest over the edge. Don't add to it. Cut the caffeine when you are anxious.

And then there is hydration.

Our ancestors would have been shocked if they witnessed how we have access to the privilege of clean water and yet still cause our bodies unnecessary strain by being dehydrated. As I write this to you, I just noticed how thirsty I am because I've been sitting at my desk writing for a while. Are you?

So often when we are busy and concentrating on all our mounting responsibilities, we can forget to drink enough water. Many times, when we consume coffee or other caffeinated drinks, which act as diuretics, we don't notice the imbalance as more liquids exit our bodies in the form of urine.

Feeling thirsty causes our system significant stress without us realizing.

The human body is approximately 60 percent water. Without replenishing that base regularly, we feel tired and our energy levels decrease. When tired, we are more prone to stress, and when we are even mildly dehydrated, our stress response goes off and floods our bodies with cortisol once more.

 Stress Hack The National Academies of Science, Engineering, and Medicine recommend that women drink three quarts of water a day and men drink four quarts (one gallon) per day, including the water in your food.

To make sure you stay adequately hydrated, renowned functional medicine doctor and author Dr. Mark Hyman suggests squeezing the juice of half a lemon or lime into your water with a pinch of sea salt. This ensures that water is being absorbed and is properly hydrating your cells.

He also emphasizes the importance of getting enough electrolytes in our diet to ensure we stay hydrated, which can be found in fruits and vegetables—bananas, avocados, and sweet potatoes are rich in potassium; vegetables like spinach and kale have both calcium and magnesium. All are useful for our hydration.

Another habit to observe is alcohol, which, when the body is stressed, becomes counterproductive to our needs. I enjoy a cold glass of wine as much as the next person, but I know when I am under stress, although a drink may be the first thing I feel like having in the evening, it is actually the one thing that I should try to hold off on until my system is relaxed again.

The feeling of relaxation alcohol initially brings is very temporary, as the presence of alcohol puts more stress on our systems. It also, while believed to help us fall asleep, actually results in poorer sleep quality and, once again, higher inflammation in the body. Too much alcohol also wears down our B vitamins, which are critical for the functioning of our adrenal glands. All of this adds more stress to our poor bodies.

Moderation is key. The next time you feel like pouring yourself a glass of something to relieve your stress, ask yourself what active relaxation (things like . . . walking, meditating, journaling, stretching, breathing, coloring) you could try out first.

Become aware of what you are putting into your body. Choose what nourishes, hydrates, and fuels it, and avoid what stresses it. More water, less caffeine; a balance of protein, fats, fiber, and carbs with less refined carbs; and finally, limit alcohol, especially when you are stressed. Your body is not a garbage can. Healthy foods don't have to be expensive, and filtered water is virtually free.

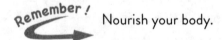 Nourish your body.

And then help it to . . .

Digest

When stressed, our digestion is told to stop so that its resources are dedicated to fight or flight. This is why, when stressed, our digestive systems can suffer.

As a result, anger, fear, sadness, anxiety, and other negative feelings trigger symptoms in the gut.

The brain and gut have a direct connection to each other, a connection that goes both ways.

Just as the thought of a delicious meal alone can send a signal to release stomach juices before food has even gotten there, a troubled digestive system can also send signals to the brain. Our gut distress can be both the cause or the product of anxiety, stress, and even depression.[22]

The gut-brain axis is made up of several highways of communication.

Some information comes from the lymphatic system, some via messenger cells called *cytokines*, which travel through the blood, while some are sent via the vagus nerve.

A lot of information travels in a way that we had very little understanding around until recently—the bugs, bacteria, and viruses that live in our stomachs and make up what is known as our *microbiome*.

Dr. Tara Swart Bieber, neuroscientist and author of *The Source*, explains that when we suffer stress, anxiety, depression, or insomnia, the negative impact affects the balance of the gut flora. The microbiome in our gut, which is needed for our digestion, immune function, and even mood, can become unbalanced, causing fatigue, sluggishness, unexplained anxiety, low mood, digestive issues, weight issues, and even sleep issues.

 Even the microbes in our gut are influenced by our stress.

Dr. Swart Bieber suggests that probiotic foods, such as kefir, kombucha, kimchi, and sauerkraut, and prebiotic foods, such as onion, garlic, artichoke, and asparagus, help our gut microbiomes thrive. And then all our healthy habits take that further—hydration, exercise, sleep, and mindfulness all actually change the quality and diversity of our gut microbiomes.

Don't think of those as foods for you but foods for your digestive system to help you digest your food.

 Take a good probiotic supplement to support your gut and make it more resilient against stress. Ask your healthcare provider for advice beforehand.

Which leaves us with one final plea that our bodies are constantly begging for and one of my favorite things to do.

Snooze

Don't believe the slogan. The truth is actually the opposite.

Remember! When you don't snooze, you lose.

Like with all else, we don't appreciate the value of our sleep until we lose it.

Professor Matthew Walker, sleep scientist and author of *Why We Sleep*, explains that sleep loss in the brain has a similar signature to stress. So sleep deprivation in itself is a stressor. This is why it is a well-known, effective form of torture. Keep someone awake long enough and they will break. Have you been your own torturer recently?

Lack of sleep increases the activity of the amygdala, which, as we explained earlier, is your early-detection system for threats. An active amygdala concentrates more on the negative, and everything seems tougher as a result.

Walker explains that the brain, after little sleep, suffers a collapse in memory, attention, cognitive function, decision-making capacity, and the ability to learn new things. This is also associated with an increase in the levels of adrenaline, cortisol, and noradrenaline. Inflammatory markers go up, and we become resistant to insulin. This makes it more likely to develop type 2 diabetes while it causes our appetites to grow, throwing our diets off-balance as a result. Talk about stress attacking our bodies from all sides.

Furthermore, lack of sleep is felt in every cell of your body, quite literally.

The Surrey Sleep Research Centre conducted a study where the sleep for one group of participants was restricted to six hours a day, while another group slept eight and a half hours a day. Only one week into the study, those who slept six hours developed distortions in 711 genes.

About half of these genes—among them the genes associated with stress, cancer, chronic inflammation, and cardiovascular disease—went up in activity. The other half, which were associated with a balanced immune system and a stable metabolism, went down in activity.[23]

Wowzer. Sleep two fewer hours for a week and your own machine turns around almost as if to kill you.

Remember! Good sleep heals your stress.

Studies show that trauma victims are more likely to develop PTSD and depression if the trauma affects the quality of their sleep than when their sleep is unaffected.

So here's the bottom line: when you feel stressed, one of the most important things you can do is to prioritize your eight and a half hours of sleep.

Which, obviously, can turn into a frustrating catch-22, because we typically struggle to sleep when we suffer mental or emotional stress. Which is why we need to bring to your attention a few healthy sleep habits.

The hormone melatonin is released by the pineal gland to help us fall asleep. Melatonin is sometimes known as the *dark hormone* because it is secreted when we sense darkness, as a signal that it is time to sleep. But what do we normally do as modern humans when it gets dark? We swipe and type and like on little illuminated screens giving off blue light, which is proven to reduce your melatonin secretion by up to 50 percent.[24]

Dr. Rangan Chatterjee, author of *The Stress Solution*, says that even if you are someone who can still fall asleep easily after using devices, the actual quality of your sleep is damaged as you lose critical hours of REM sleep—the state of our sleep where our brains process new learnings from the day and turn them into memory.

Leave your phone outside of your bedroom.

Stress Hack Stop using digital devices at least an hour before you sleep.

What else can you do? Let us walk you through a quick list of healthy sleep habits so you can also put this book down quicker and get a nap or a good night's sleep.

If you have an active mind and find it hard to switch off before bed, I would strongly advise a "mind dump" in the form of a journaling session to get all your thoughts and reflections from the day out of your head and onto paper. This allows you to more easily process your worries and concerns, making them less likely to be swirling around in your mind, keeping you awake.

But your sleep routine starts way before it is bedtime.

For example, exposing yourself to natural light first thing in the morning, making sure your eyes get the light (so no hiding behind sunglasses), gets your circadian rhythm (your body clock) moving to the right beat, marking morning as morning and night as night, which helps regulate your sleep.

Eating your evening meal earlier, say, three hours before you go to sleep, allows your digestive system time to shut down and tell your body it's time for bed.

Stop consuming caffeine after 10:00 A.M. Can you believe it? Yes, you need to prepare for your sleep starting this early in the morning. Needless to say, keep your caffeine consumption to less than two cups of caffeinated drinks a day.

Make your room cooler. A lower body temperature helps aid sleep, as your core body temperature naturally lowers at night when you sleep.

A hot bath or shower one or two hours before bed helps to lower your core body temperature by bringing blood to the surface and allowing you to emit heat through the outer perimeter surfaces of the body.[25]

Dim the lights or light candles one to two hours leading up to your bedtime. This helps your body to secrete melatonin to help aid your sleep.

 Try this sleep tea recipe one hour before bed:

Stress Hack

- Herbal non-caffeinated tea
- 2 tablespoons apple cider vinegar
- 1 tablespoon of unfiltered honey[26]

(This is Tim Ferriss's recipe, which he got from psychologist Seth Roberts.) It is a game changer, and I swear by it to help you drift off.

Cut out alcohol if you are struggling with your sleep, or don't drink in the evening. Alcohol has sedentary properties that may help you fall asleep, but it will often disrupt your sleep cycle as the liver enzymes metabolize alcohol.[27]

Restorative yoga, remember? Just before bed, do a few poses to help relax your nervous system.

Read a calming novel (paper version, not on a device). Needless to say, avoid any action thrillers or horror stories, because those seem to go with you and continue in your dreams.

Do a bedtime meditation or a bedtime breathing exercise.

And finally, try to eliminate the reasons that get you up at night. Try to silence the noise, or use earplugs. Try to block the light, or use an eye mask. Avoid going to bed too hungry or too full. Control the room temperature so it's not too hot or too cold. Hydrate all day so you are not woken up by thirst, but perhaps stop drinking an hour before bed to avoid getting up for the bathroom in the middle of the night.

These little sleep hacks work better together. Include them all in your life. Any one left out may wake you up at night. We don't care which. Once you're awake, you're awake.

If you continue to struggle with your sleep, start to address the stress in your life with the methods we have gone through so far in this book, then don't hesitate to seek professional help to support you in getting your sleep on track.

Don't let your lack of sleep become its own nightmare. Don't let another sleep issue linger or another night pass leaving you tired and stressed. Wake up. Be aware of what you need. It's one of the things you need most to de-stress your body from whatever is causing it stress.

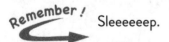 Sleeeeeep.

We have now walked you through the physical side to your stress and how to begin tackling it. But what about the nonphysical, the part of us that sits quietly within our physical selves? That is the truest part of who we are, so what about the stress we cause our souls?

7

Soul-Renity

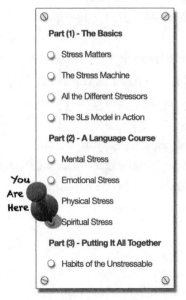

You Are Here

Define: Spirit
The nonphysical part of a person which is the seat of emotions and character; the soul.

This is the result you get when you ask Google what *spirit* is. This definition, however, is deeply contested because, for an ever-rising number of individuals in the modern world, there is no such thing. Those who associate only with the physical or follow the modern religion known as the scientific method believe in its teachings—if something can't be observed and measured by our physical instruments, it doesn't exist. For them, that spirit thing is nothing more than fiction.

Now, I, Mo, am a huge fan of the scientific method. It's what gave us civilization with all its marvels from iPhones to cookies, but I think that this basic teaching is flawed. The accurate way to teach the doctrine intended to focus on what's measurable should be reinstated as follows:

If something can't be observed and measured by our physical senses, then it still may exist, though it would not be part of the domain of science.

I knew that in my heart as I kissed the forehead of Ali—well, his physical form—after the hospital disconnected him from the life support systems. It was still the handsome look we knew when he was alive, but it surely was not my son. That body was no longer Ali. Something left. The thing that made him Ali.

It felt to the heart of a loving father who desperately wanted to hold on to whatever was left of my departing son as if what was left was never Ali. It was the shell he used to navigate our world. Like the avatar that represented him in this video game called life. His body there on the intensive care table behaved as if the player had put the controller down, abandoning the game and leaving the avatar idle to be attacked by the elements of the game. Which of course is what happens to us all just as it did to my beloved son's physical form as it disappeared in the dust in the following days and weeks.

Call that player holding the controller a spirit, if you will, or call it toast. I don't care what you call it, but it exists despite the fact that we can't measure it.

That soul exists as much as love exists. We know that because we've all, including many scientists, felt love, and yet we could never measure it or have others observe it. Germs exist, they make us sick, though for the longest time, science could not observe them. Dark matter and dark energy exist; as a matter of fact, they occupy 97 percent of the known universe, though our grandparents believed that the majority of the universe was just vacuum . . . and yes, the soul too exists.

As we ignore that soul throughout our lifetimes, it keeps holding the controller, sending us signals to guide us through the game. It communicates to us, not just leads us. It feels stressed when we don't listen, just like serious video gamers get frustrated when there is a lag between their blazing-fast movements on the controller and the movement of the avatar on the screen.

Interestingly, though, just as the real player—your soul—firmly keeps the avatar within its gaze throughout the game, the avatar too—your physical form—can choose to listen to what the soul will say. This eases the stress of the soul and allows the avatar to lead a better game. We call those who manage to establish that reverse link and connect to their spirits *spiritual.*

Define: Spiritual
Relating to or affecting the human spirit or soul as opposed to material or physical things.

It's not some kind of voodoo to be spiritual in the real world. It is the only way to deal with life, both its physical and metaphysical sides, as one complete whole.

 If science is the discipline humans use to study all that is physical, spirituality is the philosophy we need to comprehend what lies beyond what we can see.

So let's look to philosophy and wisdom now with an open mind. The spiritual part to us has often been overlooked when tackling stress. Alice here. Naturally, we have looked at what appears to be the obvious sides: the physical, mental, and even emotional; the scientific and the logical. But we only are ever complete when we look at what makes us whole. Real but not seen. So much of what we interact with every day and acknowledge is not strictly visible. So much of what we believe in is not truly proven by science. Yet we include it in our decision-making and behavior every day.

To achieve the true health and happiness we all search for, we can't simply rely on only what we can "see" in front of us but also what affects us mysteriously within and around us. I know this to be the key to really uncovering our deepest sense of calm. It has been the key not just for my clients but for myself. Which is why the spiritual side to stress is the part that can't be skipped.

Once we notice the missing piece to our internal harmony, we have the life-altering realization that we are far more than just our bodies, that this other part of us that sits within us, as us, has a profound impact on both the experience and quality of our lives.

We don't ignore the fact that certain things exist just because we can't see them. You don't doubt the air that goes into your lungs or the transcendent feeling of love you have when you look at your child or partner. You don't doubt the force of gravity to hold you down and not let you fall upside down off the earth screaming. There's no need to doubt it. Why would you? Because although you can't see it, you *know* it's there.

Yet there is a large part of us, really the truest part to us, that we often neglect or overlook as "unimportant" when it comes to our health. The world's programming of the past century has been to praise the logic of the world and to always look at the analytical, away from the sensory side of ourselves. In reality, the sensory is the missing key, as the sensory is the connective part of you. What connects you to your body, mind, and soul. What connects you to yourself.

We only need to remind ourselves that what we've forgotten is there. As Albert Einstein said, "Everyone who is seriously involved in the pursuit of science becomes convinced that a spirit is manifest in the laws of the Universe—a spirit vastly superior to that of man and one in the face of which we with our modest powers must feel humble."[1]

As one of the smartest people to walk this planet did, maybe you too can open up your mind to the idea that we are not just our bodies. That we are also spiritual beings having a human experience. When we can look at this side and realize that it is the missing piece of the puzzle to connect us to our natural calmness, we suddenly realize, *My god, is it any wonder the world is so stressed, when we are all so disconnected from the essence of who we really are?*

So, have an open mind, open yourself up to the possibility that you are not just your body. Open your heart and know that, no matter how smart we may be there is something even more important to remind ourselves.

 We can never know everything.

So how do we make decisions when some things are unproven or unknown? We resort to wisdom or to the wisdom of others. Remind yourself that the smartest and the wisest of us are the ones who humbly accept that they don't know everything and who have a hungry curiosity to explore the things they don't yet understand.

Wisdom, remember, is different from knowledge. Wisdom is more about exercising good judgment, even in the absence of complete knowledge. It recognizes that we do not know what it is that we don't know. Perhaps it is this deeper intuitive wisdom that our modern world is missing most.

THE MODERN CRISIS OF SPIRITUALITY

Spirituality can get a muddled and often bad reputation from a large part of the population today, having watched on the world stage for hundreds of years the disputes, even wars, that are carried out in the name of religion; having seen the arguments created by our unhealed human egos, telling people exactly how they "should" worship and pray.

Spirituality has been transformed by humans into something that is essentially becoming more and more un-spiritual: a controlled set of ideals that we must adhere to by a person of authority, or else we cannot possibly have any connection with the divine; an argued dispute over whose religion is "better" or "right." But does "I'm right, you're wrong" really seem that spiritual to you?

Through our human need to control, we have lost the very essence of what spirituality truly means, and in doing so, we have lost the freedom, peace, and liberation that comes with it while turning a great deal of people away from their own spiritual connection altogether.

There can be a lot of confusion for people around the many religions, beliefs, and spiritual teachings on offer today, all the many different human concepts of religion, spirituality, or even who and what we should believe.

His Holiness the Dalai Lama said he believes deeply that "we must all of us together, find a new spirituality. This new concept ought to be elaborated alongside the religions in such a way that all people of goodwill could adhere to it."[2]

This spiritual connection that we must find within us should have nothing to do with what is deemed right or wrong based on one religion's view, a certain spiritual teaching, or the polarized opinions of humanity today, if it is to truly change things for us by changing things within us.

Spirituality then must not divide us through differences of opinion.

Remember ! Spirituality should be what connects us through common ground.

Know that we are all the same; we are all here souls living as humans, no matter what we do or don't believe.

His Holiness the Dalai Lama says the concept of spirituality should be elaborated alongside the religions so that good people find solace and common ground in it, no matter what their own religious or personal viewpoints may be.

I love this, as there are many wonderful varied religions and spiritual teachings, both the old and the new. Does it mean that one is better than the other just because our beliefs created from our own experiences have decided it is so? Surely the true divinity that lives within us sees the acceptance of all and the power in the varied strengths of different beliefs and teachings, in both religion and in life.

It's hard to ignore that there are faults in the implementation of most religions and spiritual teachings, but instead of focusing on what's missing, wisdom would invite us to find the beauty in each.

Christianity teaches us to love our neighbor as thyself, love our enemy, and forgive those that have wronged us. Buddhists don't acknowledge a supreme God like other religions but instead focus on achieving enlightenment, a state of inner peace and wisdom. Hindus believe in wonderful concepts such as karma and reincarnation, meaning that our actions in this life affect not only what will come back to us now but what life we could later come back to in the next, making us more aware of our choices and their effects. Muslims have a set of principles to adhere to, such as prayer, fasting, and even pilgrimage. They also believe in finding peace through the surrender and flow of life seen as the will of God. How beautiful. Sikhism bases its three tenets on an honest living and an honest day's work, sharing with others what life and God have given to you and living life fully with the awareness of the divinity within each of us. This is also similar to one of the teachings of Judaism, that all humans are linked to God through the divine spark that's within all of us, and we must nurture this god spark and search deeply for truth.

All of these points are beautiful. All of them have a role to play in our own spirituality and in strengthening our lives.

Remember !   Find that which sits true to your own sense of
spirituality.

Find that which makes you feel most connected to yourself. Feel free to be you.

YOUR SPIRIT, YOUR SPIRITUALITY

The true beauty of spirituality is that it is defined by *your* own unique connection to the divine and does not need to adhere to any man-made ideologies. I have my own personal definition as well . . .

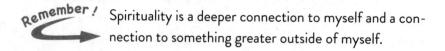

Remember !   Spirituality is a deeper connection to myself and a connection to something greater outside of myself.

For me that something greater is God, a divine power. But I'm not here to tell you what yours is or "should" be. That something greater can be in whatever form that comes for you.

Perhaps you are someone who doesn't believe in a God, a higher power, a universal creative intelligence at work, but you feel a deep connection with nature or doing something for others in need. That is your sense of a deeper connection to something outside of yourself that also helps you to nurture the deeper one within. That is your sense of spirituality.

Or you may be someone who has developed a deep connection to God, to a higher power, and that is something you have unwavering faith in, that a greater intelligence is at work—not as a being sitting in the sky but as a creative force far beyond the scope and logic of the human mind.

From this connection, you see divinity in nature, in the coincidences and synchronicities of the outside world, in the help and kindness of the people who show up *just* as you need them.

You even find the spark of divinity within yourself, the peaceful stillness hidden deep within the alcoves of your heart, feeling a deep sense of connection—within you and around you.

Or you may be someone who has always had a wonderfully strong sense of God through following a religion. So the structure of that religion, its particular beliefs and teachings and what it brings, is what you find most powerful, is what works for you, guides you, nurtures your spiritual connection, and keeps you on track and feeling connected to God. That's wonderful too. It's your choice of spirituality.

Whichever path you choose to navigate life as—an atheist, a person of faith, or simply someone who is curious about what lies beyond our physical form—it doesn't matter. As long as you are able to connect to something nonphysical within yourself and something outside of you.

Your spirituality is about finding the balance of what works for you so that you feel the calmest and most connected you can be.

Over are the days when we needed a shaman or priest to tell us how we should be. We alone get to decide how our own spirituality unfolds. We get to decide what that connection looks like.

 Remember! Spirituality is a personal journey.

. . . as much as it is a collective exploration.

So don't be afraid to go against the grain, and decide what your own spiritual journey is all about. Just don't give up on the truest part of yourself because others described it in a way that doesn't match your own. At the end of the day, we are spiritual beings, so learn to live like one.

Ask yourself now:

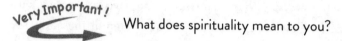 What does spirituality mean to you?

Put aside the concept of religion for a moment or whether or not you even believe in a God, and ask yourself what *spirituality* actually means to you.

What's your stance on the presence of something greater than yourself? How connected do you feel to the world around you? Do you take care of yourself beyond your physical form? Have you heard messages from that nonphysical self before? How did you respond?

I ask a lot of people I meet this question, because I truly believe that until we know our answer to this, we can't truly know ourselves.

When you can really answer that question, when you really know what it means to you, it's only then that you can start to nurture your connection to it.

THE SOUL IS CALM

The word *calm* gets thrown around a lot these days, used in wellness apps and famous commercialized slogans like "Keep calm and carry on." *Calm* has become the modern-day wellness buzzword, constantly being broadcast on social media and podcasts. It has become something we all strive to be, while also being something that the majority of us often feel very far away from. It has become like a holy grail of achievement within our well-being.

Of course, feeling calm is an important and necessary aim for all the many reasons we have talked you through. The idea of feeling calm is also something that we have spoken about in this book, but the problem lies not in our wanting it but in the way we go about searching for it. We spend the majority of our time looking for calm all around us in any way we can, when the natural cave of calmness that we seek sits silently within us in our hearts, in our centers, in our souls.

We can train the mind to be calm; we can soothe and calm our emotions and put our bodies into the calmest setting of "rest and digest." But the natural teacher of this sought-after feeling, the one that needs no training for this sense of serenity, lies within us. Not in our minds but in our centers, as the part that many of us are unfamiliar with—our souls.

Although, like anything that has been around for a while, the soul has its own wear and tear from the past, or what the ancient Vedas would describe as *samskara* (scars of the soul), the energetic imprints of unhealed trauma in mind and energy. Its truest nature always remains as peaceful.

The soul holds an understanding far greater than the limited perspective of the human mind. It knows a peace and a stillness that transcend human understanding. A stillness that is unaffected by the irrational worries of the mind, the roller coaster of our emotions, and the pains in our bodies. It waits quietly for us to stop frantically looking around for the answers and instead have the courage to sit and listen to what is being whispered to us from within. What it is trying to quietly guide us to amid the outer chaos of our lives.

Remember !   In the chaotic battle of life, your soul is your greatest ally.

There are many struggles in the world that we have to face as humans. Life's greatest challenges can be thrown unexpectedly at us at any time. We have to overcome them, and we all have the resilience within us to do so, but where we falter is relying solely on our human side, solely on ourselves. We have been given something to guide us through it all, an inner compass and a calm and powerful resource within us. Our souls not only know what we are here for, what our greatest strengths and gifts are, but how to overcome our greatest stresses and challenges.

But we disregard or miss their guidance, from our unwillingness to just be *still*. To look that little bit deeper. To go beyond the human side of us and to learn to connect to something far greater within us. Something that can be found when we step away from outward distractions.

When we connect to that calmer part of ourselves, everything changes. When we take the time to nurture this connection, then we start to see a calmness unfold from a much deeper place than just the mind and the body. We start to notice it from within our energy too. From within our hearts, from within our centers.

Above all, spirituality is about relieving suffering, whether that is out in the world or relieving the suffering deep within ourselves, the suffering that causes us to not show up in the world in the way we were destined to, in the way that matters. This suffering can only be relieved when we go that one level deeper to our souls and we finally develop our spiritual connection. When we finally remember who we are.

The art of life is to unlearn all the things that have caused us to forget our true nature. To unlearn everything that has held us captive in our fears and societal programming, everything that goes against the real essence of our true selves, our souls, our spirits.

Picture Superman in the chaos of a natural disaster caused by a supervillain, bullets flying all over the place, planes falling from the sky, and panicked people running everywhere, while Superman stands calmly assessing the situation and makes the best out of it, knowing that he has the superpower to always be okay. The super(wo)man part of you is your soul. Let it be in charge.

FEELING SPIRITUALLY STRESSED

I came to realize what it meant to be "spiritually stressed" at a defining time in my life. This experience made me realize that it was the missing piece—the last thing holding so many of us back from becoming unstressable.

To me, spirituality is a greater connection to myself and something greater outside of myself. That greater connection outside of myself is to a higher power, to a divine energy, to what I understand to be God. It is this connection that not only allowed me to have faith in my hardest times but to also have a deeper understanding of myself in my smoother ones. To be spiritually stressed, however, is when I believe we find ourselves disconnected.

It was a time in my life when everything around me felt like it was continually falling apart—my half sister had just passed away, and I was in total "control mode." My dad had just been told that they had found tumors in his body again, only weeks after her funeral, but he was refusing to do anything about it.

I was battling every day with the idea that I had to fix and control the situation. I needed to get him to see a specialist quicker and to get a plan for treatment. I had to get him to stop drinking and to see a bereavement counselor for his grief, and I had to get him to start talking and open up to us, his daughters and wife, who were still here and who loved him dearly.

I would call him every day asking the same questions . . . "Have you spoken to the specialist yet?" "When are you going for your next appointment?" "What are you going to do?" I was like a parrot on repeat.

This continually repeated conversation irritated him and upset me and was the cause of great stress for both of us. I felt heartbroken, panicked, and anxious. *How can he be so selfish?* I thought. *How can he not care about the rest of his family who are still here and really want and need him around?*

He, on the other hand, had already done the dance with cancer before. Now in his seventies, he wasn't about to spend potentially the last decade of his life in the hospital again.

He had surrendered. *He*, as we all do deep down, knew in his heart what was best for *him*.

He'd always said his cancer wouldn't grow quickly enough at his age to be a real issue. And you know what? He turned out to be right. As I mentioned, what took him wasn't the cancer but a giant burst stomach ulcer, accumulated from severe stress.

Through it all, while his body was stressed, what was stressed to the extreme on my side was my spirit. I was spending so much time looking at the world outside me, trying to control every outcome, obsessing on my need to fix what was beyond my ability to control.

When we are spiritually stressed, we feel out of control and like we will never regain control of our lives again. This illusion is what keeps us stuck in stress, because we all know that really, we were never in control to begin with. Something unforeseen can happen to any one of us at any moment. But we desperately try to control the uncontrollable or change the unchangeable.

We get stuck in resistance, and this resistance then is reflected in our own selves, in the way we feel internally, like we are fighting against something so desperately that we have no power over it.

We feel like nothing is right, everything is going wrong, that we have no solace and no calmness within ourselves, as what we are resisting is taking up every moment of our thoughts and emotions.

Whether it's grief, heartbreak, or redundancy—we all go through periods where we resist what will be. We hold on to what is gone, and we reject the inevitable. The stress we feel then is different from the pains in our bodies or the rushing thoughts when our stress is in our minds. It feels more overwhelming, prominent, and debilitating. Yet we keep going.

Are you experiencing any of this right now? It may be worth a few minutes of your time to put the book down and reflect. Take your time and ask yourself: *Am I currently resisting the inevitable?*

I found that moment of reflection after months of internal torment, months of trying to control the uncontrollable. Only then, I started to realize that what I was doing was not only causing me a lot of stress, it was also straining the relationship with my beloved dad while not making things any better.

So I chose to prioritize our relationship for the little time I knew I had left to spend with him. I stopped asking *him* about it, and I turned and asked my soul instead.

I sat in stillness. I turned inwardly and asked my intuition, and eventually, when I listened, I let go. I found peace in accepting the uncontrollable and took advice from my soul instead of my ego.

HOW TO STRESS A SOUL

Our spiritual stress is created when we are not even *trying* to listen to our souls. When we are not listening to what it is trying to show us through life unfolding in front of us. When we are resisting the events that are happening and we are looking outward to try to change the unchange-able.

We are stressed and suffering when life isn't going the way that we think it should be. But we are not seeing the way it is *trying* to be, as we are so caught up in our human need to control, rather than our spiritual nature to surrender. We miss what our souls are trying to tell us that will help us through this difficult time.

We try to figure everything out through our human nature, and then we find that we falter. It's not meant to be fixed on a human level but understood on a soul level.

This means that we may not yet see the answer in front of us, as to *why* things are the way they are. But one day, we will, and one day, if we have managed to listen to our souls' guidance and to what life was trying to show us at the time, we will understand why.

Remember ! The wisdom of the soul is the part of us to turn to when the hurricanes hit our lives.

It is the only part to look to when we don't know which way to turn. The part that is connected to the divine.

But our spiritual stress is triggered by our unwillingness to listen to what life is trying to show us, and our unwillingness to try to connect to our souls and listen to what wisdom they have for us as life in all its confusion unfolds. We don't listen to what our souls are wishing to tell us that we really need to hear.

LISTENING TO LIFE

When I surrendered to the fact that this need to try to control was causing me huge stress and adding to my dad's, I yielded to the fact that while we can't always change what goes on around us, we *can* change what goes on within us.

Remember ! When we can't change the situation, we are being challenged to change something within ourselves.

So I faced the truth that I needed to change my reaction. Because I was not just feeling stressed, I was spiritually stressed—I wasn't spending time with myself and my soul for guidance. I wasn't surrendering to what was and having faith in the situation around me. Instead, I was trying to constantly control and look outward to get answers for something that was uncontrollable.

From looking continually outward, I was getting stuck in fear and control, and I was only getting more and more stressed and upset as a result.

When we spend time listening to the dialect of our souls, so that we can make room to hear the guidance they offer, then we can have a level of connection with ourselves that allows us to make the choices that cause us the least stress and create the most happiness. To understand ourselves on a level that allows us to truly know what is right for us, not what we have been told by those around us "should" be right for us. Or what the fears of our mind would have us believe are right for us.

When we miss this connection and don't surrender to what it's whispering to us, we become spiritually stressed, as we are totally out of alignment with our true selves, our souls.

When we deny our soul sides, we deny the very essence of who we are authentically. And when we ignore these sides to us, we cut ourselves off from divine guidance and the wisdom they have to offer in our most troubled times and beyond.

No baby's first full sentence is ever "I'm so stressed!" Our natural default setting is one of calm and happiness. The soul's natural essence is untampered with by outside fears and circumstances of this world. This essence inside of us is peaceful, free from anxiety and fear. It is really the opposite of stress.

It's the ease we feel when we are connected to ourselves on a deeper level, the flow of life we experience when we are not in resistance and trying desperately to control, trying to make it how our mind thinks it *should* be rather than how life knows it will be.

It's the voice of calm guidance that lies within every single one of us. Our connection to both the divine around us and the divinity within us. Whether we choose to get to know it and listen, however, is another story, one we continually write for ourselves.

Had I spent time in those initial months of despair to make a conscious effort to connect to the calm guidance of my soul, then I would have heard the message it gave to me much sooner, which was quite simply: *Let go—this isn't your fight.*

When I finally heard this internal message, I surrendered and accepted what was playing out in front of me.

What I didn't know at the time was that this eventual surrender and the acceptance I found from listening to my soul's wisdom would be the most precious gift I have ever given myself, as it was the gift that gave me the last two years with my dad as they should have been. Not arguing about what he "needed" to be doing. Not continually worrying about something that I truly could *not* control. But simply being with him in what was.

Had I never stopped and listened and acted on this guidance, then I would have missed it. I would have turned what I didn't know were the final months I would ever spend with him into a wasted turmoil of stressed yelling and control, arguing over something that didn't even take him from us, instead of enjoying what we had left of being father and daughter, of being great friends, which he and I always were.

But had I carried on as I was—I can say with certainty that as I wrote this two and a half years later—I would have had the deepest regret still with me had I not acted on the wisdom of my soul.

LISTENING TO YOU

This side to our spiritual stress comes from when we don't take the time to connect and listen to the soul, to learn its language and not only uncover the truth of who we are and what we really want but the wisdom it holds that guides us to where we need to go. Leaning instead only to the outside world to fill this void.

The second angle to our spiritual stress, then, really boils down to our human arrogance, or should we say ignorance. It's what happens when we have actually taken the time for connection, when we have gotten to know ourselves on that deeper level, when we have turned within ourselves for the calm guidance of our souls, when we've opened up the conversation between ourselves, our authentic truth, the divine, and our intuition—but then we just totally ignore the guidance we are offered.

We ignore the niggles telling us that our job is not where we are supposed to be. We brush off the feelings that our relationship is not right for us, because we are too afraid to be on our own. Or that a relationship *is* right for us, but we're too scared to jump in for fear of being hurt.

We resort back to our human egos. To our fear-based mind, our own insecurities. Or the outside pressures of what society, family, friends, and the people around us expect of us.

We weigh the logic instead of the deeper knowing. We go against our own happiness and fulfillment to conform to the normal. Or we ignore the messages we hear because we are too stuck in fear to act, getting locked into a continual cycle of what is wrong for us rather than what is meant for us.

When we know who we are beyond the labels the world has put on us, but we still don't live true to that authenticity, we allow ourselves to constantly get caught up in making choices based on the outside pressures and the societal expectations of others, the choices that go against who we truly are and what we know is right for us deep down.

From this, we once again cause ourselves spiritual stress, because we are going against what our own souls are trying to guide us to, what our truest essence is, what they know is for our highest good and our greatest happiness, away from the fear of our mind and opinions of the outside world.

Have you been feeling like something is niggling at you recently? That something is missing in your life? Or something has been wanting to get your attention but you have just ignored it and ignored it? What are you turning away from out of fear or doubt?

What are you pretending to enjoy simply because you *think* you should?

A SOUL SLAP

These things don't quite feel "right" as we are fighting our own authenticity instead of embracing it.

So our souls will then try to get our attention by making us feel uncomfortable, to show us that this is not in our highest interest, this is no longer the direction for our highest good. We feel like something is missing, something isn't as it should be—quite simply because it's not.

Sometimes when life has desperately sent us whispers, it resorts to giving us stronger signs. Signs that that person is no longer right for us. Signs that the job we are doing is not what is going to bring us the success *and* fulfillment we rightfully seek. Signs that we are simply on the wrong path.

But what do we do? We ignore these signs, these whispers and nudges. Brushing them off until—*wham!* Life sends us a massive side slap just to try to get our attention, the kind of slap we can't ignore.

The redundancy from our job we have been hating for years but have always been too scared to change. The breakup from the person we no longer find happiness with but are too scared to start over again. The car crash that injures us and forces us to slow down and look after the health we have been neglecting for our high-powered job.

The soul slap can be shocking, but it is often necessary, as we are human. Sometimes it takes a really good shake to get our attention, to get past the fears of our minds.

But the reality is, if we can only learn to connect and listen to our souls' guidance and then have the courage to act upon it, even if just one step at a time, then we can avoid this kind of stress a lot more, as we will be living true to ourselves, living true to the unique authenticity of our own souls.

One of the bravest things we can do in this life is to have the courage to live as who we truly are.

Remember! There is nothing more spiritual than being the real you.

But if we never take the time to sit and get to know ourselves, so that we can live from this place of authenticity and align our choices and actions with it, then we naturally become spiritually stressed as we become so far removed from the authenticity of our souls and become lost as ourselves.

When we are disconnected from this side of ourselves, whether we have something largely stressful going on in our lives or we don't, we can never truly feel our best. How can we, when we are constantly listening instead to the fears of our minds, rather than the guidance of our hearts?

Your soul transcends all the labels you have. It doesn't care how the outside world perceives you or what society wants from you. It looks at who you are without all of that. Who are you beneath all the labels you have taken on from the outside world? The mother, the doctor, the son, the lawyer.

What energy do you want to bring to the world?

Not the energy behind the many masks you wear but the authentic energy that guides you to your greatest joy and truest gifts. What might you be holding yourself back from? What are you really being *guided* to?

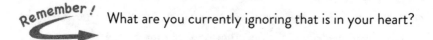

Remember! What are you currently ignoring that is in your heart?

SPIRITUALLY CALM

How can we be calm when we are going against the guidance our souls are offering us for our highest good? When we are in resistance rather than allowing? When we are conforming rather than doing what we know we *truly* need? When we are constantly looking only to the outside world for solace, relying on the outside world's outcomes for happiness—outcomes that are more often than not beyond our own control?

When we finally connect to our souls on a level that allows us to stick to our decisions unwaveringly, we trust without a doubt what is right for us, as we finally remember the truth of who we are.

When we return to that place of inner quiet, for guidance on good days and solace on our hardest, then we can finally access a calmness that goes beyond the mind, a calmness that is instilled in our hearts and our energy too.

From this place, you will find that although you feel the pains of life, you don't wallow in the suffering of it, that a strength far greater than what we can build on a physical level is born, the strength of an unwavering faith in ourselves and something greater outside of ourselves that is always guiding us to our greatest possibilities. From this place, our *deepest* calmness can finally unfold.

This faith, like all things in life, will be tested sometimes. But when we connect to the soul, we find that we will always come back to it.

What is it about connecting to our own spirituality that connects us to a deeper level of ourselves?

Why is it that this level cannot be found by merely going through the motions of our minds or looking to the outside world alone? Why is it only from this place that this *next level* to our calmness and happiness can be found?

When we are feeling spiritually calm, we feel centered and connected. We feel assured in our choices because we know they are for our highest good, not just our easiest option that gives a temporary high or comfort now. We feel steadfast and calm from within our centers, as we know that we are not meant to have it all figured out right now, we are not meant to solve the harder puzzles of life with our minds; we are merely meant to go with the flow of what life is trying to guide us to in this moment. To have the courage to see where that guidance may end up taking us. To trust.

When we are in this state, we surrender to the flow of life while also creating our lives.

Remember !   You'll know you are spiritually calm when your heart aligns with your choices.

When you are able to let go of the fears of your mind and look to the wisdom of your heart, the longing of your soul, you will find that life's greatest challenges become your greatest learning experiences. Your day-to-day happiness will increase because you are following the path that was designed specifically for you, from your soul, not the one that you merely felt you *had* to follow because your family or society had told you that was that.

You finally feel a calm confidence that even if everything is not exactly as you want it to be yet, you are moving forward to something that will be greater than you can imagine. That life is filled with infinite possibilities, and the restrictions we create are largely in our minds.

Wouldn't you want that bliss to be the life you live every day, to feel assured and calm deep from within your center, knowing that you are being guided by your soul, not the limits of your fears?

All you need to do to achieve that state is to relearn how to truly listen to your soul and step away from fears of your mind.

THE LANGUAGE OF THE SOUL

The mind and the soul are like two people living in the same house who speak a totally different language. The mind is like your friend who has a split personality. On one hand, they can be calm, rational, and open-minded, able to see beyond judgment and look at things from a different perspective. On the other hand, your mind can become a totally different person—unkind, fearful, constantly caught up in the negativity around them, the stress of the outside world, and harshly judging both themselves and others. We call this the *negative ego*.

Don't get me wrong—the mind is not two people. It's just the same person motivated by two different things, sometimes fear and other times reason. When fear is the motivator, ego kicks in, and when reason kicks in, intellect takes over.

Regardless of which side of the mind is speaking, it's your brain, not your soul. You are not your thoughts. But these two sides to the mind are the reason why the soul can often find it hard to just be heard.

Why are we so hung up on the pressures of the outside world? Why are we not seeking solace in the part of us that possesses all these qualities naturally?

Why are we not prioritizing taking time to really connect to and understand our souls?

The ego is one of the main reasons behind this. We get hung up on this fear-based voice, on the negativity bias of our own minds. Our hardwired brains are looking for the threats to our survival. So we get hung up on what they perceive as a "threat" from the tiny actions and even opinions of the outside world.[3]

Then when we manage to break away from this way of thinking, the ego chimes in and convinces us that this is the wrong thing to do and that we are in fact doomed if we suggest otherwise, if we suggest that we have a different way that might cause us greater happiness. If we suggest that we might want to do something differently, our egos cause us to doubt ourselves, trying to hold us captive in the illusion of safety within our fears, rather than let us be free in our true spirits, free in yourself to be and feel exactly what you wish to. After all there is a reason for this.

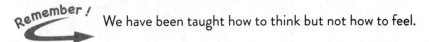 _Remember !_ We have been taught how to think but not how to feel.

But there is another friend who doesn't want to scream to get your attention, who knows that what they have to say is of great—if not much greater—value, far greater than the fear-based voice of the ego. But they are not going to stoop to the level of the ego just to get your attention.

They know that their voice will be heard eventually, that their guidance will be sought out by you when you are ready to hear it. Whether that's by taking time to engage in a private and quiet conversation, or whether after you have taken many wrong turns listening to the irrational advice of your ego, you eventually succumb to the idea that listening to it isn't working and you need to turn instead to a different friend.

So you turn to your friend who has been waiting for you to come to them when you are ready, awaiting you with open arms, zero judgment, calm assurance, wisdom, and compassion.

Of course this friend is your soul.

Remember ! The soul doesn't speak the language of fear; the ego does.

The only challenge you have here is that this wise friend speaks a different language.

THE VOCABULARY OF A SOUL

The soul speaks in the dialect of kindness, compassion, patience, love, connection, and wisdom.

It is not here to judge you or others. It is the part of you that connects rather than separates.

Anytime you find yourself in thoughts of separation, in thinking that it's you against the world, this is not your soul speaking. Anytime you find yourself full of judgment toward yourself or others, this is not your soul speaking. Or anytime you feel fearful and alone and you find yourself getting caught up in your fear-based stories, this is *not* your soul speaking.

The soul's nature reflects all the greatest qualities of humanity combined, our divine nature.

The compassion we give the friend who is struggling. The kindness we show a stranger in the street. The calmness we emit that makes another who is in angst feel at ease. The lack of judgment we have toward others, rather than the gossip we get caught up in for a momentary high. The sudden steady wisdom that comes when we need guidance most. The forgiveness we give to someone who has wronged us. The love we give without any expectation of anything in return.

This is the language of the divinity within all of us. These incredible qualities are at the heart of true humanity, that so often get lost in the angst and stress of the outside world, that are so often overlooked and cast to one side as "unimportant," as society has deemed that intellect, competition over creativity, and power are of greater value if we are to succeed in the game of life.

The truth, of course, is the opposite. These driven qualities have their place, but it is these peaceful qualities that are needed for us to not just exist but to truly live well.

They are the qualities that change things both on the inside and the outside; the qualities that create a ripple effect of good, with no measurable end; the qualities that cause us to *feel* good within ourselves and make others feel good around us.

This isn't spiritual hearsay; it's scientific fact. Studies show that daily acts of kindness have the ability to reduce our stress,[4] with a study by Harvard University showing that gratitude and actively being appreciative for things increase our happiness levels.[5]

So if these spiritual traits of the soul are the same qualities that are scientifically proven to show positive change in our health and happiness, then why are we not consciously tapping into them in every waking moment?

All spiritual teachings value the connection to the heart rather than the head. In Islam, for example, the Koran describes those who are happy in life as those who have hearts with which they reason. Sufism teaches that love is the sole connection to the divine and all the metaphysical. Buddhism instructs years of meditation practices just to get out of our heads and into our hearts of compassion, because *feeling* is the language of our souls. It is the way they speak to us and through us.

 Your heart is the conduit of your soul.

Your heart is your center for a reason. It's not just the center of your biology, it's the center of yourself. The home of your soul.

Now you know how your soul is trying to reach you, you understand a little of the language it speaks. Now, it's time to bring it all together.

PRACTICE, PRACTICE, PRACTICE

 We have trouble listening to our souls because we've been trained to not notice how they speak, to truly feel our feelings and then give them our attention.

We spend so much time putting on a pedestal the opposite of our sensory side and our ability to feel deeply, celebrating our rationale, intellect, our drive. But something that is equally if not more important is our intuition.

 Intuition is the words of your soul.

It's the bridge between you and your higher self, in whatever way you relate to that. It is the part of you that "knows" and feels, rather than intellectualizing, weighing up the pros and cons, or dwelling in your fears. It is the part of you that is connected to your soul's innate wisdom of what is truly right for you, the part that always knows what you *really* need to make you your happiest and most fulfilled.

Sometimes we don't want to hear the messages it has for us, because we are too stuck in the fears of our minds, not ready to hear them, let alone act upon them. But intuition is always there trying to guide us, even if we are not yet ready to listen to what it has to say.

You have to think of your intuition as a muscle. Like any muscle, if you don't strengthen it and don't take time to maintain it, then it gets weaker. But if you go to the gym and continually work on it, it only gets stronger.

Our intuition is like this: when we ignore it, it gets weaker, when we listen to it and act on it, it gets stronger.

The problem is that so many of us today are not even aware of when our intuition is speaking. So we end up just brushing it off and ignoring it. It then gets weaker and weaker, and the cycle of unease continues. We begin to feel lost, uncertain, lacking clarity or direction, and of course—stressed.

Pause for a moment now and ask yourself: When was the last time you acted on your own intuition? When was the last time you checked in with it for guidance? And when was the last time you ignored it? When was the last time you pushed aside your senses to listen to others rather than what you *knew* deep down yourself, only later to frustratingly realize you should have listened to your intuition because *you* knew what was right for you all along?

ACCESS TO YOUR INTUITION

When we start to understand our intuition, we understand that in order to hear it, we need to feel it.

There is no spiritual work without the emotional body and no intuition without the sensory side to your physical body.

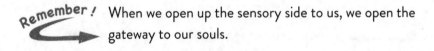 When we open up the sensory side to us, we open the gateway to our souls.

We begin to understand and learn the language of our own intuition, and just as we have different vocal voices, we have different intuitive voices too.

Our uniqueness as human beings ties into our uniqueness as spiritual beings. Your intuition's way of communicating with you may be totally different from the way a friend's intuition communicates with them. Does that make it wrong? Absolutely not. It makes it unique. It makes it yours.

Remember ! You've ignored your intuition every time that you have spoken yes but have felt no.

There was a deeper part of you making you feel a certain way to try to guide you, while your mind was on autopilot listening to your fear. That deeper *knowing* is intuition.

When we continually go against our intuition, then we start to betray a part of ourselves. Through this internal betrayal, we cause ourselves spiritual stress, as we don't feel we are in the flow of what is right for us. We can't feel completely at ease, as we're not totally connected to the truth within ourselves.

To open up our intuition fully, we need to become aware, aware of how it tries to communicate with us through the sensory, aware of when we are ignoring it, and aware of how to actively connect to it as and when we need.

Learning to use our intuition is like having an internal GPS system to keep us on the right track, where we can use our logic to complement it, not to take away from it. We can use our intuition as the anchor point to our choices by learning to feel into what is right for us, not just thinking about what "should" be right for us from within our minds.

The first side to actively using your intuition is to notice how your body tries to show you when it's guiding you. Shamans believe that the body is far wiser than the mind, that when we can connect to our bodies, we can gain incredible insight into what we need.

Remember ! Wisdom doesn't come from the restrictions of our minds, it comes from the knowing of our hearts.

The senses in our bodies, the feelings we get from deep within, these senses are what we use to connect to our intuition—the bridge to our souls.

If our intuition is a bridge to our souls, then our bodies are a bridge to our intuition. The body can be used to connect to our intuition by getting in touch with the feelings and senses it is giving us. From this, we can start to learn how our intuition is trying to communicate with us through our own gut feelings.

BODY BRIDGING

A great starting point to connect to your intuition is a shamanic exercise. I like to call it the *body bridging* exercise, which Shaman Durek, a sixth-generation shaman, spoke about in his book *Spirit Hacking*.[6] In it, he brought to the Western world some of the ancient shamanic tools that we can all use ourselves to help us connect more deeply to our spirits. He wrote about how one of the ways we can connect to our intuition is by actively communicating with our bodies.

Body bridging is an incredible way to communicate with your body and see what it is telling you in the form of simple yes-or-no answers through sensory feelings.

Stress Hack

We first become familiar with our bodies' yeses or nos, and then we can actively use them ourselves for guidance when we need a yes or no for something specific.

- Find a quiet place to either sit or stand.
- Relax your body, take a few deep breaths, and close your eyes.
- State out loud with conviction (it must be out loud so your body can hear), "Body, show me a clear *yes* so that I can feel it."
- Take a deep breath and scan your body from head to toe for sensations (it doesn't matter how subtle they may be or how strange they may seem).
- If you don't notice anything yet, then repeat the process.
- When you have noticed a sensation in your body as a response, then state out loud, "I feel *X* in my *Y*" (e.g., "I feel a tingling in my throat").
- Then state out loud, "Thank you."
- Repeat the process again for the opposite way around to show you the sensation of *no*. Say out loud, 'Body, show me a clear *no* so I can feel it."
- Note where the yes and no in your body language are held.

Repeat this process over the course of a week so you can really get clear on what your body's yeses and nos to you are.

Start to become more in tune with this sensory part of your intuition. I have had many clients say to me that they have actually felt the sensation of their yes or no multiple times before, but they ignored it, not knowing at the time what it was.

Once we become aware of how our intuition is trying to communicate with us through our bodies, then we can start to ask yes-or-no questions to our souls and see what is communicated back to us.

Repeat the above process, by asking your intuition out loud a yes-or-no question and then seeing which sensation comes up. You will then also start to notice when these sensations are coming up without you even taking the time to sit down, connect, and ask.

Remember that this isn't about it coming back with some elaborate, long-winded answer, like the kind you would get from a friend or the fear of your ego. It is about it coming back with a clear and simple *feeling*. The feeling of *yes* or the feeling of *no*.

By beginning to open up your own awareness toward your intuition, then you can more easily notice it as you go about your life, when you are being warned against something that's not right for you or being guided toward something or someone that is.

Take the time to try out this exercise and get to know your body's intuitive language. You may be pleasantly surprised at what you find.

SOUL APPOINTMENT

Something I found is great to ensure that I am connected and in communication with my soul is to create an appointment with it, to value it enough to carve out a specific time for it, just as you do when you take time to exercise because you value your physical health. I call those *soul appointments*.

In order to thrive in this world, we have to value our spiritual health as greatly as the other parts of us. So making it a nonnegotiable part of your week is key to accessing a deeper, steadier calmness.

In this appointment, you can start to really explore the nuances of your soul through opening up the channel to ask it the questions that you need guidance on that week.

You want to create a quiet space for connection. That may be out in nature on your own or a space in your home where you won't be disturbed and you can light a candle to help get you into a tranquil space. Even if that means you have to lock yourself in your bathroom just to create this space of quiet, do it! It's that important.

Once you have created a space of calm and quiet, you can then begin the appointment.

First get a piece of paper out, and write down everything you would like to have guidance on at the moment, anything that you are currently unclear or feeling confusion around, anything that you want advice on.

Once this is all out of your mind and on paper, you can now do an exercise to help you get out of your head and drop into your heart space, which is where we access our souls, beginning with a process I created called *intuitive questioning.*

By using this process, you are more easily able to tap into the wisdom of your soul, the deepest part of you, to become aware of the things that it is telling you that you need to do at this time and connect to its serenity, if only for a moment.

Find somewhere quiet. Create a quiet space of stillness, and let's guide you through it.

/Stress /Hack   THE INTUITIVE QUESTIONING PROCESS

- Sit down somewhere quiet with your back supported and get comfortable. Place your palms facing upward and rest them in your lap.
- Connect to your breath for three deep breaths using the four-four-eight breath sequence.
- *Breathe in through your nose for a count of four, hold for four, breathe out of your mouth for eight.*

- *(Repeat three times before relaxing back into your own breath pattern, continuing to breathe deeply in through your nose and out through your mouth.)*
- Place one hand over your heart and the other hand over that hand, and continue to breathe deeply.
- Bring your awareness first to the energy in your mind, the upper part of your head, and just notice it without judgment. What does the energy currently feel like inside your head?
- Breathing deeply, concentrate now on bringing that energy, that awareness that is placed on your mind, and move it down through your body, intentionally bringing it down through your head, into your throat, into your chest, until you drop your awareness into your heart space (where your hands are placed).
- Once you have reached your heart center, place your awareness now on the energy of this space.
- Notice the space within your body that your heart takes up.
- Notice how it feels. Does it feel tight or easy, light or restricted? Just breathe deeply into this part of your chest for a moment, expanding it with every breath.
- Now that you are more connected to this part of you, you can begin the intuitive questioning process.

For this part, you can either use specific situations that you need guidance on, or you can ask general questions for guidance. I often use the following structure.

- With your hands still over your heart, continue to breathe deeply.
- State confidently either in your own mind or out loud (whichever is most comfortable):
    * *Soul, what do I need to know about X?* or *Soul, what do I need to know most right now that is for my highest good?*
- Keeping your awareness on your heart center, notice what the first message that comes to you is from *this* space. Don't try to control it or judge it; just allow it.

- Once you feel you have received the message (listen for the first simple and clear one, and stop if your mind starts to go down a loop of confusion). Take a deep breath and state out loud or in your mind, *Thank you.*
- You can then move on to the next questions, repeating the same process:
  * *Soul, what do I need more of?*
  * *Soul, what do I need less of?*

Note down your answers afterward, and don't be surprised if you find yourself laughing at some of the answers you get. The soul likes to keep things simple and clear, and sometimes we can find that the answers only make sense when we read them back later.

You can create your own questions, or you can follow this simple structure. The important thing is to keep it simple, taking notice of what the first answer that comes to you from your *heart space* is, not your head. Keep a note of them.

This form of spiritual connection allows us to connect to our souls in an active way. But the soul is always whispering to us, just as life is.

 It's our job to learn to get out of our own way (our heads and fears) and to start to pay attention.

CRUCIAL CONVERSATIONS

The whispers it sends, the compassionate, kind, nonjudgmental, and forgiving energy that lives within us can be harder for us to access on the days that get the better of us; the days we all have because we are human; the ones where you just want to shout at someone, disappear, or curl up in a ball and cry, as life has just gotten to be too much.

No human being on the planet has never not had one of these days. Multiple, in fact. It's part of our human experience to have highs and to have to navigate lows in the ebb and flow of life. How quickly we are able to come back from those moments, however, largely comes down to how quickly we can remember that we are first and foremost spiritual beings having human experiences.

There is a spirit within you far greater than anything that may be going on around you. The spirit that lives in us is what we must turn to on the days that we want to press Control-Alt-Delete. It is what naturally possesses the qualities we need most in those moments. The qualities we need to give to *ourselves* on those days.

To be kind to ourselves when we have a terrible day. To not judge ourselves when we make a mistake. To be compassionate after we have a moment of fear or anger. To forgive ourselves for simply being human.

WHAT WOULD MY SOUL DO?

The soul exudes the greatest traits of our humanity, the nature of what we all strive to be yet deep down already are. But how can we align ourselves with these great qualities when we are constantly being bombarded with the harsher ones of the world around us? When we have people around us judging and gossiping? When we have a boss snapping at us telling us we have done a bad job? When we have a partner who is irritating us when they are unable to meet our needs that day?

How in those continually unfolding moments of stressors can we find it in us to align with the higher values and essence of our souls?

It begins by being mindful of when we are getting caught up in the opposite traits, when we notice that we are continually irritated, when we notice we are gossiping or judging, when we notice the negativity that we have found ourselves in. It is *then* that we can pause, take a deep breath, and simply ask ourselves this question.

Stress Hack   What would my soul do?

Once we ask this question, we naturally separate ourselves from our egos and allow ourselves the space to look from a higher perspective. From there, we can answer just as we would when we know what the actions of someone we admire would be in this situation.

We can look at how far away we are from our soul selves and ask ourselves away from the chatter of our egos. What would our souls do? What would the part of us that is kind, compassionate, calm, and wise do?

By pausing, breathing, and asking, we give ourselves the power to choose again—to choose again from a place of alignment with our spiritual nature.

Ask yourself now, how can you bring more of your soul qualities, more of the peace of the divine, into the smaller actions of your day? What extra kindness, compassion, love, and gratitude can you give today that you don't already?

Go that extra step to consciously bring more of those divine attributes into your day, and watch how your days get better. Knowing that when those tougher moments come, you have the power within you to pause, breathe, and ask yourself, *What would my soul do?*

The more we notice when we are not aligned with our divine traits, the more we can aim to consciously embody them. We can wake up and simply say *thank you* that we have woken, reminding ourselves that just that alone is a gift. We can smile at the stranger in the street. Take time to talk to the houseless person we pass by every day. We can try to gossip less, judge less, and listen to truly hear and not just reply. We can be kinder to ourselves and go that extra mile to be kinder to others.

We can start to ask ourselves in the smaller moments and the larger challenges of life simply, *What would my soul do?*

TAKE CARE OF THAT LITTLE SOUL

The famous guru Paramahansa Yogananda said, "Seclusion is the price of greatness." But is it even a price or simply a necessary gift we must give to ourselves so we can come back to our spiritual nature?

Very Important! → The soul requires seclusion.

It requires us to have those moments where we sit alone with ourselves, to actively engage with it through meditation or the above kind of processes, to simply learn to be in the company of ourselves so that we can make room to listen to it away from the chatter of the outside world. As Marcus Aurelius once said, "Nowhere can man find a quieter or more untroubled retreat than in his own soul."[7]

If we constantly deny ourselves the gift of seclusion because we're too afraid to be with the thoughts in our heads, then we will never know true peace, *true* calm. We will never know the power that silence brings and the gifts that solitude and seclusion offer us, away from distraction.

We are all human. We require connection to thrive. But we are also spiritual beings, so to thrive fully, to reach our greatest potential, we must also make room for the requirements of our souls.

The soul asks for very little, unlike the body that houses it or the mind that runs our days. It has no requirement of food, water, exercise, learning, or conversation for its strength and survival.

It simply requires some silence.

Silence so that we can learn to listen to its guidance, learn to love the beauty of us as a whole. To remember our truest nature, the unique path we are here to take and the unique gifts we have to bring to the world.

When we finally take the courage to spend time alone with ourselves, we can discover an originality within us that goes far beyond what any outside influence may have shown us. We can see ourselves for who we truly are, being guided to the greatness that our lives have to offer us.

Take the time to sit with yourself in silence every week, every day—even for just five minutes. Go for a walk alone in nature. Be alone and sit with your breath and your own internal contemplations, with no phone or other distractions around.

Sit every week in seclusion with yourself and in silence with your soul. Notice what this space can bring into your life.

NICE TO MEET YOU, SOUL

Within that space, we not only find a deeper calmness, clearer guidance, and the truth of who we really are—we can strive to live in the totality that this holy grail has to offer. We can finally learn to not just truly know ourselves but to both love and accept the entirety of ourselves too.

Self-love has become another thrown around and, to be honest, mildly annoying buzzword of the twenty-first century. *Love yourself. Don't forget your self-love. #SelfLoveSaturday.* These are some of the tiresome phrases we constantly hear on social media. But the truth behind self-love, the spiritual truth, goes far beyond what any hashtag trending on Instagram says it means.

True love of the self is not simply about taking time for self-care and bubble baths, or trying to be kinder to yourself within your mind, although these things are important and valid.

True love for yourself goes beyond this. It goes to seeing yourself *fully*, looking at your shadow side and your strengths, then having the courage to not look away when you may not like all that you see, recognizing what's there and then accepting unconditionally *all* that you are.

Remember !   The light within us is only amplified by the shadows that lie next to it.

This 360-degree seeing of the self is an elusive feat for many of us today. We may see our faces in the mirror, but never see the truth in our hearts. We may know ourselves on the surface levels of society, but never understand ourselves on the deeper level of our souls.

Without searching to fully see all of us and then having the courage to not look away, observing our flaws and imperfections as much as we do our strengths, we can never truly embrace the entirety of who we are. How can we, when we are asking others to love the parts of us that we ourselves deny?

In a romantic relationship, there is a common expectation that our partners shouldn't be the ones to try to change us, that *they* should love and accept all of us for who we are, that this is true love. But the reality is if we are asking another to do this for us, while being unable to do it for ourselves, can we ever really know true love?

Without embracing, knowing, and loving all of who we are, right down to our souls, can we ever fully love?

How can we love outside of ourselves when we deny loving all within ourselves? How can we expect another to love the parts of us that we refuse to look at ourselves?

I LOVE YOU

Those three words that we long to hear from others are often the ones that we find hardest to say to ourselves. We look at the surface, and we love one physical feature over the others. We love the way we do a certain thing or the way we act during certain moments. We love only the good that we choose to see, instead of the imperfections we desperately try to cover up.

Being spiritually stressed is in part about not knowing ourselves on a soul level, denying our authenticity, and going against what that authenticity is calling for. But then the acceptance of ourselves once we finally see ourselves truly is the bridge between our humanity and our divinity.

The divinity within all of us, the souls that we are, loves unconditionally. While that little voice in our heads may come in and tell us we are not worthy of something or someone, or not good enough to achieve something, the divinity within us accepts and loves it all. It connects us to the deepest part of our hearts. It knows a crucial lesson.

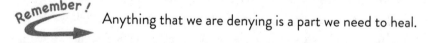 Anything that we are denying is a part we need to heal.

When we have the courage to look at what we don't like about ourselves with compassion and kindness, we can come to a place where we not only accept it but we can learn to love it, not because it is our favorite part of ourselves but because we finally have the realization that without it, we would not *be* ourselves.

There are more than 8 billion people on this planet—8 billion souls. Every single person here holds different gifts, their own different superpowers. Yet among these powers, we all hold one that is exactly the same, one that both connects us and lets us stand out on our own.

The power that out of the 8 billion souls here, not a single one is the same as you.

Not a single one holds the exact same soul blueprint as you, the exact same life experiences, and from this the exact same gifts and more.

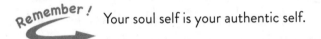 *Remember!* Your soul self is your authentic self.

No one is the same as you, once you only take the time to discover and love the entirety of who you *really* are.

COMPLETE WHILE INCOMPLETE

We all have room for growth. It is said if you're not growing, you're dying. While that may sound dramatic, I find it to be totally true. When we are not growing in some way, if only minutely, we begin to feel stagnant in ourselves. Life becomes monotonous, and we become stuck and start to feel unfulfilled.

Our growth doesn't just depend on the outer growth of our actions and accomplishments, or the relationship we find ourselves in that pushes us to face our own fears or the new skill we learn that challenges us. It is also centered in our spiritual growth, to expand and raise our consciousness.

Once we become committed to our own growth—mental, physical, emotional, *and* spiritual—we can discover ourselves on an entirely new level, uncovering gifts, traits, and resources within us that we never knew we had, while also discovering the things we have yet to heal that are holding us back.

But you don't have to suffer your own critique, feeling like you are not enough while you work on that growth—because this kind of growth is a lifelong quest. You're amazing as you are right now; you can be better, but that doesn't mean you're not enough as you are.

A place to begin in your quest for growth: self-love.

A large part of our spiritual growth is this love of the self. When we can grow enough to say that we love the entirety of who we are, we have managed to align with our spiritual nature of kindness, acceptance, compassion, and love. This nature has to start with the self if it is to succeed in being carried into the world.

Start with how you treat yourself and how willing you are to look at yourself on a more intimate level. Look at the cracks, the shadows, and the flaws, and love and accept them as much as you can the parts of you that you're naturally proud of and want to show to the world, even accepting the parts that you need to work on, without judgment.

Part of the spiritual journey is to know yourself fully and to then love yourself completely—flaws, cracks, and all. Perfection is found within the beauty of imperfection. When we can see the beauty of the flaw, we can see the growth it has brought us and the gifts it has given us.

But why must we look these imperfections in the face? Why can't we just ignore the parts of us we don't like and carry on in blissful ignorance?

Remember !   When we deny the parts of us we don't like, we don't get rid of them—we strengthen them.

We end up creating false personas that glitter over the cracks, putting on the masks we wear to hide these truths, for fear of being judged because we have already unconsciously judged ourselves.

But if we're not willing to learn what these parts of us are, to see them all clearly and love them unconditionally, to peel back the layers of who we aren't meant to be and instead uncover the truth of who we came here to be, then how can we ever expect to reach our greatest potential when we aren't willing to see our shadows?

The idea of the shadow self was popularized by psychiatrist and psychoanalyst Carl Jung. It is composed of the parts of ourselves that we reject, that we often don't know are there, as we refuse to look at them.

Shadow work is about self-examination, and when integrating this, we can reach a level of love that is more in line with our divine selves than our human selves, no longer dependent on a love that loves only the good but a love that sees and accepts the whole and is willing to grow from it.

One way the shadow shows us it's there is when we find we are triggered by someone that we find distasteful or irritating for some reason. Try out this exercise as a starting point for looking at your own shadow and see what you might find.

Stress Hack

IN THE SHADOWS

- Think about someone who bothers you and try to gently work out what bothers you in this person that might also be in you.
- Ask yourself the following questions and write down your answers:
    * What is it about this person that I don't like?
    * What makes it irritating or difficult for me to be around them?
    * Do I find that I have some of those traits sometimes?
    * What parts of myself does this person ignite when I am around them? And how do I feel about those parts of myself?

In our lives, it is our darkest parts that we need to try the hardest to see, to accept and integrate them so that we can grow through them. As Carl Jung said, "Everyone carries a shadow, and the less it is embodied in the individual's conscious life, the blacker and denser it is."[8]

SEE, ACCEPT, LOVE

Our willingness to look at the entirety of ourselves is the starting point for an exponential type of spiritual growth—a growth that allows our perceived weaknesses to become a catalyst to the expansion of our consciousness, choosing not to hide from them but to own them instead. This can be a harder task than simply looking a little closer.

Very Important!

Most of us can look, but we never truly see.

We look at the surface, while never seeing the truth of what's underneath it—the beauty of the flaw, the lesson of the wound . . . the diamonds of the soul.

When we feel truly seen and heard by someone in our lives, it is one of the most empowering and beautiful feelings we as human beings can ever experience, to know and feel that someone truly sees us and actually accepts and loves what they see.

This feeling can be mirrored only by the feeling of truly seeing ourselves.

SAL is a tool I created to use to start this soul exploration, to start to see, accept, and love the entirety of who you really are. The more you do this, the more you will gain from it; the more you'll find that one day you no longer look at yourself and think, *I need to hide that part of myself or dim myself down to fit in.* You'll think, *How can I show that part of myself more? How can I allow myself to radiate that bit brighter?*

We see ourselves when we can look beyond what we think we are and come to discover who we really are.

We accept ourselves when we can look past our strengths and beauty and find the wounds and flaws that we can grow from, that make us both unique and wise.

We can love ourselves when we see all of this in its entirety and we are finally able to be grateful for *everything* that we are.

SAL

This **see-accept-love** method aims to help you see who you truly are and start to learn to accept and love everything you see.

Stress Hack

We will not rush through this. As a matter of fact, I recommend that you work through this method over a period of three days (or longer, if you like). Savor it and give it all you have so that you can allow each stage to fully integrate.

Stage 1: See

Success at the end of stage 1 will be to see all of you. See every trait, quality, strength, weakness, and fear.

- Sit quietly somewhere and write down on a piece of paper all the things you believe are your strengths, best qualities, and gifts.
- Then ask two people you love and trust to do the same.
- Reflect on both yours and their answers.
- Then write down all the things that you don't like about yourself, the things that you believe are your weaknesses, and the fears that hold you back.
- Then ask two people you love and trust to do the same.
- Reflect on both yours and their answers.
- Are they different or similar? Are there parts on either side that you yourself didn't see?

Stage 2: Accept

- Looking back on your answers for both sides, note down which parts you find hardest to accept, both in the good and the perceived bad.
- Which parts do you not agree with?
- Ask yourself now, why don't you agree? Or why might you find these parts the hardest to accept?

- Then ask yourself what you might need to forgive yourself for in order to accept these parts of you.
- Write a list of forgiveness to yourself and read it back and say it out loud to yourself, "I forgive myself for . . ."

Stage 3: Love

- Looking at what you have written down above, first ask yourself what it is that you love about the good that both you and others have seen?
- Then ask yourself what the perceived bad has shown you about yourself and why you could also love that?
- Write down a list of eighty things that you love about yourself (from the physical, personality traits, gifts, etc.). This can take a number of days, but don't stop till you reach it.
- Keep your list and read it back to yourself on the days that you really need reminding why you are as great and unique as you are.

SAL helps us to get connected to ourselves on a deeper level by helping us to see the entirety of who we are. When we begin to uncover the truth of who we are, it is then that we can reach our greatest potential.

YOUR DIVINE POTENTIAL

When we can see and love our whole selves, we realize that our divine potential knows no bounds.

We can be and create whatever we want, whether that's within ourselves or in the outside world. I believe that people who create great things never do it alone; there is always some form of divine guidance at play. Even in our hardest times.

What if everything in your life—every trauma, hurt, and blissful experience—wasn't random?

What if the good and the bad had in fact all gone exactly to plan, even if that plan wasn't quite your own?

Along with our unique talents, we have also been given our own unique experiences, our own lessons learned. But if we don't then share all that we have learned, by accessing our greatest potential and then going out to give it to the world, then just as when we bake a batch of delicious cupcakes and don't share them with those around us, we are being selfish by not sharing the potential within us.

I believe we all have a divine obligation to go out into the world and to serve in only the way we can—by trying to actively seek out our own divine potential. Ancient Greek philosopher Socrates spoke about the concept of *entelechy*—the potentiality in every living thing. He said that every single thing, being, and person has a specific potential within them, unique to them and them alone.

So a cherry stone when watered has the potential to become a cherry tree, but it could never turn into an apple tree, as that's simply not its potential. Just as when we are trying to be something that we are not, we find we falter, as it's not who we *truly* are.

Remember !   It is your choice alone whether you choose to activate your own greatest potential or not.

Just as a cherry tree will not grow and have fruits if it is put in stones rather than soil and watered, you won't reach your greatest potential, your divine potential, if you don't look harder at six things.

- What have you learned through your own hardships?
- What are you innately good at?
- What are you truly interested in?
- What do you love?
- What is it that you really want?
- What actually matters to you?

Reflect on these questions. Look at what will help you activate your own divine potential. Ask yourself what your heart is really trying to guide you toward.

Stress Hack

Ask yourself, away from all the labels and the outside noise. Away from your job and your relationships. Just ask yourself the most important question.

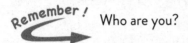 Who are you?

Who are you when everything is taken away? What makes up your essence?

SOUL-RENITY

Beyond your thoughts, beyond the chatter, a part of you that hosts a calm wisdom waits for you within, the potential of your greatness and the truth within your heart. It is the part that answers simply and clearly, that doesn't doubt or confuse, guiding you through compassion and kindness, rather than fear and judgment. It does not cause you internal conflict or increase your suffering but rather eases your pain.

Our internal conflict, our spiritual stress, comes from our disconnection to this part of us, from only relying on the swirling around of our minds and resisting the divinity within us to come through with grace.

When we don't connect to our emotions, to our hearts, then we cannot connect to our souls. If we don't connect to this part of us, then we are only living in the mental and physical realms of our world, the realms that host our fears, our need to control, our self-made restrictions, and our deepest anxieties. But when we can access this deeper part of ourselves, if only for a few moments every day, then everything changes.

We no longer make decisions that aren't right for us, because we know ourselves on a level that can't be tampered with by outside noise. We no longer always look to the outside world to change our problems or validate us, as we know that we can seek solace and comfort within the knowing of our souls. The divine connection that lies within.

We all must try to remember to not think too much and feel too little, to not push away the part of you that is the key to your true power and your divine potential.

 The power we create when we reactivate our own spirituality is a power that can't be shaken by fear or tampered with by judgment.

Knowing yourself on this most intimate level should be the goal at the forefront of your own personal mission for growth. As you grow and evolve, so should that self-exploration. As you become wiser and calmer, explore that little bit deeper.

The modern term of consciousness was originally derived from the Latin word *conscius*, which meant "knowing or aware." So to raise your level of consciousness means to raise your level of perception, to raise your level of understanding, and to see from a higher perspective—a perspective that is more aligned with the divinity within you, rather than the humanity around you. This allows you to reach a new level of spiritual wisdom that you haven't yet attained, to learn and grow both through life's hardships and life's gifts.

Create the intention to heal from the wounds that are running the show for you, to see your shadow and uncover your gifts, to go past the doubts of your mind and into the well of your heart. As Carl Jung said, "Until you make the unconscious conscious, it will direct your life and you will call it fate."[9]

Take the time to uncover the whole truth of who you are, the truth of your shadow and your fears and the promise of your gifts. Understand why certain people and things cause you more stress than others. Learn why you react to some things and respond to others.

Remember! You can only direct your life when you truly know yourself.

So get to really know yourself, uncover the hidden parts of you, and love them unconditionally. Discover your hidden strengths that lie deep within your soul, and go and give them to the world.

If we go on this mission of soul exploration, then we have to be willing to really look, see, feel, and accept all that we find. To look at what we truly desire, what makes us laugh and what makes us cry. To see who we are beyond how we have only been conditioned to see ourselves. To *feel* what is right for us and what is begging us to stretch ourselves that little bit further. To accept wholeheartedly all the things we have come to find and love them unconditionally.

Remember ! Just as the intellect grows and the body strengthens, the soul seeks.

It seeks a higher level of consciousness. It seeks to evolve, to bring you back to your truest self.

Finding this deeper soul-renity comes from an internal faith that what is inside of you is far greater than any stressor that may cause you to falter from the outside. This faith is everything—it is a faith in life, in a higher power, in yourself. Wherever you place it, just make sure you hold it.

Have faith in an ever-unfolding plan that paves the road with synchronicities and good intentions.

Have faith that your hardest times and greatest stresses are merely bringing you toward your greatest self—only when you are willing.

The skeptic in you may dismiss the magic of synchronicities as nothing but coincidences. But ask yourself next time one of those "coincidences" happen: What was it that you were thinking about when it did? What were you spending your days wishing for before this coincidence occurred?

What have you wanted so desperately to happen in the past that ended up not working out in favor of something far better, that you couldn't have foreseen in the future? Something that you could never have foreseen with your human mind, but when you look back, you notice perhaps there *was* a greater plan working for you all along?

If *you* don't know yourself on the level of your soul, ask yourself, *Why not?*

What are you afraid to see? Scared to uncover? As Marianne Williamson wrote, "It is our light, not our darkness, that most frightens us."[10]

 Spiritual freedom is being able to base your choices on the guidance of your heart rather than the fears of your mind.

To live from a place of faith over doubt. To know yourself well enough to say that you alone get to decide how you feel, no longer allowing those feelings to be controlled by circumstance alone—but by you. To feel totally free from a place that is strengthened by autonomy, empowered by knowing that you alone control yourself. You are not controlled by your reactions but rather freed by your responses.

 Sometimes our suffering gets entangled in the fates of others, but that doesn't mean our suffering should become our fate.

Take control of your mind, soothe your emotions, love your body—but whatever you do, don't forget to lead with your soul.

SUMMARY OF PART II
Speak Fluently

- We are all made up of four elements that affect how we show up in the world: our mental, emotional, physical, and spiritual selves. All these parts of our beings can be both the cause or effect of our own stress. While they all have their own language and unique system, they are also interconnected. What happens in one can affect another. The mind can create our emotions, our emotions can create our physical symptoms, and our spirits can connect to us through our emotions. We are all linked within these systems as one unique whole.

All we have to do is learn each of their unique languages and listen.

- The barrier to understanding the language of our mental selves begins with the distinction that we are not our thoughts, that there is a space within us that can observe our thoughts and, most important, direct them. Our minds are waiting for instruction and will do what we tell them to if we take control. We can learn to walk it rather than allowing it to run wild with damaging thoughts that increase our stress and unhappiness. When we take the time to direct our thoughts, we can create thoughts that enhance our lives and reject the thoughts that cause us greater anxiety and stress.

  Creating a practice within our minds is key, working them out in their own gym, just as we would our bodies. When we practice the good with our minds with things like gratitude and mindfulness, those are the things that get stronger. It is only when we can direct our minds that we can truly direct our lives. It's not the things in our lives that stress us; it's the way we think about them that does.

- The barrier to understanding our emotional selves is our inability to submit to negative feelings and fully allow them. We have been taught how to think but not how to feel. When it comes to our emotions, what we resist persists, so anytime we push away our emotional stress with distraction, we don't get rid of it—we compound it.

  When you can take a step back and become the compassionate observer of your feelings, you allow yourself to not be absorbed by them. Your emotions are asking you to get curious and pay attention to what they may be trying to tell you. The more curious you are, the easier they become to understand. Pay attention to your emotions just as you would a friend. Ask yourself where the feeling is, why it is showing up, and what you can do to ease it.

The more in tune you are with your uncomfortable feelings, the more heightened your great ones will be. You can affect how you feel through the thoughts you create and the response you give your feelings when they arise. Move your negative feelings through you so you can return to feeling at ease. Use your feelings as the compass to guide you back to your happiest self.

- The barrier to understanding our bodies is when we only pay attention to them on the brink of collapse. We don't become in tune with them when they're happy, so we don't notice the smallest beginning signs of when they're not. We then don't give them the right fuel to run properly and neglect their basic needs. Our bodies are like cars: they require certain maintenance to run well and the correct fuel to run properly. Learning what that maintenance is and how to release the stress from them is key to them functioning well. When we are not in tune with the sensory sides to our bodies and their basic needs, then things start to break down. And if our bodies are speaking (screaming), it's really time to pay attention. Our bodies can be stressed by the actions we take as much as the actions around us.

We can overcome this by being mindful of how we are treating our bodies, while actively diffusing the stress from them, then listening to their pleas—move, restore, stretch, relax, breathe, fuel, digest, and snooze.

- The barrier to understanding the language of our souls is that we search for our answers outwardly rather than inwardly. We get lost in the fears of our minds and the opinions of our outer world, rather than our deeper knowing within. We turn away from the truth of our hearts, and we don't look deeper at who we are beyond the expectations of others, what we truly love and want. We try to solve everything in our minds, and we don't pay attention to the feelings and guidance our souls are offering to us.

Our intuition is the bridge between us and our souls, our hearts are their homes. When we can learn to listen to the intuitive feelings we are being given, connect to the truth of our hearts, we find the truth of ourselves. We do this by making space and time for our souls just as we do for our bodies, to sit with them in stillness and pay attention. When we slow down, we give space for connection to our souls and something greater. When we relinquish control, we allow space for soulful surrender. Learning the language of the soul begins with feeling and then paying attention.

Part III

Putting It All Together

The true superheroes of the modern times are those who manage to stay engaged, productive, and successful as they navigate the fast-paced, stressful alleys of the modern world without suffering chronic stress and burnout. They are those who succeed at what they set their minds to, without having to pay with stress as the inevitable price for their success.

We call those the unstressable. They abide, relentlessly, by seven habits that make them who they are.

8

The Unstressable

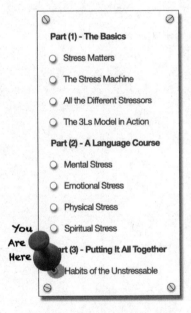

To be unstressable, we do not need to avoid the world as a monk or nun would do; we just need to behave in ways that evade the reasons for the types of repetitive stress that wear us down. As we have seen in this book, the habits and techniques that can reduce our exposure to stress and the skills and abilities that we can use to deal with it are practically countless. Each and every one of us relies on a different variety of those techniques and methods to find a path to a less stressful life. In our research, we have found, however, that those who tend to be the calmest even when exposed to the most stressful life circumstances, the ones who are fully engaged in life while extremely productive and successful, usually live by seven habits. Those habits seem to be ubiquitously present among all those who happen to be unstressable.

The unstressable keep the target of an unstressed life squarely within their gaze at all times. In addition to having these habits, the unstressable view every stressful experience as an opportunity to learn. They constantly cycle through the three *L*s model: limit, learn, listen. They revisit what stressed them, question what they missed, and think of ways to remove that stressor from their lives and of ways to increase their abilities to deal with it if it ever crosses their path again. Every one of their habits seems to address one side of the three-*L* triangle. They are constantly attempting to reduce the reasons that can cause them stress. Be the stressors internal or external, micro or macro, the unstressable never carry the TONN. As they suffer stress, they listen attentively to their minds, hearts, bodies, and souls. They understand the language, those vital parts of what makes them human, and they respond when they get the message and deal with the stress. As they do, they reflect and learn to become better the next time. They take note of the skill that helped them navigate the harshness, embrace it, and use it the next time a similar form of stress attacks them. You can see them mature gracefully with age. You notice their wisdom in how they see life for what it is and how they handle its events with calm and grace. Once they do, they restart the three-*L* cycle, look at the stressors in their lives, and reduce.

Let us share those seven habits with you here and encourage you to make them your top priority and include them in every facet of your everyday life.

1. THE UNSTRESSABLE KEEP AN INVENTORY AND REDUCE

Stress does not kill if we know how to use it correctly. As a matter of fact, a bit of it can drive us to do a little more than we would without it. Be a little more focused. Put a bit of extra effort in. But too much stress can, and does, kill. It leads to chronic anxiety, depression, and burnout, and it leaves us unable to deal with life with our optimum performance. The top priority of all unstressable is to limit their exposure to stress wherever that exposure originates from.

Some of the stress we face in life comes in the form of traumatic, unexpected events that hit us with hardship, harshness, and pain. Events like losing a loved one or being laid off from work unexpectedly on a Monday morning are entirely out of our scope of control. There is no escaping the stressful effect they have on us. No one, even the best of all unstressable, can do anything about those but learn to navigate and cope with them.

Other than those events, however, the unstressable learn to remove all other stressors and weed them out of their lives regularly so they don't grow, don't last, and don't impact them negatively beyond the short term.

Those other stressors constitute the majority of all the stressors that we face every day—small nuisances like being stuck in traffic or running out of coffee when you need it most on a Monday morning. Those events can stress you, and if you let them, they can pop up in your life in the hundreds of instances every single day. The experienced of the unstressable know that every single one of those minor external stressors can surely be avoided.

If we make it our priority to ensure that we avoid the little stressors by, perhaps, taking a different path through our commute or turning that traffic jam into an opportunity for listening to a podcast we wouldn't have had the time to, there would not be any need to struggle with those undesirable stressful events. The unstressable make it a habit to take stock and remove the events they can from their lives as soon as they observe them surfacing.

Beyond those, every other stress is generated not by the world around us but by our brains. We either obsess about certain concepts, how stupid we think our boss is, or how unfairly treated we feel we have been by our last lover, and think about them over and over until they lead us into depression or anger or despair as the stress mounts up to burn us out without life actually doing anything to upset us, perhaps, other than an event that took place a long time earlier in our past. Often we even obsess about events that life has not even created in the first place. We imagine them, worry about them, obsess over them, and make them the centers of our lives until our thoughts harm us a lot more than the event would ever have even if it did happen. Which it didn't. But not the unstressable. Those who have vowed to live a stress-free life never let their brains hijack them into obsession. They see through the illusions and turn their thinking positive and objective.

Beyond those big obsessions, which are easy to spot, it is the mounting of little negative thoughts that drown us. We worry about endless little things, too many of them, when none of them truly even deserve our attention in the first place—a silly comment on social media or the way someone looked at your shoes as if to disapprove.

If it's generated by their brains, the unstressable immediately take charge and stop the negative thoughts. They insist that their brains think useful thoughts and avoid brain cycles that make them feel bad without making their world any better.

Whatever you do, if you want to be unstressable, take charge and limit the duration and the number of the stressors that you allow into your life. Whether those are small events imposed on you by life or the thoughts that you generate yourself, never let the stress linger, even if it means that you stop everything else and spend the time working through your de-stress plans.

When our stress lingers, our physiology suffers a stress response that is originally designed to make us run away from danger or address it head-on within minutes or, at most, hours. We were not designed as humans for our stress to linger and last for weeks. Take charge of your stress and stop it before it takes on a life of its own. Without allowing stress to linger, you will always be okay.

2. THE UNSTRESSABLE RUN LIFE THE WAY A CEO WOULD

Those who live unstressable never sit down to interact with life as observers. They don't sit and wait for things to happen. They are in charge of their own destinies and in charge of their own states of mind. They hope for things to be easy but know that life will sometimes send a curveball their way. When it does, they don't sit back and complain. When things go wrong, they don't act as the object of the event. They are the subjects. They take charge. They make things happen like a CEO runs a business. They know that they're the boss because they engage with challenges in a positive and objective way.

Over the years, experienced CEOs gain the skills, courage, and determination to make life right when things go wrong. When any part of their business doesn't go according to plan, they ask to be fully informed of the truth, and then they ask for action to fix things or at least make them better.

As the CEO of your own life, you should do the same. When an event in life stresses or challenges you, you need to ask three questions.

Is it true? That's the first and most important question you can ever ask. The unstressable know for a fact that what their brains tell them is not necessarily always true. Your brain, at best, only attempts to tell you what it thinks is true. Blurred by its own assumptions, your emotions, conditioning, and beliefs, your brain could be quite a long way off the truth.

When life is difficult or things go wrong, your brain tends to err on the side of caution. It tends to exaggerate, and it tends to search for the negative it believes that it should protect you from. When it looks for it, it finds it. Often what our brains tell us is not true, but that does not stop them from making scary and sad claims that make us unhappy.

The unstressable are always armed with the question *Is it true?* when their brains tell them something negative. They ask their brains explicitly, *Is that true, brain? Is it true that my partner doesn't love me anymore? Is it true that the world is going to end? Is it true that if I lose my job, I will be homeless and starve to death? Is it true that the Uber driver disrespected me? How could he disrespect me if he doesn't even know me?*

If the answer to this question is *No, it's not true*, then drop it. There is no point being stressed about anything that is not true.

However, if it is true, then it's time for the next question: **What can I do to fix it?**

The only reason our brains keep us hostage with negative thoughts is because they want us to take action so that they can make us safe and improve our lives. To end the thinking, make the world better, and remove the stress, there is only one thing to do. If something that is stressing you is true, do something about it. Ask yourself, *What can I do to fix it?* The unstressable start to use logical thinking that can improve the situation, instead of wasting their brain cycles on incessant thoughts that only make them feel bad. When they find the answer, they immediately engage in doing what they need to do, and the stress goes away because taking action is linked to positively thinking about what is possible and does not leave space in their heads to think negative thoughts. At the same time, the bonus they gain is that the problem they're facing starts to be resolved and things start to get better.

Even when there is nothing the unstressable can do to fix the stressor facing them, they still engage. They know that part of life's harshness, sometimes, is final in its nature.

If you've lost your job, you've lost your job. That's it. There's no going back. If you've scratched your car, it's scratched. There is no way you can go back in the past and erase the accident. There is no way you can erase the damage unless you can work on fixing it. What should you do, then, when faced with finality? You ask yourself the third question: **Is there something I can do to make my life better despite what happened?**

The third and most effective question for the Jedi Masters of all who are unstressable is: *Can I accept what happened as the new baseline of my life? Not because I'm weak but because I'm strong enough to recognize that this is what it is. And then can I commit to make things better, despite the presence of something that I wish was not part of my life?*

The unstressable will constantly search for a way to make life better. Even if they lost their job, they will find a way to do some part-time work until they find another one. They may use the time to rest and reflect, or they may simply use it to do the spring cleaning. They know that finding another job will take time and that if they try their best, they will get there as quickly as possible. So what's the point of sitting in the corner, complaining and feeling sad for themselves and stressed about their current reality? This stress doesn't add to their ability to solve the problem. In fact, it takes away from it.

3. THE UNSTRESSABLE LIVE A JOYFUL LIFE

Living an unstressable life is not just about avoiding or coping with stress. It equally is about including joy, calm, and comfort proactively in one's life. This does not mean expensive vacations or fancy dinners. Joy is found in the simplest of pleasures, and the best things in life are free.

Those who learn to live unstressable include sufficient portions of rest, connection to loved ones, fun activities, joyful food, as well as reflection time and hobbies into their calendars on a daily basis. They spend time in nature, slow down frequently, and listen to music.

They understand that those activities deserve as much priority as getting another piece of work done. They immerse themselves in them and give them time. When a conflict arises and work competes for the time they had originally allocated to unwind and enjoy life, they will not just sacrifice their joyful time; they will make sure sufficient time is found for it at another opportunity before they let something else replace it.

When we make our well-being our priority, we include joyful activities into our calendars and block the time for our self-care needs in our calendars first—before work and the stress of life grab hold of every minute of our days.

When we feel pleasure and calm, our parasympathetic nervous systems engage to signal that everything is okay. Feel-good hormones are secreted, and the stress hormones are flushed out of our bodies, leaving us not only feeling amazing but also ready to engage with the challenges of life when they arise, to achieve and win in life.

Instead of just fighting stress, working all the time, spend as much of your time engaging in the true joy that life can bring. Life is only what we choose to make it, so make yours as memorable a story of joy as you can.

4. THE UNSTRESSABLE LIVE FROM THE HEART

Our hearts are our centers. They're the truth of our beings and the compasses of our lives. Living unstressable begins with being in touch with that center. It begins with knowing that if we weren't meant to feel, quite simply, we wouldn't.

When we learn to connect with our feelings on a more intimate level, it's only then that we can get to truly know ourselves, and only when we know ourselves can we begin to create a life worth living—a life that's informed by who we *really* are and what we really want.

The unstressable know that it's not just the mind's job to understand how to create a joyful life but also the heart's. Their hearts' guidance allows them to create the lives they ought to live, guiding them through feeling, not just through logic.

They understand that their feelings are not their enemy but their greatest ally. They embrace the feelings they may not want to feel as much as the ones that they do. From this, they start to experience life to an unmatched level of depth, living from a place of truth and authenticity. They learn to navigate through life from a greater perspective and a much deeper wisdom, knowing that their own ability to feel deeply also allows them to connect to others more fully.

When we fully connect to our emotions, we can then learn to understand them. From this place, we can use them—to guide us, to grow us, to inspire us—while also better allowing others to understand us as well.

The unstressable strive to be the ones that feel the most deeply. Feeling fully becomes their strength. They view their ability to embrace emotions as an achievement to be proud of, not a hindrance on their paths to success. As they let their emotions live, they manage the actions that are triggered by them, so they don't need to fear them. The more they feel, the more curious they become. They know themselves better than anyone.

When we are brave enough to embrace our negative emotions, the freedom that ensues makes us experience heightened positive ones. The yin and yang of feeling goes hand in hand with our acceptance that everything in life has polarity, including the feelings within us. There is no one on earth who can escape sadness or pain, stress or struggle. Our ability to manage our emotions doesn't come from being lucky enough to never have events that trigger our negative ones but from being wise enough to know how to handle the negative feelings when they arise.

The unstressable know that the same society that tells us to hide away our feelings is the one that is the most stressed and unhappy it has ever been. Bottling up emotions is not working, not understanding our emotions is not helping. The unstressable choose to feel free to feel—and free to show those feelings.

They know that if they're not fully feeling, then they are not truly living, that without embracing their feelings, both the good and bad, they can never reach their ultimate potential. They understand that they can learn from the depths of their hardest emotions and live from the height of their greatest.

They know that living from the heart is the only thing that makes life worth living in the first place, that a feeling is always there for a reason, there as a clue. They use their feelings as their guides, alerting them to change something or to treasure something, acknowledging they are what keeps us at our best by showing us when we are at our worst.

The unstressable speak the language of emotions fluently. They have learned to observe their feelings, understanding they have the power to create them, keep them, or release them.

The unstressable pay attention to how they feel, without judgment. They realize that this is one of the greatest skills we can ever learn. They are the masters of their emotions, they love them and learn from them, never allowing unprocessed emotions to be just another reason for their stress.

5. THE UNSTRESSABLE KEEP A HEALTHY LIFESTYLE

We all get one body and one body alone. Those who live unstressable appreciate this; they don't wait for their bodies to tell them they've been pushed too far. They nurture them and give them the things they need when their bodies tell them.

They make sure that they move their bodies every day, if only for a leisurely stroll. They eat the foods that fuel them and aid their digestion. They know that they can enjoy life with balance, that they can eat well and also treat themselves, that they can exercise and work, but also must relax.

They know how to relax properly, beyond the standard TV marathon, and take time to practice active relaxation, as they know this will nurture them when stress has taken hold. They meditate, walk, and stretch. They dance, they laugh, they breathe.

The unstressable know that breathing deeply is something they can do whenever anxiety or stress has taken hold; they keep the simplest of breathing techniques in their minds and know that at any time they can use them, both around people or silently alone. They don't just use breathing to reduce stress; they use it to prevent stress.

They build relationships with their bodies that allow them to notice the earliest ache or pain. They listen to these early signals and act on them, seeing what can be done through simple changes to their lifestyle. They know that their bodies can manifest their emotional stress, that their unprocessed emotions can turn up as a sudden trouble, ache, or pain. So they ask themselves what emotions they may need to deal with to help ease their bodies. They are aware that they are totally linked through body, mind, and soul.

They don't delay listening when their bodies are asking them to pay attention. They don't allow the physical symptoms of stress to simmer and strengthen. They take control of their stress and deal with what they need to in their bodies as and when it arises. They know that when the body talks, it's time to listen. They try their best to make sure they are supporting their bodies so there's no need for them to scream.

They make their sleep a priority and refuse to fall into the trap of getting less sleep to try to get more done. They know that the more rested they are, the more productive they will be. They take their sleep as seriously as they do their work. They make sure that they wind down at bedtime and don't challenge their sleep by being on their devices in bed.

They treat their bodies when they can, they massage them, they stretch them, they move them. They know that the more well looked after their bodies are, the stronger their minds will feel, while also being aware that their minds can have an effect on their bodies all on their own. They keep their thoughts around their health positive and don't get lost in the trap of creating something negative in their bodies through thought alone.

They are careful not to miss the simplest things that activate their bodies' stress response all on their own—they hydrate themselves, they sleep, they don't fill themselves full with sugar and alcohol during their most stressful weeks. They release the stress from their physical systems; they don't sit simmering at their desks waiting for it to miraculously change.

They know that if they look after their bodies, if they nurture them and move them, then life will move better for them too.

6. THE UNSTRESSABLE SET BOUNDARIES

Every unstressable knows that, left to its own devices, life will bombard them with stressors. Work will ask for every last ounce of their effort and attention. People will ask for every free minute of their time, and the regular pace of everyday life will consume them in long commutes and chores that leave no space for them to enjoy life. The modern world always attempts to leave them stressed repeatedly beyond repair. To prevent the mounting load of stressors, the unstressable learn to become really good at setting boundaries.

They regularly check the time and effort that they give to people and work. They are honest in their assessment about which of those stress them while bringing no benefit to their progress and goals.

They regularly rank the events that stress them in order of their intensity and the value those bring to them, and they weed out the useless stressful ones, not only by removing them once but also preventing the possibility of future stress by setting boundaries that prevent those events from affecting them again. They learn to say no. They know that saying yes to every request that comes their way not only reduces their ability to perform as best as they can, but it also takes up their precious time and leads them into a corner where they can no longer do the things that really matter, which leaves them frustrated and stressed.

The unstressable also take stock of what adds value to their lives— the time they dedicate for their own well-being, hobbies, reflection, and connection with nature, their families, friends, and loved ones. They plug those events into their calendars first, and they protect them as if their lives depended on it. Because they know they do. When someone or some event competes for the time they have allocated to their own well-being, the unstressable refuse to give up the time they allocate to taking care of themselves and their needs. They say no and see how the world responds. Often, whoever is demanding the time will find another slot of time that works. If they don't, the unstressable will find another slot for their joyful activities to fit in first before they remove them to allow time for anything else.

The unstressable fiercely protect their boundaries. When those boundaries are crossed, they say a simple no, and they don't even feel the need to offer justification.

They always end up with fewer engagements and activities than the rest of us, but they perform those engagements impeccably. They enjoy them tremendously, and as a result, they progress much further in life without feeling drained from the stress that results from doing too much.

A typical skill of the unstressable is that they learn to respect the boundaries of others too. They encourage those that they love to set boundaries, and once they know the limits set by another, they tend to respect them just as much as they want others to respect their own.

Stress, as per the stress equation, is the result of external stressors applied to our ability to deal with them. Nothing eradicates stress better than preventing the stressor from occurring in the first place. Setting sufficient boundaries to protect your well-being is probably the biggest investment you can make to enhance your ability to deal with the stress of everyday life so that you become unstressable.

7. THE UNSTRESSABLE RELATE TO MORE THAN THIS WORLD

Those who live unstressable live in connection with their souls. They know that the deeper sense of calm and peace we seek cannot be found through the mind and body alone, that there is a force both within and around us that is waiting to be tapped into, and once we find our own connection to it, then everything changes.

They know that they can never truly know themselves if they do not have a connection to their souls—that all their greatest gifts, answers, and wisdom lie in this part of them. They see that when life turns upside down, the first place to seek guidance and comfort is within them, in their own spiritual sanctuary. They know that when life seems totally unfair, it is not their job to try to control the uncontrollable but rather to surrender to what is trying to unfold and see where it ends up taking them.

They have a relationship with their souls that is as active as the one they have with their bodies. They nurture their spiritual health as much as they do their physical health, knowing it's just as important.

They are tuned in to their intuition, they consult it rather than brushing it aside. They make it a priority to sit in silence for guidance, even for just five minutes a day, knowing that this stillness is what will bring them back to the clarity they need—the actions they need to take, the people they need to speak to, the ideas they need to act upon. They make their relationship with their intuition an ongoing practice, so it strengthens and grows.

The unstressable know that when their intuition speaks, it's time to pay attention. They know that even if the fears of their minds are trying their hardest to override it, that intuitive feeling holds something that they need to know, need to act on. They are able to decipher between the voice of their egos and the whispers of their souls. They are able to act on their souls' guidance, even when sometimes it makes little sense; they know when they just "know."

The unstressable *see, accept, and love* all that they are. They extend the same kindness to themselves as they do to others, living from a place that embodies the divinity within them, extending kindness, gratitude, and joy, and moving away from judgment.

They try to live in alignment with their spiritual natures. Even when the world is trying desperately to make them act purely as humans, they don't allow themselves to live in this space for long. They notice when they are stressed, when they falter, and they pull themselves back to their spiritual truth in their hardest moments by simply asking, *What would my soul do?*

They realize that there is a divine potential within them that is theirs and theirs alone. They spend their lives seeking to evolve this part of them, to seek to be in alignment with the wishes of their souls. They are acutely aware that the more they learn, the more they realize they do not know, that sometimes the question is not meant to be answered but experienced. That there is always a force that is guiding them both within and around them, paving the way for synchronicities to unfold. That sometimes their only job is to get out of their own way and surrender to what is already trying to emerge.

Most important, the unstressable know that their spirituality is something to be treasured, not feared, and they have no need to fear it, as they know that their spirituality is theirs and theirs alone.

They live from a place of confidence that no matter what life throws at them, they can always fall back on the guidance and wisdom of their spiritual connection and the grace of their souls.

Before we leave you, let us remind you that our world is not going to reduce the stress that it applies on each and every one of us anytime soon. It is up to each of us to choose a lifestyle that keeps us stress-free and increases our skills to handle the world we live in, through knowing these four parts of us.

Join the gang, be one of our heroes, and become unstressable. Show your commitment and sign up to our members community at Unstressable .com to get a total of fifteen dollars off the first month—likely the price you paid for this book—when you enter the promo code **IAMUN-STRESSABLE**.

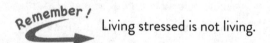 Living stressed is not living.

Stress is a process. To reverse its effects, you need to be in charge of the gears.

 It's not the stress that burns you out and kills you.
It's letting it linger that can take your life away.
And it's not the events of the world that stress you.
It's the way you deal with them that does.

Notes

This Is Not an Introduction

1. "America's #1 Health Problem," American Institute of Stress, https://www.stress.org/americas-1-health-problem.
2. Megan Hull, "Mental Health Disorders," Recovery Village, August 24, 2023, https://www.therecoveryvillage.com/mental-health/stress/related/stress-statistics/.
3. "At 6.7% CAGR, Global Sleeping Aids Market Size & Share Expand to USD 101.7 Billion by 2026: Facts & Factors," Global News Wire, March 17, 2021, https://bit.ly/3xcgk4E.
4. "Stress: Statistics," Mental Health Foundation, https://www.mentalhealth.org.uk/statistics/mental-health-statistics-stress.
5. "The Science of STRESS," South Louisiana Medical Associates, https://bit.ly/2SmdWti.
6. "Stress in America™ 2020," American Psychological Association, https://www.apa.org/news/press/releases/stress/2020/report-october.

1: Welcome to the Machine

1. "SBNI Lunch Lecture Series-The Neurobiology of PTSD," YouTube video, 50:49, posted by Cottage Health, April 7, 2016, https://youtu.be/hrIUPOtmeyQ.
2. *Britannica, s.v.* "Mechanics of Solids," https://www.britannica.com/science/mechanics-of-solids/History.

2: Trigger (Un)Happy

1. Jitender Sareen, "Posttraumatic Stress Disorder in Adults: Impact, Comorbidity, Risk Factors, and Treatment," *Canadian Journal of Psychiatry* 59, no. 9 (2014): 460–7, https://www.ncbi.nlm.nih.gov/pmc/articles/PMC4168808/.
2. "How Long Does Depression Last?," Healthline, https://www.healthline.com/health/how-long-does-depression-last#Depressive-episodes.
3. Rodney J. Korba, "The Rate of Inner Speech," *Perceptual and Motor Skills* 71, no. 3 (199): 1043–52, https://journals.sagepub.com/doi/abs/10.2466/pms.1990.71.3.1043.

4. Nate Klemp, "The Neuroscience of Breaking Out of Negative Thinking (and How to Do It in Under 30 Seconds)," *Inc.*, https://www.inc.com/nate-klemp/try-this-neuroscience-based -technique-to-shift-your-mindset-from-negative-to-positive-in-30-seconds.html.

3: Carrying That TONN

1. Lorna Collier, "Growth After Trauma," *Monitor on Psychology* 47, no. 10 (November 2016), https://www.apa.org/monitor/2016/11/growth-trauma.
2. Richard G. Tedeschi, "Growth After Trauma," *Harvard Business Review*, July–August 2020, https://hbr.org/2020/07/growth-after-trauma.
3. "We Touch Our Smartphones at Least 2,617 Times a Day!," *Economic Times*, July 14, 2016, https://economictimes.indiatimes.com/magazines/panache/we-touch-our-smartphones-at -least-2617-times-a-day/articleshow/53211326.cms?from=mdr.
4. Josh Howarth, "Alarming Average Screen Time Statistics (2023)," Exploding Topics, January 13, 2023, https://explodingtopics.com/blog/screen-time-stats.
5. "SLO MO REWIND: Nir Eyal on Becoming Indistractable," YouTube video, 1:16:21, posted by Mo Gawdat, January 7, 2023, https://www.youtube.com/watch?v=BzBhWPZrT7A.

4: It's in Your Head

1. "Festive Fatigue: December Is the Most Stressful Month of 2022 for Half Your Workforce," Visier, December 8, 2022, https://www.visier.com/company/news/festive-fatigue-december -most-stressful-month-of-2022/.
2. "27 Holiday Stress Statistics + Tips to Survive the Festivities," Everlywell, https://www .everlywell.com/blog/sleep-and-stress/holiday-stress-statistics/.
3. Zoya Gervis, "Couples Have Seven Arguments During the Holiday Season, Study Finds," SWNS Digital, September 6, 2021, https://swnsdigital.com/us/2018/12/29791/.
4. "Blue Monday: What Is It and Where Did It Come From?," Croud, January 6, 2023, https: //croud.com/blog/blue-monday-what-is-it-and-where-did-it-come-from/#:~:text='Blue%20 Monday'%20is%20a%20day,formula'%20for%20the%20January%20blues.
5. "Debunking Blue Monday," Centre for Suicide Prevention, January 13, 2016, https://www .suicideinfo.ca/debunking-blue-monday/.
6. Dave Radparvar, "Neurons That Fire Together, Wire Together," Holstee, https://www .holstee.com/blogs/mindful-matter/neurons-that-fire-together-wire-together#:~:text =%E2%80%9CNeurons%20that%20fire%20together%2C%20wire,gratitude%20can%20 be%20so%20powerful.&text=Neuropsychologist%20Donald%20Hebb%20first%20used- ,formed%20and%20reinforced%20through%20repetition.

5: Feel to Heal

1. Kendra Cherry, "The 6 Types of Basic Emotions and Their Effect on Human Behavior," Very-well Mind, December 1, 2022, https://www.verywellmind.com/an-overview-of-the-types-of -emotions-4163976.
2. Yasmin Anwar, "How Many Different Human Emotions Are There?," *Greater Good*, September 8, 2017, https://greatergood.berkeley.edu/article/item/how_many_different_human _emotions_are_there.
3. Brené Brown, *Atlas of the Heart* (New York: Random House, 2021).
4. Sarah Regan, "The 8 Types Of Love + How To Know Which One You're Feeling," mindbody-green, December 28, 2022, https://www.mindbodygreen.com/articles/types-of-love.

5. "Brené Brown: The Call to Courage | Official Trailer [HD] | Netflix," YouTube video, 1:10, posted by Netflix, April 10, 2019, https://www.youtube.com/watch?v=gr-WvA7uFDQ.

6. Dr. Kim and Dr. Hilary, "Emotions Are Energy : The Bodymind Connection and E-Motion," Authenticity Associates, April 7, 2022, https://www.authenticityassociates.com/emotions-are-energy/.

7. "The 90 Second Life Cycle of an Emotion," YouTube video, 4:49, posted by WUSA9, May 26, 2021, https://www.youtube.com/watch?v=vxARXvljKBA.

8. Meg Coyle, "The 90-Second Rule You Can't Afford to Ignore," One Body, https://onebodyinc .com/the-90-second-rule-you-cant-afford-to-ignore/.

6: Your Hips Don't Lie

1. Bessel van der Kolk, *The Body Keeps the Score*, read by Sean Pratt (New York: Penguin Audio, 2021), Audible audio ed., 16 hr., 15 min.

2. Ye-Seul Lee, Yeonhee Ryu, Won-Mo Jung, Jungjoo Kim, Taehyung Lee, and Younbyoung Chae, "Understanding Mind-Body Interaction from the Perspective of East Asian Medicine," *Evidence-Based Complementary and Alternative Medicine*, 2017: 7618419, https://www.ncbi .nlm.nih.gov/pmc/articles/PMC5585554/.

3. "Louise Hay on Health," Louise Hay, https://www.louisehay.com/health/.

4. "Clear the Lungs and open the mind with TCM," SHA Magazine, September 20, 2018, https: //shawellnessclinic.com/en/shamagazine/clear-the-lungs-and-open-the-mind-with-tcm/.

5. Penny Sarchet, "The nocebo effect: Wellcome Trust Prize Science Writing Essay," *The Guardian*, November 12, 2011, https://www.theguardian.com/science/2011/nov/13/nocebo-pain -wellcome-trust-prize.

6. Kara E. Hannibal and Mark D. Bishop, "Chronic Stress, Cortisol Dysfunction, and Pain: A Psychoneuroendocrine Rationale for Stress Management in Pain Rehabilitation," *Physical Therapy* 94, no. 12 (2014): 1816–25, https://www.ncbi.nlm.nih.gov/pmc/articles/PMC4263906 /#:~:text=Under%20normal%20conditions%2C%20cortisol%20binds,acts%20as%20 an%20anti%2Dinflammatory.&text=However%2C%20prolonged%20or%20excessive%20 cortisol,mechanism%20underlying%20insulin%2Dresistant%20diabetes.

7. "Inflammation," Cleveland Clinic, https://my.clevelandclinic.org/health/symptoms/21660 -inflammation.

8. "How Your Heart Works," British Heart Foundation, https://www.bhf.org.uk/informationsupport /how-a-healthy-heart-works#:~:text=Each%20day%2C%20your%20heart%20beats,vessels%20called%20your%20circulatory%20system.

9. Ursula Barth, "How Many Cells Are in Your Body? Probably More Than You Think!," Eppendorf Handling Solutions, May 12, 2017, https://handling-solutions.eppendorf.com /cell-handling/about-cells-and-culture/detailview/news/how-many-cells-are-in-your-body -probably-more-than-you-think/.

10. Mark Fischetti and Jen Christiansen, "Our Bodies Replace Billions of Cells Every Day," *Scientific American*, April 1, 2021, https://www.scientificamerican.com/article/our-bodies-replace -billions-of-cells-every-day/.

11. *Britannica*, s.v. "White Blood Cell," https://www.britannica.com/science/white-blood-cell.

12. Serusha Govender, "Is Crying Good for You?," WebMD, https://www.webmd.com/balance /features/is-crying-good-for-you.

13. Nikolai A. Shevchuk, "Adapted Cold Shower as a Potential Treatment for Depression," *Medical Hypotheses* 70, no. 5 (2008): 995–1001, https://www.sciencedirect.com/science/article/abs/pii /S030698770700566X.

14. "Exercising to Relax," Harvard Health Publishing, https://www.health.harvard.edu/staying -healthy/exercising-to-relax.

15. "How to Build Self-Confidence," MindTools, https://www.mindtools.com/selfconf.html.
16. "Relax," Harvard Health.
17. "Walking: Trim Your Waistline, Improve Your Health," Mayo Clinic, May 19, 2021, https://www.mayoclinic.org/healthy-lifestyle/fitness/in-depth/walking/art-20046261.
18. Kerstin Uvnas-Moberg and Maria Petersson, "Oxytocin, a Mediator of Anti-Stress, Well-Being, Social Interaction, Growth and Healing," *Z Psychosom Med Psychother* 51, vol. 1 (2005): 57–80. German. doi: 10.13109/zptm.2005.51.1.57.
19. Jorge E. Esteves, Laura Wheatley, Clare Mayall, and Hilary Abbey, "Emotional Processing and Its Relationship to Chronic Low Back Pain: Results from a Case-Control Study," *Manual Therapy* 18, no. 6 (2013): 541–6, https://pubmed.ncbi.nlm.nih.gov/23756033/#:~:text=Chronic%20low%20back%20pain%20(CLBP,%2Defficacy%2C%20catastrophizing%20and%20depression.
20. "Breathing to Reduce Stress," Better Health Channel, https://www.betterhealth.vic.gov.au/health/healthyliving/breathing-to-reduce-stress.
21. James Nestor, Breath: *The New Science of a Lost Art* (New York: Riverhead, 2020).
22. "The Gut-Brain Connection," Harvard Health Publishing, July 18, 2023, https://www.health.harvard.edu/diseases-and-conditions/the-gut-brain-connection.
23. Rangan Chatterjee, *The Stress Solution* (New York: Penguin, 2019).
24. Chatterjee, *The Stress Solution*.
25. Susie Neilson, "A Warm Bedtime Bath Can Help You Cool Down And Sleep Better," NPR, July 25, 2019, https://www.npr.org/sections/health-shots/2019/07/25/745010965/a-warm-bedtime-bath-can-help-you-cool-down-and-sleep-better?t=1647354192687.
26. Tim Ferriss, "5 Tools for Faster and Better Sleep," Tim Ferriss website, https://tim.blog/wp-content/uploads/2017/05/5-tools-for-faster-and-better-sleep.pdf.
27. Eric Suni and Abhinav Singh, "Light and Sleep," Sleep Foundation, September 1, 2023, https://www.sleepfoundation.org/bedroom-environment/light-and-sleep#:~:text=In%20response%20to%20darkness%2C%20the,that%20this%20hormone%20facilitates%20sleep.

7: Soul-Renity

1. Albert Einstein, *Albert Einstein, The Human Side: Glimpses from His Archives*, ed. Helen Dukas and Banesh Hoffman (Princeton, NJ: University Press, 2013).
2. Vladislav Šolc and George J. Didier, *Dark Religion: Fundamentalism from the Perspective of Jungian Psychology* (Asheville, NC: Chiron, 2018).
3. Pam Rutledge, "The Brain Is Hardwired to Doomscroll: Can You Stop It?," Fielding Graduate University, June 10, 2020, https://www.fielding.edu/news/the-brain-is-hardwired-to-doomscroll-can-you-stop-it/.
4. Elizabeth Scott, "Helping Others Can Increase Happiness and Reduce Stress," Verywell Mind, October 26, 2020, https://www.verywellmind.com/stress-helping-others-can-increase-happiness-3144890.
5. "Giving Thanks Can Make You Happier," Harvard Health Publishing, August 14, 2021, https://www.health.harvard.edu/healthbeat/giving-thanks-can-make-you-happier.
6. Shaman Durek, *Spirit Hacking: Shamanic Keys to Reclaim Your Personal Power, Transform Yourself, and Light Up the World* (New York: St. Martin's Essentials, 2019).
7. "Quote by Marcus Aurelius," Goodreads, https://www.goodreads.com/quotes/326583-nowhere-can-man-find-a-quieter-or-more-untroubled-retreat.
8. Carl Jung, *Psychology and Religion: West and East, Vol. 11* (Princeton: Princeton University Press, 1975).
9. "Quote by C.G. Jung," Goodreads, https://www.goodreads.com/quotes/44379-until-you-make-the-unconscious-conscious-it-will-direct-your.
10. Marianne Williamson, *A Return to Love: Reflections on the Principles of* A Course in Miracles (New York: HarperOne, 1996).

Acknowledgments

To Elizabeth Beier, Brigitte Dale, Brant Janeway, Amelia Beckerman, Sophia Lauriello, and all of the incredible team at St. Martin's; to Katy Denny, Cara Waudby-Tolley, Maya Conway, Annie Rose, Siobhan Hooper, and all of the wonderful team at Bluebird; and to our friends and literary agents Michael, Julien, and Lyndsey. Without all of you this would have never seen the light.

To our readers, followers, and members for being with us on our mission.

And to our friends and family for all of your continued love and support, without which we would not be unstressable.